A Guide to Instructional Television

A GUIDE TO

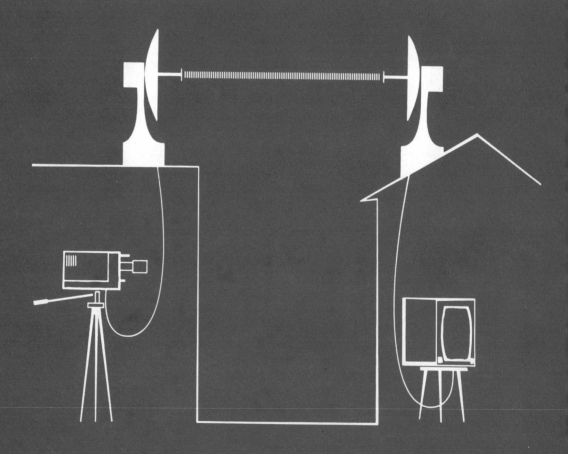

INSTRUCTIONAL
TELEVISION

edited by

DR. ROBERT M. DIAMOND

Director of Instructional Resources

University College

University of Miami

McGRAW-HILL BOOK COMPANY

New York

San Francisco

London

Toronto

A Guide to Instructional Television

Preface

A Guide to Instructional Television is designed to fill the present need for a single reference for administrators, teachers, students, and laymen interested in exploring the possible applications of television within a particular school or school system.

While there is obviously much duplication among the current instructional television projects, there is also a wide variety of specific applications. School districts facing almost identical problems have successfully used television in ways that have differed in both development and procedure, the choice of techniques having been based on factors unique to particular districts at particular times.

For teachers and administrators it makes little difference whether a telecast is received from a local community or commercial station, from an airplane circling overhead or from a satellite. What matters is the program's application within the classroom, its contribution to student learning, its quality of presentation, and its cost to the district.

An attempt has been made here to cover the broad spectrum of the uses of television in education with emphasis on the elementary and secondary school levels. Some examples from higher education have been selected for their potential application to the other levels of instruction.

It is probable that many examples will suggest immediate application in a majority of school districts. On the other hand, obviously, what will make sense in one school system may be wasteful and impractical in another. It should also be recognized that television will not have a place in all subjects on all grade levels. For some areas of learning, the particular objectives, the number of students, or the method by which certain material may best be taught makes the use of the medium impractical.

Nevertheless, in many areas television, wisely used, can increase both the effectiveness and the efficiency of the teaching.

When exploring the various applications of television in education, we find that in actual practice, while the grade level and subject matter may vary, the problems faced and the uses of television tend to fall into several basic patterns.

For example, the technique of using television as a simple magnification device in a biology laboratory has immediate application in all other courses where the teacher without television must repeat a demonstration several times if all the students are to see. A series of television programs designed to bring a subject-matter specialist into the classroom will have the same potential for improving the instruction whether the course be biology, music, physics, or French. In effect, it is the teaching problem that determines the particular use of television, rather than the grade level or the subject matter.

The authors of the chapters in this book have been selected because of their experience with instructional television in its many forms. Some are administrators, others are teachers. In those chapters discussing specific application of the medium, the authors have been asked to cover several points as specifically as possible: the problems that were faced, the rationale behind the selection of television as a possible solution, how the medium was used, and finally, what happened, what worked and what did not, and why.

Part I, "Single-room Television," is concerned with the extremely practical, but often overlooked, use of television as a magnification device within a single classroom, laboratory, or lecture hall. The four chapters included in this section have implications for most schools, since the cost is minimal and the variety of uses unlimited.

Most television projects are concerned with large numbers of students; these applications are covered in Part II, "Studio Television," comprising seven chapters which fall into three general subject areas. The first group of chapters focuses on the administrative choice between open- and closed-circuit television. In these examples five superintendents and administrators present the logic behind their selection and then describe briefly what they did and what the results were.

A description of how one school district used television to solve commonplace guidance problems follows in Chapter 10, "Guidance and Television." Chapter 11, "Television in the Secondary School," discusses the wide variety of applications of television within junior and senior high schools, highlighting the scheduling problems involved.

Part III presents several examples of administrative uses of television—uses which are practical and effective, yet often overlooked. Examples include television in the administration of standardized tests and in the field of in-service education.

Part IV attempts to place instructional television in its proper perspective. Television is not the answer to all the problems facing education. It has often been misused and sometimes oversold. The role of evaluation within any television project is discussed in Chapter 15, for only with proper evaluation can we determine whether we are succeeding or failing in any particular application of the medium. Chapter 17, "Television: Part of the Answer," discusses the relationship between television and other communications media, ranging from simple projection techniques to programmed instruction.

In Chapter 18, "Instructional Television: Its Potential and Its

Problems," the editor makes a calculated guess about the future of television in education, with a close look at the major problems now standing in the way of its extensive use and effective utilization.

The Appendixes are designed for administrators or teachers who are planning to use television within a school or a school district. This material is not intended to be a complete equipment or production manual, but rather information that will save time, effort, and dollars as equipment and production techniques are explored.

Included in the Appendixes are brief chapters on the problems of introducing television into a school or a district, purchasing equipment, the selection and role of television teachers, and the preparation and function of the teacher's guide. A Glossary has been included as well as an Annotated Bibliography that lists books and other sources of information which take over where this book leaves off.

Instructional television is in its early stage of development. Each year new technological developments open up completely new areas of application. While we can speculate, there is no way of foreseeing the implications for educators in the availability of low-priced, highly portable video tape recorders, new inexpensive transmission facilities, or inexpensive wide-screen projectors.

At present the ideal interrelationship between self-study, student-teacher interaction, and large-group instruction on the one hand, and television's role on the other, is still unknown.

The ultimate role that instructional television will play in the entire spectrum of education is still to be determined. Television is neither a panacea nor a passing fad. It is the hope of the editor and the authors that the material in this book will assist the reader in achieving a perspective view of television in its proper and valuable role in education. It is also hoped that *A Guide to Instructional Television* will enable those who choose to use the medium to gain new insight into its specific applications for their local instructional programs.

Robert M. Diamond

Acknowledgments

A Guide to Instructional Television is the cooperative effort of many individuals. First and foremost the editor's thanks go to the chapter writers who, despite full schedules, were kind enough to prepare their manuscripts for publication.

The editor also expresses his appreciation to Presley Holmes and Hideya Kumata for permission to quote from their writings, and to his former colleagues at San Jose State College, Dick Lewis, Jerry Kemp, and Gaither Lee Martin, for their suggestions during the preparation of this book.

For their contributions to the Glossary the editor's thanks go to Philip Lewis, Kathryn Kendig, Gaither Lee Martin, Glen Pensinger, and William Johnson.

The chapter writers gratefully acknowledge the assistance they received from Eunice Bishop, Olwyn O'Conner, John Rhoades, John Woodward, Lyndy Wade, Myron Schussman, Richard Dewey, and Mary Jane Lewis.

And finally a word of thanks is given to Barbara Lindsay and Margaret Griese for their editorial help and typing, and to Dolores Diamond, who sacrificed a husband so that this manuscript might be completed.

Photo Credits: In large part the photography and graphic illustrations are the works of Margaret Murray, Sue Pfaffl, Richard Szumski, and Daryle Webb. Unless otherwise indicated, all photographs are printed with permission of the Instructional Television Center, San Jose State College.

Contents

Contents

part I

Single-room television

INSTRUCTIONAL TELEVISION is usually thought of in terms of a fully equipped studio, a television teacher, and students in many scattered classrooms viewing the telecast. Because there is a natural, though unfortunate, correlation between cost and publicity, we tend to ignore the usefulness and creative possibilities of the less expensive "single-room" television, where the teacher, TV camera, receivers, and students are all in the same classroom, laboratory, or lecture hall. Yet in this direct classroom context, television has proved itself an exciting and practical audio-visual technique with elements attractive to administrators and to teachers.

The cost is low. In the last few years inexpensive equipment has been developed by several manufacturers. A complete installation, including camera, lenses, camera stand, and receivers, is now available for less than $1,200. The equipment requires little additional subject lighting beyond normal classroom levels. Where highlighting is desired, or when a room is exceptionally dark, a 60- or 100-watt bulb in a movable lamp bracket is usually sufficient.

In investigating television in education, there has been a tendency to emphasize its effects upon learning while overlooking one aspect that may have equally important administrative implications: the effect of television upon teaching efficiency. It is in this area that single-room television is having its most dynamic effect. In many classrooms and laboratories, teachers are now forced to repeat demonstrations and presentations in order that all may see; in some instances, valuable material is actually omitted to avoid this waste of time and effort. By simply eliminating the need for duplicate presentations, television has been able to reduce the time needed for certain lessons by as much as 70 per cent. It can be anticipated that, as a result of this saving of time, it may be possible to increase course content or to reduce the time allotted to those courses where the single-room television technique has constant application.

The equipment is easy to operate, dependable, mobile, and unlimited in its applications. The entire installation can be set up in a matter of minutes by most teachers. Moreover, administrators introducing the equipment find none of the resentment and hesitancy on the part of teachers which is often associated with the introduction of studio-based programs. In fact, for many school districts and colleges, this simple type of operation has been an

3

excellent method of introducing the use of television. Often more comprehensive programs and facilities follow as a natural development.

Of all audio-visual techniques, television is the only method that will with any success enlarge three-dimensional objects. Yet television cameras can also magnify and transmit pages of books, small photographs, microscope slides, and, by the simple process of adding a light box, transparencies of the type used with an overhead projector. Thus the television camera can, in effect, often replace both the overhead and the opaque projector. There is, of course, the color limitation; however, instructors using television equipment have found little need for color in a majority of demonstrations.

Only with the flexibility provided by single-room television equipment is it possible for a teacher to present to his entire class demonstrations using simultaneously two- and three-dimensional materials and his own personal commentary. Experience has already shown that the applications of television as a simple magnification device are limited only by the creativity of the instructor using it.

Most important, single-room television brings the many advantages of the medium to the classroom situation of direct student-teacher interaction. Trump[1] and others who are exploring new teaching configurations base much of their approach upon the assumption that certain subjects can best be taught and certain teachers can best teach within this situation. With single-room television, it is possible for the teacher to use television techniques and at the same time to adjust pacing, content, and approach to his particular students' needs.

In laboratory demonstrations, there is strong indication that when the student has the opportunity of manipulating the same materials he is seeing on the screen, there will often be significantly greater achievement on the part of the low-ability student. Students of high ability, when motivated, tend to learn under any conditions. Experiments in this area tend to support much of the early research on student participation with the use of film.[2]

Single-room television has been used in a wide variety of courses and with many materials. Four examples are highlighted in this volume. Each explores one particular use that will suggest applications in numerous other courses.

In two of the four examples, the course involved an initial problem of repeated demonstrations with resultant inefficient use of the instructor's time. The chapter on typing describes a project wherein two cameras were required; the project resulted in outstanding improvement of typing speed for the entire class. The fourth chap-

[1] J. Lloyd Trump and Dorsey Baynham, *Focus on Change: Guide to Better Schools.* Chicago: Rand McNally & Company, 1961.

[2] William H. Allen, "Research on Film Use, Student Participation," *Audio-Visual Communication,* R 5:1957, pp. 424–425.

ter highlights the use of single-room television as but one of a variety of techniques used within a large lecture hall. This particular application has immediate implications for those districts exploring large-group instruction as part of a team teaching project.

It is only when the camera is in use that we can fully explore the applications of single-room television within a particular course. The wide variety of uses, combined with low cost and simplicity of operation, makes this approach to instructional television a probability for most schools within the near future.

chapter 1

Television and the teaching of typing

Edward C. Kelly

In this chapter Dr. Kelly describes a unique application of television within typing classes that not only resulted in increased learning but also reduced the number of teaching hours required. The techniques used have practical application in all courses training students in machine operation.

Recently, this writer had the experience of using closed-circuit television as a replacement for the traditional techniques used in teaching basic and advanced typing. From this project four basic conclusions have been reached: one, the use of television as a simple image magnifier speeds up mastery of the touch system of typing; two, television offers an excellent means of developing high-speed typists; three, the correct procedures for typing letters, manuscripts, and other office forms can be covered more quickly; and four, television gives the teacher an excellent opportunity to correct poor techniques.

A single television camera was connected directly to two 21-inch receivers located in the front of the room. The camera was of the type where all the controls and generating equipment are located within the camera unit. The teacher, in the rear of the room, had his desk on a raised platform enabling him to observe every student while seated at his demonstration desk. After some experimentation the camera was mounted on a boom arm that could be easily moved to a position behind, above, or alongside the teacher, and was operated by the instructor without technical assistance.

LEARNING TO TYPE BY TELEVISION

A camera was focused on the instructor's keyboard while the students imitated his stroking of the keys. In this manner the entire keyboard was mastered in one 50-minute period. In addition, such processes as operation of the margin stops, tabulator bar, and

Dr. Kelly is Assistant Professor of Business and Economics at San Fernando State College, Northridge, Calif. The project discussed in this chapter was conducted at the University of California at Los Angeles.

Single-room television

In the teaching of speed pacing within the typing class the television camera is focused on the paper at the point where the keys strike (see insert). (University of California at Los Angeles)

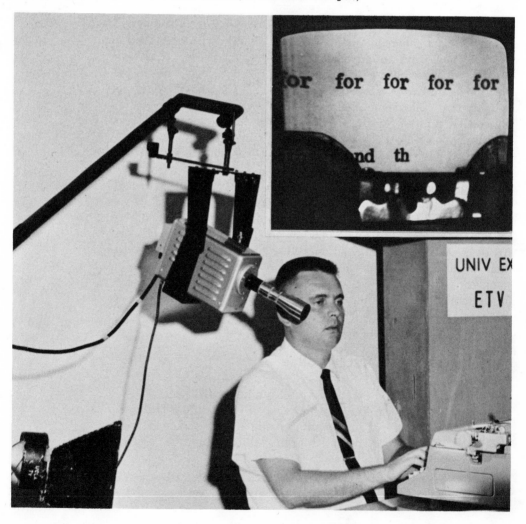

backspacer were quickly learned by the students by viewing the monitors at the front of the room.

Because this instructor was located in the back of the room on a platform, he was able to observe the stroking[1] technique of every student. Corrections could immediately be viewed by the students on the television receivers. The traditional procedure of walking to the student's seat was unnecessary. Not only was the teacher's time saved, but the students were able to concentrate on improving techniques without the emotional distraction of direct correction by the teacher.

The results of this teaching method were startling. Instead of the usual three to five periods required to learn the touch system of typewriting, students mastered the fundamentals in a single class period. Furthermore, because television magnification allowed the students to follow actively the details of the teacher's technique, the amount of remedial work later in the course was sharply reduced from that usually required under traditional methods.

Television and speed development. When the camera was focused on the instructor's typewriter carriage, each letter typed appeared on the two monitors at the front of the room. Thus, if the letter "t" was struck, the students immediately copied it from the monitor. After being instructed to copy all material that appeared, the students were paced. If a sentence was typed at 20 words a minute, the students in order to keep up were forced to type at 20 words a minute. In the advanced class where this technique was used, six of the twenty students reached at least 100 words a minute for one minute. Three students obtained a speed of 100 words a minute for five minutes with fewer than ten errors.

Teaching letter placement, manuscript typing, and office forms. Television made it possible to cover such subjects as letter placement, manuscript typing, and the completion of office forms in less than 50 per cent of the time normally required. For example, students copied from the letters as they were typed by the instructor. Oral comments were made concerning each part of the letter. Subsequent testing indicated that students learned letter placement after one exposure to this technique. The same procedure was used on all types of production materials commonly taught in high school and college typewriting classes. In every instance the time required to complete the unit was reduced by at least 50 per cent.

Correcting poor techniques through television. In order to develop proper techniques for stroking the typewriter keys, each student was instructed to type on the typewriter at the instructor's desk while the television camera was focused on her hands. While the class

---

[1] Stroking is the technical term for hitting the keys.

watched, suggestions were made for improvement. Changes in stroking technique were readily apparent to the student as well as other members of the class. Further, individual fingers were magnified on the screen, thus aiding in highlighting particular stroking faults. Many faults which might otherwise have gone undiscovered were quickly corrected by this technique.

TECHNICAL FACTORS IN TELEVISION TEACHING OF TYPEWRITING

The techniques described were developed over two semesters of experimentation within one beginners' and one advanced typewriting class. In addition to these approaches, certain technical factors were involved in the experimentation, such as attempts to eliminate the use of a cameraman or assistant, ascertain the maximum amount of light allowable, and discover whether or not a stationary camera was feasible.

Need for a cameraman. At the outset of experimentation with the use of television as a blackboard replacement, a cameraman assisted the instructor during preparations for the class as well as the actual conducting of the class. Materials and procedures to be televised were rehearsed and suitable cues determined. Through the introduction of preplanned drills of short duration not requiring the use of the television circuit, the instructor was able to take over the work of the cameraman and, in effect, eliminate the need for assistance. This procedure did not reduce the effectiveness of the learning process.

Lighting factors. Perhaps the most difficult problem to overcome during the experiments with television involved the room lighting. Originally, the room was kept in darkness in order to allow the students to read directly from the monitors. This presented a problem, because students had difficulty in locating home row[2] on the typewriters. In addition, students could not read printed materials or ascertain whether or not they were striking the correct keys. This problem was first overcome by switching the lights on and off. With this technique the students complained of having to adjust their eyes constantly to the change in light.

After extensive experimentation, it was found that by using venetian blinds and brighter lighting over the instructor's platform the lights in the room could be left on.

Use of a stationary camera. Though it was possible to eliminate the need for a cameraman, use of the movable equipment required the

[2] The "home row" comprises the middle row of letters on a standard keyboard.

instructor to delay the instruction process while time was taken to adjust the camera for desired results. This delay was eliminated by the use of a lightweight portable camera attached to a specially constructed stand which allowed the instructor to adjust the angle of the camera without leaving his seat. In this manner, the camera could be focused on the instructor's hands and then quickly moved to the carriage as desired.

From the experiences this writer has had with the use of television in the typewriting classroom, he has come to the conclusion that three basic advantages exist over the traditional approach in teaching this skill. First, valuable time is saved in the high school or college typewriting classroom. Second, these techniques can make it possible for large numbers to be taught typewriting at the same time. The number of students in this type of class is limited only by the size of the room and the number of typewriters. Third, with the use of television it is possible for the instructor to become an improved teacher with students performing better, and, as mentioned above, this improvement can be reached under reduced instructor time.

chapter 2

Television in the anatomy laboratory

Robert E. Richter

A college anatomy laboratory, like many others of a similar type, required repeated demonstrations on the part of the instructor. The inexpensive application of television as a simple magnification device, as described by Dr. Richter, has immediate implications not only for other science courses but for any situation where small objects or printed materials comprise part of the demonstration.

Students majoring in Physical Education and in Recreation at San Jose State College are required to take a three-unit course in Functional Human Anatomy. Both lectures and laboratory work are included, the latter being designed to train students to recognize and identify anatomical structures of the human cadaver.

PROBLEM

Several factors have combined to make Functional Human Anatomy a problem for both students and instructors. First, while the course is high in academic content and expectations, it tends to have a student population whose interests are more practical than theoretical. As a result, the attitude on the part of many students is negative. Second, a large amount of material must be covered in a class limited to five hours a week—two in the lecture hall, three in the laboratory. And third, under conventional teaching methods, the types of materials used in the laboratory require that demonstrations be repeated several times during each of six weekly three-hour laboratory periods.

Because of the important content of Functional Human Anatomy and the special problems involved in teaching the course, a committee of department heads and instructors in the biological sciences and in physical education has for several years given it special attention. From time to time, changes in approach have been attempted. In view of the time limitation and the generally

Dr. Richter is Associate Professor of Biological Science at San Jose State College and holds a doctorate in veterinary medicine.

low level of the students' ability, it was decided in 1959 to convert from a dissection laboratory to a demonstration laboratory.

Following this recommendation, instructors used for laboratory purposes a human cadaver, previously dissected by students. Supplemental anatomical parts and models, when available, were distributed among the students for individual study. However, the bulk of instruction was given by the teacher to groups of eight or ten students. This necessitated at least three presentations during a laboratory period. While the first group was watching a demonstration, the other two groups had to "mark time" for perhaps a full hour of the laboratory period before they were able to view the cadaver or the dissected specimens. Waiting groups became bored and restless.

Furthermore, the three demonstrations occupied nearly all of the laboratory period, leaving little or no time available for work with individual students. And by the end of the third demonstration, the instructor was so tired—both in mind and in voice—that he could hardly generate enthusiasm for individual help, even when a few brief moments were available. Yet for best results in a course such as this one, it is imperative that the laboratory work be conducted at least in part on the individual level, where it becomes possible to prod the slower students and challenge the brighter ones.

After many consultations with students and numerous meetings of instructors, department heads, and related faculty, it was decided, as one possible solution, to use television as a simple magnification device within the laboratory.

EXPERIMENTAL DESIGN

To explore this approach, the 128 students were divided into two groups of three sections each, one using the experimental television method, the other the conventional demonstration method. Sections were equated for ability and past performance. The two instructors involved taught under both control and experimental conditions. The course itself consisted of fifteen 3-hour laboratory sessions.

Where applicable, the human skeleton was used, with the students having specimens at their desks for individual study. Instruction on musculature incorporated both cadaver demonstration and limb dissections by the instructors. All remaining systems were taught primarily with mounted specimens or models, the students being required to observe the organs or systems in the cadaver as well.

In the experimental sections, television was used in the following manner: the equipment consisted of a single direct-wire television

13

camera mounted on a special stand designed at the college for this purpose. One 17- and two 23-inch television receivers were used. A single 40-watt bulb on a movable bracket produced all the additional lighting required for most of the demonstrations. Two lens combinations were used—a hand-operated zoom lens or a 2-inch lens mounted along with a standard wide-angle lens on a turret head of the camera (see illustrations, pages 16 to 20).

The total cost of all equipment was under $1,500. The equipment was set up by a student assistant immediately prior to the laboratory meeting, and the instructor was completely responsible, without technical assistance, for its operation during the laboratory period. With television cameras of this type, all the controls and generating equipment are built into the 16-pound camera, which is connected directly to as many as eight standard television receivers.

The two 23-inch receivers were placed on movable carts located on each side of the instructor's desk. All students were seated at their benches in such a manner as to be within the ideal viewing distance of a set of this size, and were able to see at least one of the sets without any interference. The instructor faced the class, with the camera mounted within easy arm's reach. The 17-inch receiver was used as a monitor by the instructor during the demonstration. The instructor demonstrated by pointing out structures of a specimen as students followed the demonstration on one of the television screens. If materials were available, the students had identical specimens at their desks with which they could follow the demonstration. Students could—and did—ask questions of the instructor at any time during the presentation.

RESULTS

In reviewing the effects of television as a simple magnification device within the laboratory, several significant results were obtained.

Time reduction. First, the time needed to complete a majority of the demonstrations was drastically reduced—in some cases by as much as 70 per cent. For example, what had been a three-hour laboratory demonstration on the human skull was completed in approximately fifty minutes. The instructors were then able, for the remainder of the period, to work with students individually; in addition, it became possible actually to increase the amount of material covered. Improvement was made in several units in both the time factor and the content coverage.

Limitations. It was found, however, that television was not practical in all the units within the course. In the study of muscles, it is important that the student first associate muscle groups before learn-ing the individual muscles. It is therefore necessary that large areas of a cadaver be used in the initial presentation. The equip-ment used did not provide sufficiently clear differentiation and contrast between individual muscles and ligaments, primarily be-cause of the inherent limitations of the inexpensive television equipment. With more expensive studio equipment, however, such detail can be adequately presented.

Student achievement.   A comparison of student achievement under the two methods proved most interesting. As usual, the motivated, high-ability students did well; such students do well regardless of the mode of instruction. It was discovered, however, that less able students, when they had identical materials at their desks, per-formed significantly better under the experimental conditions than in the control sections. This improvement was perhaps due mainly to the students' active participation in the demonstration; it may also have been due, in part, to the additional time available for individual instruction and follow-up when television was used.

Student reaction.   The class as a whole seemed more responsive when all students received instruction simultaneously. The prob-lem of restless waiting groups was eliminated. In general, students were more attentive in the televised portion of the laboratory peri-ods. The television screen seemed to command more concentration.

Among the many students questioned about the experiment, there were some who did not approve of the method. The author feels that their disapproval was probably caused by the experi-mental nature of the study. The instructors, during the early labo-ratory periods, were learning how to use the equipment, and there were some moments of confusion and delay. However, continued use brought about improved and smoother presentations. After several periods of use, we experienced little difficulty with the actual manipulation and operation of the equipment.

In conclusion, we found that television, when used within the laboratory as a simple magnification device, was worthwhile and rewarding. Most of the problems which arose could be solved by making changes in the presentations. Large objects, for example, tend to be extremely difficult to handle. Smaller dissected areas should be used, thus making it possible to handle the camera and the materials simultaneously and with ease. The equipment need not be used continually in all presentations; it should be on hand for use when it is needed and when it can best do the job. In addi-tion, specimen materials should be placed in the students' hands to achieve the best results; television instruction is not as satisfac-tory when the student is limited to watching the screen and taking notes.

Single-room television

Without television the teacher has to repeat a demonstration before two or three groups of students.

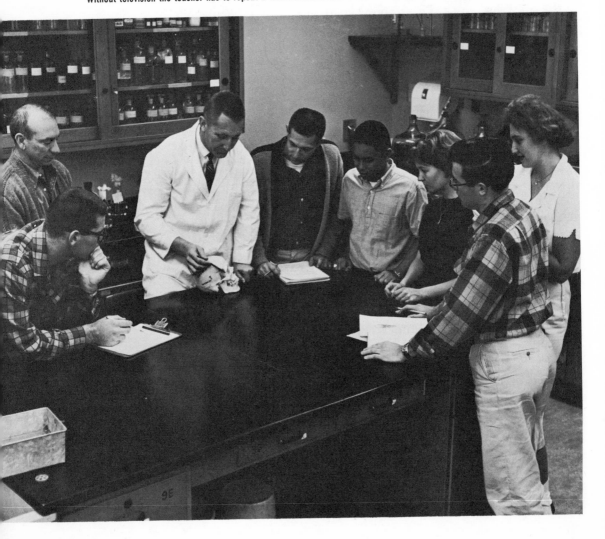

With television all the students in the class can follow the demonstration from their desks. The instructor, in the front of the room, may change pace and answer questions, and he needs to complete a demonstration only once.

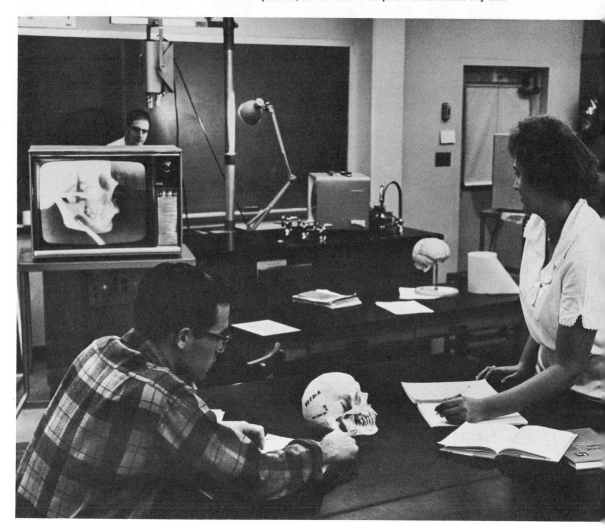

Single-room television

For simplicity of operation a zoom lens is often used. This lens allows the instructor to change the magnification of the image with a minimum of effort.

(Opposite) Students see the demonstration clearly from their desks. When possible they manipulate materials similar to those being viewed on the television screen.

Television in the anatomy laboratory

Facial region of the human skull

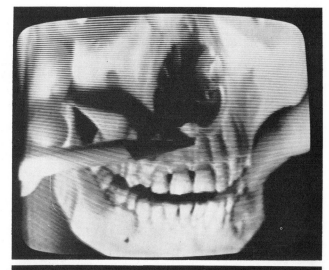

Cross section of the human brain

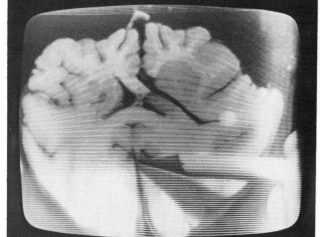

Top view of the frontal sinuses

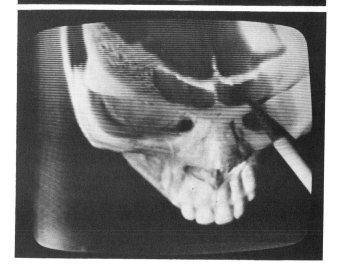

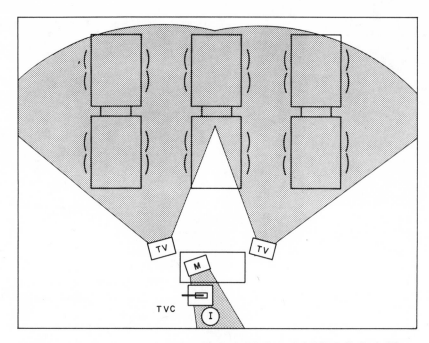

Two 23-in. television receivers are located at either end of the instructor's table in the front of the room. The instructor (I) faces the class while manipulating materials under the television camera (TVC), using a small 17-in. portable receiver (M) as his monitor.

Inexpensive television has a definite place in the anatomy laboratory. Although it may not be applicable to all units, it is useful in many. Demonstration time can be markedly reduced, allowing for a greater amount of individual instruction and for the inclusion of more material within the course. Instructor fatigue is reduced and the instructor's time and energy more effectively utilized. There is a strong indication that television as an image magnifier will result in significantly greater achievement on the part of the low-ability student provided that he can actively manipulate materials similar to those being shown on the screen.

It can be anticipated that, in time, television equipment of this type will become a permanent part of the standard laboratory equipment in schools and colleges.

This chapter is based on Robert M. Diamond's "The Effect of Closed-circuit Resource Television upon Achievement in the Laboratory Portion of a Functional Human Anatomy Course," unpublished doctoral dissertation, New York University, 1962, in which Dr. Richter was one of the two participating instructors.

chapter 3

Television in the art class

Robert R. Coleman

*In this chapter an experienced teacher describes the many applications of
single-room television within art teaching. A wide range of techniques is
covered, including the teaching of jewelry making, basic design, and
composition.*

Traditionally art, as a visual subject, has been taught through a
visual means. There are often limiting factors that art teachers
have accepted and have been forced to live with. From experience
we have found that some of these problems can be reduced or even
eliminated by the use of a television camera, operated by the instructor, within the art classroom.

THE PROBLEMS

Major problems facing the art teacher concern methods of demonstration and methods of keeping students' attention focused.

Demonstration of small drawings.   In any group larger than five or six
students, small drawings must be enlarged in order to demonstrate
by traditional means. Enlargement, however, changes the character of design and of sensitive relationships, so that the subtle
values, the relational qualities in small drawings are often lost.

Demonstration of three-dimensional materials.   Most three-dimensional
visual materials, such as carvings and small pieces of jewelry, cannot be made larger because of their physical makeup. Demonstrations in such cases must be limited to a few students at a time;
otherwise, students sitting more than a few feet from the instructor may receive only a vague notion of the message. The instructor
is thus faced with the unappealing alternatives of presenting demonstrations which adequately reach only a few students or of

Dr. Coleman is Associate Professor of Art at San Jose State College and has used television within a wide variety of subject offerings over the past three years.

repeating demonstrations again and again, thereby lowering his own enthusiasm and ability to project.

Visual distractions.   In the traditional art studio or laboratory there are many visual distractions, things that fight for attention and lessen the effectiveness of any presentation.

Excessive interaction.   Student interruptions, reactions, or questions may sidetrack demonstrations. While good teaching requires that an instructor respond to his audience, too much interaction reduces the total effectiveness of the lesson.

EQUIPMENT AND TECHNIQUES

To help solve these basic problems at San Jose State College we turned to the single-room television camera. A camera unit was set up in such a manner as to allow it to be operated by the person conducting the demonstration. The camera was usually mounted in such a way that students watching the screens had the same view of materials as the instructor did (see illustrations, page 25). Similarly, all hand work, drawing, tracing, designing, etc., was televised from above the instructor's head or over his shoulder, giving students a "first-person" view. It was possible, with careful depth-of-field adjustment, to show simultaneously a three-dimensional object and the drawing that was being made of it. Soft black pencils were used on ordinary drawing paper for many demonstrations. A zoom lens made it possible to move rapidly from long shots into close-ups for minute detail.

Photographs were also used. Adjustment of lights so that they hit the working surface at an angle usually kept glare or light bounce from hitting camera lenses. Even with this precaution, it became necessary at times to adjust the picture because of the reflection. A dulling spray was also used on photographs to cut glare. Tracing paper laid over photographs was used as a surface to draw on. In working on this kind of surface it was found that watching the television monitor instead of the paper surface made it possible to see more of the photo. Somehow the light striking the surface of the tracing paper gives it a milky film, but the television camera looks through to the photograph with only a slight haze showing. The drawing is done by watching the hand and pencil line on the television screen, which gives the instructor the feeling of working by remote control.

Sequential drawings on tracing-paper overlays provided excellent opportunities for the student viewers to see the intimate and subtle qualities that this method affords. No large drawing for the same size of audience (twenty to thirty students) could possibly give this.

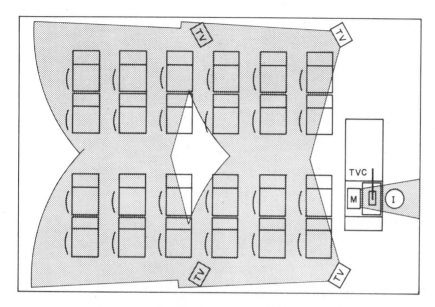

Within the art class four 23-in. receivers are used to allow for maximum viewing on the part of students. The instructor (I) faces the class when using the single-room television camera (TVC) and has a small 17-in. portable receiver for his own use (M).

For the twenty-four students stationed in most of our class-rooms, two television monitors with 21-inch screens proved adequate. A third small screen (usually of the portable variety) was set up directly in front of the instructor for his use.

ADVANTAGES OF TELEVISION

Focus of attention.   Television provides a strong focus of attention. In a semidarkened room the television picture keeps and dominates the attention of the students with a minimum of distraction.

With television it becomes possible to emphasize a single point, direct the student's attention to a particular area, and avoid unrelated considerations.

In a design class where the author was working with nature as a source for design a drawing was made of the small vertebra of a steer. Each phase of the observation and sketch was pointed out during the demonstration. The work was with the "percept-concept" activity at that moment. Under standard teaching procedures, drawing the same object on a large drawing board was less dynamic, since the drawing and the object were of necessity separated. The use of television also eliminated the distractions caused by extra pencils, extraneous materials, and the instructor himself.

The television camera is located in such a position as to afford the students an unobstructed view of the demonstration with a maximum of magnification.

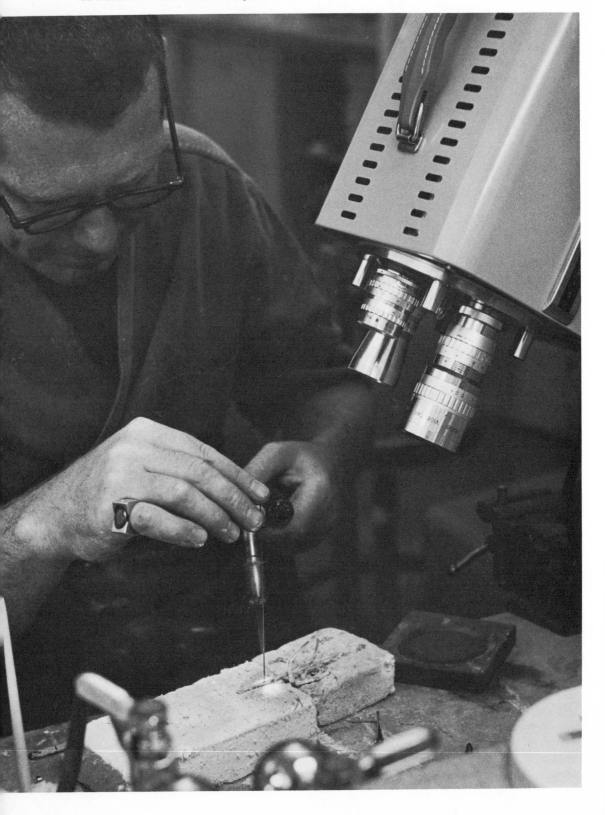

In a design class the camera is mounted to provide the students with a view identical to the instructor's. The instructor follows his demonstration on a small television receiver located directly in front of his materials. The stand being used was designed by the Sound View Supply Company of San Jose, Calif., to allow for a maximum variety of camera positions with a minimum of instructor effort.

Details clearly seen. Details can be observed by the entire audience, in first-person viewing, as only the one demonstrating might see it under traditional techniques.

As an example, in a recent jewelry demonstration on the techniques of soldering, the author was able to present the clear and exact picture of all the visual items the craftsman sees—fluxing, positioning of the solder, and heating and flowing of the molten solder. This picture, in fact, was clearer than one viewed with the naked eye, for the zoom lens attachment enlarged the items sixty-four times. A piece of solder less than $\frac{1}{16}$ inch square was enlarged to over 2 inches square on the viewers' screen.

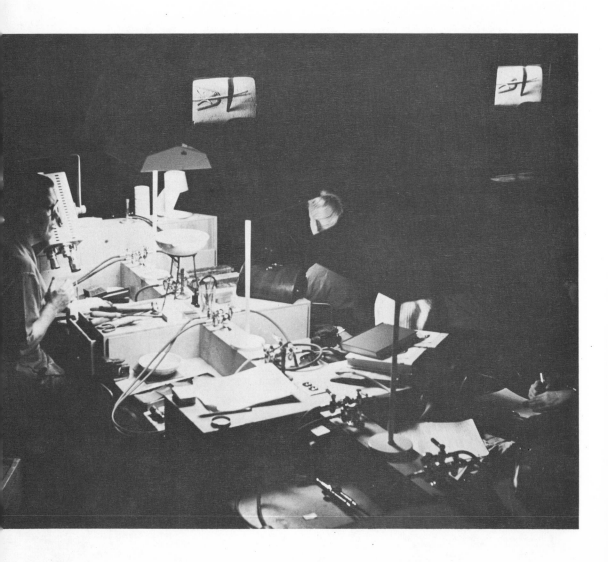

In drawings, subtle movements and sensitive transitions were easily controlled and naturally rendered with the kind of considerations that would be done on one's own drawing. Here again the entire audience was able to have a clear first-person view of the artwork in an enlarged state.

Point of view—near-far.   Differences in point of view are made possible by using lenses of varying focal length or by using the zoom lens. By a simple change in the lens setting the student may see first the overall picture and then, immediately after, a small fragment of it.

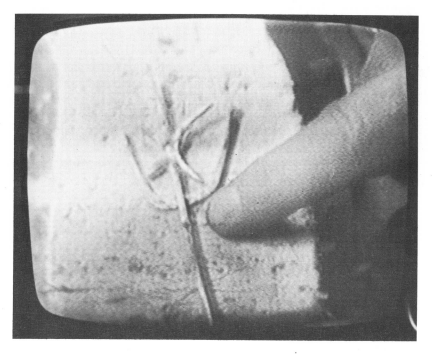

A jewelry demonstration as viewed on the television receivers

(Opposite) In the jewelry laboratory the demonstration by the instructor (left) is clearly seen on the television receivers by the students at their seats.

Such a method has been used to advantage in working from a photograph of tree roots and rocks used as source material for design. The picture seen as a whole gave an impression of great activity, but also of busyness and confusion. By reducing the field of vision with the zoom, thus enlarging a fragment of the area to the entire screen, it was possible to show details. The addition of tracing overlays allowed clear indication of the natural rhythm and diagram balance and the selection of areas for emphasis. As a visual technique for television instruction, the tracing overlay not only allows the instructor to select and draw certain points but also acts as a wholly transparent veil over the surface. We found that the image on the television screen could be clearly seen through tracing paper which, viewed directly under television lighting, had an appearance of milky frost that was difficult to see through. In many instances, the author found it easier to watch the television monitor and draw than to look directly at the pencil and tracing paper. A similar phenomenon was noticed in the three-dimensional demonstration of jewelry soldering. Television lights seem to make the gas-and-air flame almost invisible to the naked eye. But because the camera picks up the action against a darkened background, it is possible with television (using side lighting) to see the flame and follow what it is doing. It has now become standard practice to watch the television screen while soldering—a kind of remote-control soldering, so to speak.

First-person view.   The first-person view of the work—obtained by using the camera over the shoulder of the demonstrator or above the work (if it is on a flat table)—proves an advantage for the student viewer. He is able to put himself in the situation of the demonstrator; the methods used thus become, in a real sense, a part of the viewer's experience.

TELEVISION IN A DIRECTED EXPERIENCE

In the jewelry laboratory the author has used television as a device in a directed-problem presentation where linkage and chain making formed the assignment. The introduction outlined the general problem, while allowing the student time to feel at home with the materials, tools, and finished products before him. The demonstration was divided into many parts: selection of a mandrel, wrapping of wire, cutting, fitting, joining, grouping, soldering, and finishing. Each section was followed by student activity. Such how-to-do-it exercises do not leave much room for creativity, but they do provide a one-time experience which builds a set of skills that can be employed creatively at a later time. Moreover, the individual activity of bending wire, using the saw, working with pliers, and handling the torch were shown to the entire class in a single television presentation. Before the television program was developed, as many as *ten* demonstrations were used to take care of the *same* number of students.

THE NECESSITY FOR ORGANIZATION

The message of an art lesson can be a pure one provided that the theme is set and sequential ideas are developed to a follow-through.

The preplanning required for television presentation usually means that the purpose of the lesson is well organized. The sequence of visuals is planned so that the message is complete. While the instructor can still sense the response to his lesson because the viewers are present in the room with him, the organization allows only a minimum of augmentation. As a result one is inclined to follow through with the complete preplanned outline, thus avoiding the pitfalls of sidetracking.

The television screen is almost inflexible in its demand for well-organized lessons. On one occasion the author was using television to present a lesson in design when a new thought occurred to him. He began to rummage through the piles of photographs and papers that were off camera. For a period of nearly three minutes the class was looking at a blank screen. The punch was lost because the timing was poor. Therefore, it is essential that all materials to be used on camera be well organized and available, so that the presentation moves smoothly and quickly.

When the work is done on a table and the television camera is being operated by the demonstrator, it seems to be a good system to have visual materials in folders which can be moved slowly on camera and, just as slowly, off camera to the other side. All work in front of the camera should be done so that it alone gives the message. If things are thrust in from the side or off camera, they disturb and are at times hard to understand.

SOME CONSIDERATIONS

While the "self"-operation of the television equipment may keep the instructor very busy, it gives him the opportunity to time his work and to move through his presentation as classroom response dictates. With the zoom lens, especially, there is a wide variety of visual impressions which can be executed.

When television is used for such activities as jewelry demonstrations, where three-dimensional objects and physical movement are so demanding as to shot position and treatment of focus and size, it is desirable to have a television technician or cameraman help-

29

ing. Before any presentation is made, a general run-through of what is to be done should be discussed with the operator. The author has found that in addition to the regular lecture a running commentary on what you are trying to put over is helpful for the camera operator.

In working with a cameraman, the demonstrator must watch the monitor as much as ever to be sure that what he says goes with the picture the class sees. Care must be taken, also, to keep the hands out of the way. When the author gave the first demonstration of a jeweler's saw, pliers, and tweezers, the remarks came back that the entire demonstration gave the class the impression that *thumbs* can be posed in many ways—and that thumbs are effective shields against seeing what is going on.

In each of the art classes there may be special considerations which are unique to the particular subject, but *all* the visual arts can gain by its use.

With each new experience television in the classroom is found to be a more versatile tool. During a semester up to one fourth of the demonstrations are done by television. Single-room television is used in conjunction with such traditional tools as the slide projector, movies, chalk-talk demonstration, and displays.

In discussing this application of television with the students we find that most of them are enthusiastic. Chief among their reasons for approval is that television gives them a chance to see in detail what the instructor is doing. A few have objected to the impersonal aspect of "the box," but with the instructor in the same room as the students and therefore able to answer questions as they come up, this reaction seems invalid. Some students just do not like television in any shape or form, but these are few and far between.

CONCLUSIONS

Single-room television has many applications within the art class, both for two- and three-dimensional materials. It may be used in a wide variety of ways to support a lecture visually, magnify demonstrations, show how-to-do-it techniques, reinforce concepts, or provide directed teaching.

If the equipment is available, closed-circuit television is a welcome addition in the art classroom. It is generally easy to use and simple to connect. It lends variety to the instructional program and provides valuable assistance in the transmission of small-detail items that are usually impractical for more than two or three students at a time. Single-room television can dramatically reduce the time required for certain demonstrations by eliminating the need for repetition.

chapter 4

Television in large-group science instruction

Robert L. Hassur

*Over the past few years, spurred on by experimentation with various
redeployment and team teaching plans, many schools have turned to the
large-group lecture as a standard part of the teaching configuration. This
chapter highlights the use of the single-room television camera as but one
of a series of audio-visual tools within a science lecture to several hundred
students.*

Over the past decade there has been a dynamic increase in the use
of the large-group lecture as a teaching technique. This has been
particularly true in the field of science, where the number of
skilled teachers is limited, the time needed to prepare a particular
presentation is often extensive, and the materials required are
often in limited supply. Moreover, team teaching, recently introduced in many schools particularly at the secondary level, necessitates the use of the large-group lecture technique.

The teaching of science under situations of large-group instruction poses many problems because of the great dependence upon
visualization. Many of our basic principles can only be taught by
actual demonstration. For large-group teaching it becomes necessary for the school to purchase or construct large-scale demonstration apparatus. Often the responsibility for construction is left
to the teacher and requires considerable expenditures of time and
effort. Many objects, furthermore, are not easily enlarged without making some sacrifices in accuracy and detail.

When using the conventional magnification techniques, it is
often necessary to turn off the room lights. This handicaps the
instructor and the student, for whom note-taking becomes extremely difficult.

For demonstrating materials to a large group we have several
alternatives. We can eliminate the use of large-scale demonstration
devices and visualization of any kind, but this would have a dis-
astrous effect upon the teaching. We can rely solely upon the standard audio-visual devices now available. With slides, filmstrips,
overhead and microprojectors one can often do an excellent job.
These usually require special equipment and room facilities, as well

Mr. Hassur is Assistant Professor of Science Education at San Jose State College and
has used the single-room television camera extensively within his own teaching and
has also taught in-service science over open-circuit television.

as time to prepare or preview the materials to be used, and in the end they are limited in their potential. A third choice is to combine single-room television with selected audio-visual devices.

USE OF TELEVISION

For the past four years we have been exploring the application of single-room television within our large science classes. For our specific application the lecture hall is arranged in the following manner. The television unit is located next to the instructor in the

In the large lecture room the single-room television camera (arrow) is but one in a series of audio-visual devices used by the instructor.

front of the room (see illustration, page 32). The camera is mounted on a rolling overhead stand which allows for vertical and horizontal adjustment. Two movable lamp brackets with two 150-watt floodlights are connected to the vertical shaft of the stand and usually give more than adequate light. The camera is connected directly to one 17-inch monitor for the instructor's use and to four standard 23-inch receivers for the class. We have found that these sets, when properly located, can adequately serve between 100 and 200 students. There is one on each side of the demonstration table in the front of the lecture hall, while the other two are

The television camera (TVC) is mounted on a movable stand behind the instructor's table. A 17-in. receiver (M) on the table serves as a monitor. Four 23-in. receivers are used, two in front of the room on movable carts and two mounted from the ceiling (see illustration of ceiling mount). Note use of overhead and film projectors.

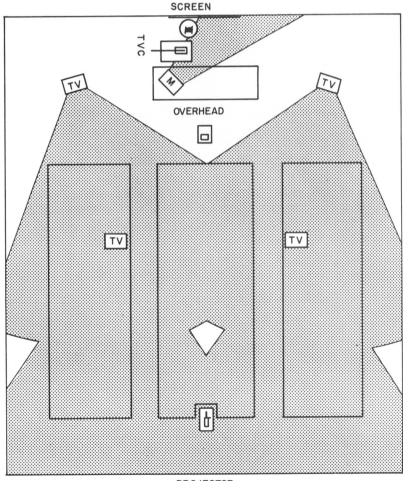

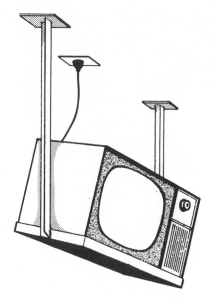

The ceiling mount used within the science lecture hall. Sets are turned on by a switch located in the front of the room. Both ceiling receivers are permanently wired to the instructor's table, where they receive the output line from the television camera.

suspended from ceiling mounts approximately one-third of the way back in the room.

The camera unit is set up and operated by the instructor, who connects and adjusts the unit before the beginning of the period. It is then left turned on with a blank screen ready for use during the class period. Mention should be made of the two lens configurations used. For most demonstrations a zoom lens with its easily adjusted field of vision is preferred. However, we have found that, while easier to operate than a turret head with several single lenses, the zoom lens, by its character, does lose some fine definition. For this reason, when very fine detail is required, in studying rock texture for example, a series of regular lenses is used, usually in a combination of 1-, 2-, and 4-inch focal lengths.

As a rule the instructor is limited to the few minutes between classes for setting up the television equipment. It is therefore imperative that the unit be designed so that it is as simple as possible to set up and operate. The television technicians at the college have been exploring several camera mount designs. The most recent and the most effective has the camera unit and stand mounted permanently on a movable cart. The monitor for the instructor's use is built into the cart and when needed swings up in much the same way as a desk typewriter. To simplify the problem further, the camera unit is preadjusted and all connections between the camera and instructor's monitor already made. This leaves the instructor with only two basic last-minute preparations to make: one, plugging into a 120-volt wall socket for camera, lights, and monitor power, and two, connecting the camera unit to

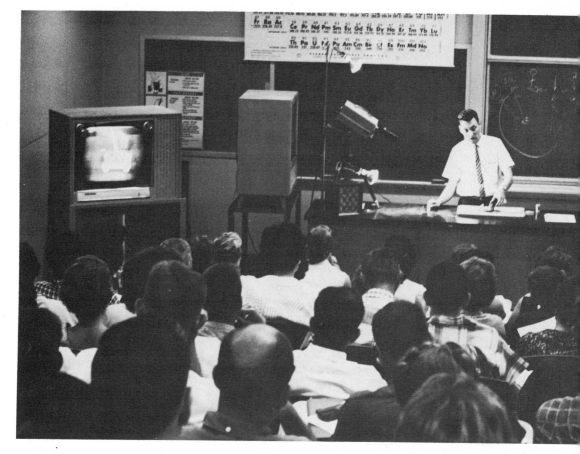

The use of the single-room television camera enables each student to have an unobstructed and detailed view of the small materials being used by the instructor.

the master junction box feeding the four television sets in the classroom.

From experience we have found that the proportion of time devoted to the use of single-room television will vary from lesson to lesson. For some group lectures there will be no practical use for the unit; for others television will be used for a single demonstration lasting no more than a few minutes. Occasionally it will be used continuously. Television has been used both in conjunction with other audio-visual devices and alone.

We have found single-room television to have both advantages and disadvantages. On occasion, a presentation we thought ideal for television proved impractical because of difficulty in manipulation, poor color contrast, technical limitations—for a variety of reasons. Others, given little chance for success, proved to be highly effective and an exciting addition to our instructional program.

35

SUCCESSFUL APPLICATIONS

Perhaps the best way to indicate the advantages of the single-room television system is to cite a few examples of how in several science areas it improved the overall instruction.

Biology. In the study of human physiology the television unit was used to demonstrate the use of a standard sphygmomanometer in measuring blood pressure. Close-ups of the equipment and the method of attaching the cuff to the patient were effectively

Television is used to show a wide variety of materials within many subject areas.

The gooseneck barnacle

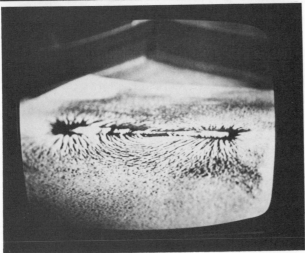

The magnetic lines of force around a bar magnet

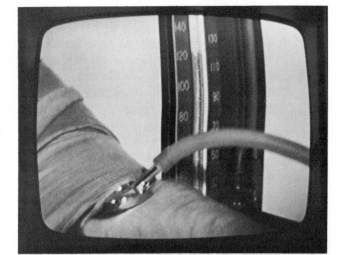

The technique of measuring blood pressure

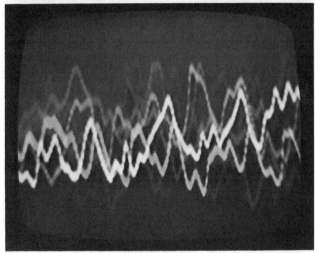

Sound waves on an oscilloscope

The effect of water temperature on
dissolving sugar cubes

shown. A special microphone was attached to the stethoscope used by the instructor, which enabled the students to see the pressure change on the manometer and also to hear the change in the sound of the pulsebeat when the diastolic and systolic pressures were reached (see illustration, page 37). Every one of the students in the large lecture hall could actually record the blood pressure of the subject as if they were taking it themselves. Normally when working with small groups this same exercise requires an hour or more for the instructor, each student sharing a number of expensive instruments. With television, less than fifteen minutes is required.

Physiology. An area in the field of physiology in which the television system was found to be very helpful was a demonstration of the techniques for typing human blood. The television camera was used for close-ups of the microscope slide preparation. Then the camera was coupled with a standard microscope with extra-bright substage illumination. In this way the students got a lab-technician's-eye view of the clotting of blood in response to the testing serums. The student response was overwhelming. Actually seeing the blood cells clotting was much more effective than all the blackboard and flannelgraph diagrams in the world.

Physical sciences. The effect of the temperature of a solvent on the dissolving rate of a solid was very effectively shown by the television system. A close-up was shown of two labeled beakers, one of hot and the other of room-temperature water (see illustration, page 37). Sugar cubes were added, and students could time the rate of breakdown and solution of the sugar in each container.

To demonstrate single-replacement reactions in chemistry usually calls for a large-scale operation with great quantities of solutions. Using the television system, on the other hand, standard, even semimicro, glassware is sufficient. Adding a coil of copper wire to a crystal-clear solution of silver nitrate produces in a few minutes mounds of white mossy silver forming on the wire as the entire solution darkens with copper nitrate.

Physics. In the field of physics the television system makes possible many demonstrations which would normally be far too small to be attempted in a large lecture hall. These include a study of the air currents around a candle flame in a convection box. Dense smoke introduced into the system could be seen to rise above the candle as cooler air laden with smoke rushed in from all sides to take its place.

Televising the oscilloscope trace of a sound which the students can also hear is an easy way of showing the relationships between its frequency and pitch and the amplitude and volume of sounds.

The presentation of Ohm's law, a basic concept of electricity, to large groups of students is more easily done by utilizing the magnification potential of the single-room television system. Using a simple resistance board and inexpensive lab-type meters, students can easily record, by means of television, sufficient data to derive the equation for Ohm's law. This same technique would be nearly impossible without television; that is, unless huge, very expensive demonstration meters, visible from the back of the room, were available for use.

Climatology.   In the study of weather perhaps the most difficult area of instruction is the construction of weather maps and their use in weather prediction. Using television as an opaque projector, weather maps—isobars, fronts, and all—can be constructed, starting with a blank weather map. Of course this can also be done with transparencies on an overhead projector. Where television really has the advantage is that the latest weather map, hot off the presses, can be placed in front of the camera, and each student can examine it under the direction of the instructor's pointer. Transparencies for the opaque projector, on the other hand, take some time to prepare.

ADVANTAGES

Among the advantages of the television medium for large-class instruction are its great flexibility of use and the fact that it can and should be used with full room illumination. With simple modifications the basic camera setup can be switched from wide-field magnification to very close up. With high magnification each student can get an almost firsthand view of the specimen, instead of being content with squinting halfway across the room at a shiny plaster model.

In addition to simple magnification the television system can easily be used with full room illumination as an opaque projector, as a high quality microprojector, and as an overhead projector. This is not to say that all other audio-visual devices are now outmoded, for many of the specially designed devices such as an overhead projector are better than the television system.

LIMITATIONS

In our experimentation and use of single-room television we have had our successes and our failures. With added experience we have been able to gain a better understanding of this new teaching tool, and with this understanding has come an awareness of its limitations and problems.

The instructor problem. For all instructors, television is a new device for use within the classroom. It seems foreign and strange when first used. The average instructor has taken several periods of use to become accustomed to the technical details. We have found that for some this adjustment has been simple and almost immediate, for others much more difficult.

It is imperative that the instructor prepare much of his demonstration in advance. Many of the materials must be pretested on the television camera. This is particularly true when using high magnification, the microscope, or very shiny materials—all of which require special lighting. It is therefore important that the instructor allow himself enough time to complete these final preparations.

Technical assistance. Although equipment problems have been few and far between, and the teacher himself usually operates the unit, there have been several times when skilled technicians were required. This may involve special lighting, special lenses, or the use of audio-visual equipment in conjunction with television. In the ideal situation a technician will be available to assist the instructor during the setup period when help is required.

The skilled technician can also be of invaluable assistance in training the instructors in the use of the equipment. This training program deals with such problems as lighting, set adjustment, lens selection, and proper camera angles.

Lighting. While lighting problems were generally simple, there have been times when direction and angle were critical for contrast. This was particularly true of preserved specimens, where lighting was made more complex by glare from the containers. We have found it advisable to remove the specimen from the bottle or, when possible, to have it in a flat-sided glass container.

It has continually been amazing to those of us using the television camera how important and how critical the lighting problem can be. There are numerous instances where moving a light an inch or two in one direction will spell the difference between a clear picture and a vague outline. When using glossy prints under the camera, we have been able to eliminate the glare by placing a small piece of nonglare glass on top of the picture. While not noticeably dimming the illustration, it did eliminate lighting problems caused by glare. Dulling spray has also proved effective in reducing glare, but care must be taken in using it on models and specimens so as not to damage the finish.

Color. Obviously there are times when color is a basic ingredient for the success of any demonstration. This is particularly true of many chemical demonstrations and enlargements of colored pictures or models. For this reason there are many times when television just cannot be used. One way around this problem is to select chemicals or illustrations whose colors are distinguishable as shades of gray. Or, particularly with chemical reactions, the large containers of colored chemicals can be shown to the class as the demonstration proceeds. We have found that with a little help from the instructor the students are able to make a mental color interpretation of the black and white television images.

TELEVISION USED WITH OTHER AIDS

The television camera has become an integral piece of audio-visual equipment in our science lecture hall, and as such is rarely used alone. It has been indicated before that quite often an instructor will use the television camera along with slides, film clips, and the overhead projector. While the television unit can act as an overhead projector when set up with a light box, it is often too time-consuming to change from a series of close-ups of several specimens on the television camera to a light box that necessitates camera movement to cover the entire field. It is much simpler to move to an overhead projector, already set up, that has the added advantage of color. But we must admit that as an audio-visual medium, television is very flexible and of great potential.

From our experience there is little doubt that single-room television has helped us approach the ideal 1:1 ratio of pupil to teacher that we try hard to achieve in our science lectures. What its long-range role in the instructional pattern will be we do not know. However, we expect that as more effective techniques for its use are discovered it will become as standard a piece of equipment for most lecture halls as a slide or motion-picture projector.

part II

Studio television

T HE BASIC PROBLEM facing education today is one of logistics: more information to teach, more students to teach it to, with relatively fewer teachers to do the teaching. The most dynamic applications of instructional television have been designed to help cope with this problem. The specific uses and the complexity of the operations have varied greatly from district to district, but the rationale behind the uses of television is generally consistent:

1. Delegating to television those particular aspects of courses that can be effectively presented on the TV screen makes it possible to reduce markedly the amount of duplicated effort on the part of teachers and to increase time teachers can spend working with small groups or individual students.
2. Television permits a more effective utilization of available specialists.
3. Television allows for improved utilization of the specific talents of the individual teacher within a district by allowing for specialization.
4. There are basic advantages inherent in television teaching that can effectively improve a particular presentation (see pages 49 to 55).
5. Video tape and kinescope allow for the storing and retelecasting of outstanding presentations that would otherwise be lost or unviewed.
6. Once television is in use, there are other applications that, while not of primary concern, can directly affect efficiency within the district.

However, studio production, when done well, takes time, talent, and, obviously, money. For example, one half-hour telecast was analyzed as to the time required to put it together. Involved were the television teacher, producer, director, visualization specialist, engineer, and several student assistants. While this particular lesson, in elementary school science, may have been more complicated than many, it certainly could not be considered far out of the ordinary. The hours involved were as follows:

Preparation time for single half-hour telecast

	Hours
Television teacher	22
Producer	13½
Director	12½
Visualization specialist (graphic artist–photographer)	20
Engineer*	8
Student assistants†	15
Total hours	91

* Time includes setup and teardown of set.
† Includes two cameramen, floorman, and assistants for the visualization specialist.

Not only is there the expense of staff time involved, but there are also the expenses of graphic-photographic supplies and of equipment maintenance and depreciation. Many of these costs can be cut; the director-producer function can be combined, the amount of visual assistance reduced, and the number of rehearsals limited. However, such reductions must not be made at the expense of well-prepared, stimulating lessons.

The administrator wishing to use studio presentations as part of his program has two alternatives. He can join with other school districts in the use of an existing local community or educational television station, or he can develop his own studio operation.

Programming available through the local station is perhaps the best educational buy for the dollar now available to most school districts. At a nominal yearly charge (normally ranging from 75 cents to $1.50 per registered pupil) the district can receive an entire range of in-school telecasts. Often of the highest quality and prepared by centers in many parts of the country, such series will cover a wide variety of topics on many grade levels. Along with the in-school telecasts, teachers using the lessons within their classrooms will receive study guides for each series and often will have an opportunity of viewing telecasts designed specifically to help them utilize the prepared programs. For this fee the school district may receive weekly as many as twenty series and over forty individual programs.

For some school districts, the community or educational station may not be available. Moreover, in areas where there is a station, the district may find that it needs programs that are not available, or the station's coverage may not meet specific local curriculum, administrative, or scheduling problems. Any existing community-wide station must limit its coverage, obviously, to those particular areas where there is basic curriculum agreement among participating districts.

Since high-quality studio production does take time and cost money, the administrator contemplating the development of a district-operated facility must estimate in advance the cost of the project, and then equate this expenditure with other possible alternatives.

Every television operation has a "break-even" point, a point at which the total cost per viewing student is equal to the cost for the same basic lesson when taught under standard classroom procedures. The number of students needed to reach this point may be as low as 150 or as high as 1,000 or more, depending upon the complexity and staffing of the project.

The administrator exploring the potential of television within his district must determine first his educational objectives, and second, the type of installation he will need (see Appendix B) and the required staffing. Quite often a comprehensive studio operation will simply be too expensive for a particular school district. When this proves to be the case, the district can still explore the single-room applications as discussed in Part I.

The following chapters present the experiences of school districts, often facing the same basic problems, using television in a wide variety of ways. Chapters 5 and 6 are examples of effective closed-circuit operations, one on the district level, the other state-wide. In Chapter 7 the superintendent of a financially distressed district describes a television operation that has proved to be a major factor in solving certain basic instructional problems. The reasons one district turned to the local community station rather than develop its own production center are covered in Chapter 8, while Chapter 9 provides an example of a district which took the opposite approach and developed its own educational station.

Chapter 10 highlights the various applications of television within a district-wide guidance program. The final chapter in this section, "Television in the Secondary School," explains how one district has used television within its secondary program, an area where scheduling problems have often curtailed the use of television.

An attempt has been made to include the widest assortment of successful applications, both open- and closed-circuit, in school districts both large and small, rich and poor. The number of students involved ranges from a few hundred to several thousand. In each case the application has proved both educationally and financially sound to the individual school district concerned, to its teachers, and to its administrators.

PICTORIAL ESSAY

When given enough time for preparation, the television teacher can locate all the materials that will assist in the presentation of a lesson.

The teacher has the use of such devices as the magnetic chalkboard . . .

and movable acetate overlays.

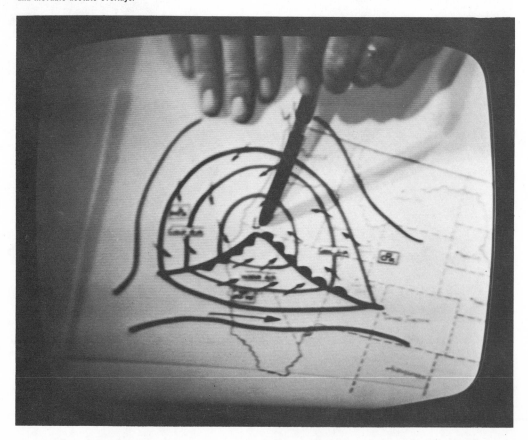

The television teacher has the inherent advantage of television itself, image magnification.

Studio television

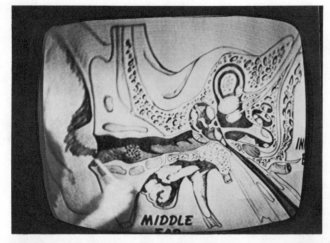

The television teacher has the assistance of skilled graphic personnel. Films and slides are prepared as they are needed, and many complicated charts can be simplified to emphasize the material being highlighted by the teacher.

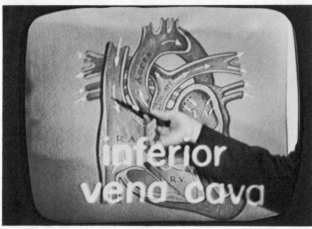

With television there is the potential of using supers to reinforce terms or definitions.

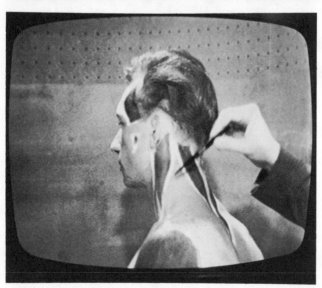

The creative graphic artist may develop special techniques for a particular lesson. Muscles are actually painted on an individual to demonstrate body movement and leverage.

An overhead camera technique was developed that enabled the television teacher to teach sentence structure and punctuation by manipulating words and punctuation.

And, finally, television means that the talent and creativity of the finest teachers may be combined with a skilled production team to provide the best possible presentation to an unlimited number of students.

(Anaheim School District)

(Opposite, above) The television teacher also has the support of outstanding guests and specialists who are usually unavailable to the classroom teacher. (Dr. Guatelli, IBM, Plainedge Public Schools)

(Opposite, below) When video tape is used, the teacher has the opportunity to redo a particular part of a lesson and thus to improve its quality and effectiveness. (South Carolina Educational Television Center)

chapter 5

The Anaheim approach
to closed-circuit television

Robert E. Shanks

A successful television project is dependent upon many factors. Paramount among these is careful planning and sound educational objectives. In this chapter a highly effective operation is comprehensively described.

In Anaheim, California, the Anaheim Instructional Television Project is now in its fifth year, having been successfully launched on September 14, 1959, after some eighteen months of extensive study, planning, and preparation. Although school plant needs, teacher shortages, growing class sizes, shrinking school dollars, and soaring school enrollments were integral parts of the total school picture in Anaheim in 1958 (see table below), it is important to note that the board of education did not embark upon a program of instructional television with the thought that television could be used as a panacea for all their problems.

The Anaheim elementary school district growth pattern*

	1950	1960
City area, sq mi	5	30
City population	15,000	130,000
Schools K–6	5	20†
Pupils K–6	1,700	15,200‡

* Figures approximate for convenient presentation.
† Additional schools under construction or in planning stages, 1962–1963.
‡ Does not include grades 7–8, transferred to junior high program in 1954.

The decisions (1) to investigate the possibilities inherent in the use of television for instructional purposes, and later on (2) to invest district funds in this direction, were based upon an expressed wish of the school board to expend a reasonable allotment of each year's budgeted funds (from 3 to 5 per cent) in one definite direc-

Mr. Shanks is Superintendent of the Anaheim School District.

tion in a continuing effort to improve the quality of the educational program. School board members noted that in business and industry it has proved worthwhile to devote from 3 to 5 per cent of yearly expenditures for research and experimentation to improve the quality of the product, and concluded that the same principle might profitably be applied to the management of school district finances. A well-planned experimental effort, in other words, might be expected to improve the quality of the educational product.

The idea that television might be useful as a teaching tool had been briefly discussed by various members of the school board as early as 1955 and 1956. Thus the idea was not entirely new when, in the autumn of 1957, board member Arval Morris suggested that educational television be seriously considered for the Anaheim elementary school system and, with growing interest, the board members thereafter discussed this proposal on a number of occasions.

EXPLORING AND PLANNING FOR TELEVISION

In April, 1958, two of the district's board members and the district superintendent attended the National School Boards Convention at Miami Beach, Florida, primarily because the matter of educational television had been included in the program. While there they observed a demonstration of teaching by television presented by the Dade County, Florida, public schools; and also heard Dr. Alexander J. Stoddard, Consultant to the Ford Foundation's Fund for the Advancement of Education, speak regarding the potentials of television for the schools.

Reports presented at subsequent school board meetings regarding what had been learned at the Miami convention led to a recommendation by Mr. Morris and unanimous action by the board of education directing the superintendent to investigate the cost factors and the feasibility of providing for the installation of a closed-circuit television system. (A brief summary of the developmental steps will be found in the table on page 58.)

During this period, many activities that were to play a basic role in the final success of the project were under way. All available publications on instructional television were carefully studied. A series of staff meetings examined in detail the role of television within the total learning process. Course study outlines were developed for those subjects in which television was to be used. Later meetings defined the role of the project director, production staff, studio teacher, classroom teachers, and building principals. An outgrowth of these meetings was the set of handbooks developed for classroom and television teachers (see Bibliography).

As administrators, supervisors, and teachers explored instructional television, basic objectives for the Anaheim television proj-

57

Chronological development of the television project in the Anaheim school district

July, 1958—Superintendent reports on feasibility and cost estimate study. In principle, plan for closed-circuit television system approved. Further study of ways and means authorized.

October, 1958—Electronic consultant firm retained. Authorization given for superintendent and assistant superintendent to investigate and visit instructional television operations then in use (included trips to 9 districts in all sections of the country).

November, 1958—Administrators report on survey, on the Stoddard Plan for redeployment, and on the Ford Foundation's National Program for the Use of Television in the Public Schools. Modification for Anaheim's use suggested and recommendations made for grant applications to be submitted to Ford Foundation and to Title III and VII of the NDEA.

December, 1958—Final plans and specifications for district-wide closed-circuit television system being completed by superintendent.

February, 1959—Instructional television project director appointed and authorized to visit school districts currently using instructional television.

March–April, 1959—Application for grants to Ford Foundation and NDEA Title III submitted. Formal approval of instructional television project for 1959–1960 school year given by school board. Administrative arrangements and selection of television teachers and other specialized personnel begun. Contract signed for installation and maintenance of coaxial cabling connecting studio to all schools.

May, 1959—Ten district personnel attend National Workshop on Educational Television.

June–July, 1959—Final plans and specifications completed, approved, bids accepted and awarded. Construction begins. (Contract includes studio equipment, 175 television receivers, on-site cabling, and one-year maintenance of system.)

August, 1959—Employment of television teachers, production personnel, and selected classroom teachers for participation in summer television training workshop. School of Education, University of California, contracted to carry on comprehensive testing and evaluation program of television project.

September, 1959—First lesson televised.

---

ect were developed and identified. Generally these fell into three broad categories:

1. Improvement of instruction with emphasis on the areas of science, social studies, mathematics, and conversational Spanish.
2. Identification and utilization of the unique characteristics of television when used (a) as an integral part of the teaching-learning process, (b) to improve staff communications, and (c) for expanding in-service education.
3. Exploration and application of a redeployment plan to improve instruction and to make more efficient use of staff and facilities.

PROJECT ORGANIZATION

The project itself was organized as follows. For the first year it was decided to use television only on the fourth- and fifth-grade levels. Five elementary schools were selected for the redeployment plan, primarily because the principals of these schools seemed particularly fitted to assume the supervision of the new program. At these schools, large classes were to receive the televised instruction and related classroom teaching, and unusually small classes were to be established for the same pupils for instruction in the basic elementary school subjects: reading, arithmetic, spelling, handwriting, and written and oral language. At seven other schools, the same televised instruction was to be received by pupils in regular sized classrooms. While the curriculum content was to be the same, in the district's five remaining schools no television instruction was to be provided, enabling the research group to use these schools as "control classes."

The redeployment plan. The redeployment plan represents a marked departure from the traditional arrangement of the elementary school day for our fourth- and fifth-grade pupils and their teachers. It involves a regrouping and redeployment of pupils and teachers for instructional purposes. It makes use of televised lesson presentations as a regularly scheduled aid to teachers of large groups and as an integral part of the total instructional program in these large classes where pupils spend a portion of their school day. The redeployment plan has made it financially possible for the district to establish unusually small instructional groups (the skills classes) in order to provide more individual instruction in the basic elementary school subjects for these same pupils (see table, page 60).

The audio-visual classroom, for the large classes, is at least twice the size of a regular classroom. In addition to regular classroom equipment—tables, chairs, text materials, maps, globes, and science equipment—it is provided with an overhead projector, record player, slide projector, tape recorder, opaque projector, microphone connected with the television receiver amplifying systems, and from four to six 24-inch television receivers (see illustration, page 61).

The two teachers in the audio-visual resource classroom are responsible for providing instruction in social studies (history, geography, and civics), science, conversational Spanish, physical education, health, safety, fire prevention, music, and art. In the skills classrooms the three skills teachers provide instruction in the basic elementary school subjects.

The redeployment plan answers one of the perplexing problems that have plagued elementary schools for many years, that of pro-

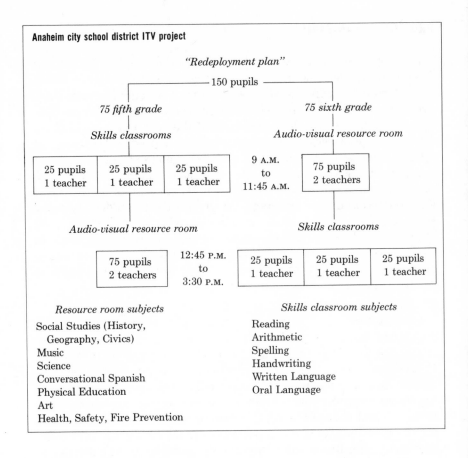

Anaheim city school district ITV project

"Redeployment plan"

——— 150 pupils ———

75 fifth grade   *75 sixth grade*

Skills classrooms   *Audio-visual resource room*

| 25 pupils 1 teacher | 25 pupils 1 teacher | 25 pupils 1 teacher | 9 A.M. to 11:45 A.M. | 75 pupils 2 teachers |

Audio-visual resource room   *Skills classrooms*

| 75 pupils 2 teachers | 12:45 P.M. to 3:30 P.M. | 25 pupils 1 teacher | 25 pupils 1 teacher | 25 pupils 1 teacher |

Resource room subjects   *Skills classroom subjects*

Social Studies (History,
  Geography, Civics)
Music
Science
Conversational Spanish
Physical Education
Art
Health, Safety, Fire Prevention

Reading
Arithmetic
Spelling
Handwriting
Written Language
Oral Language

viding a smaller pupil-teacher ratio for teaching the basic three R's without greatly increasing the cost per pupil and without creating a need for additional classrooms. Further, the plan provides a partial answer to the problem of teacher work load by dividing almost in half the number of subjects for which the teacher in the redeployment plan must make daily lesson preparation. At the same time, it brings teachers together far more effectively to exchange ideas and to learn from each other as they team up to make the most of their teaching talents.

STAFF AND COMMUNITY PREPARATION

It was recognized that success or failure of the Anaheim project would be dependent upon the way in which the project was introduced to teachers, parents, and the community at large. In the spring of 1959, a number of training meetings were held with the principals of the redeployment plan schools under the direction of the project director. It was the principal who would provide leadership within the individual school.

In the resource room the teacher has the use of maps, globes, large charts, and various types of projectors. (Anaheim School District)

Television teacher selection.   Early in the planning stages it was decided that every effort should be made to select television teachers and production personnel from among the district's teaching staff. Teachers selected were to be released full-time from all other teaching duties.

In April a memorandum announcing the openings was distributed to all certified personnel. About twenty teachers applied for the six studio teaching positions when tryouts were held in May, 1959. Applicants were required to plan for and present a complete televised lesson based upon assigned lesson topics and objectives. The teachers were given complete freedom as to teaching method and approaches, thereby best demonstrating imagination and creativity in using television as a teaching medium. A committee consisting of the superintendent, assistant superintendent, project director, curriculum assistant, and two principals observed each lesson and made the final selection. A similar selection committee interviewed applicants for the large-class teaching assignments, and for the small "skills classes" that were to be established as part of the redeployment plan.

Summer workshop. The first workshop for studio teachers, production personnel, and selected classroom teachers was held the following August. During this period lesson plans were completed and mimeographed for distribution. Television teachers practiced before the cameras, and the production team familiarized themselves with the technical aspects of the operation.

Staff orientation. During the four-day preschool orientation program, held immediately preceding the opening of school, a sample telecast was presented, teacher handbooks were distributed, and the role of the classroom teacher in introducing and following up the telecast with related classroom teaching was explained and reviewed in detail. Teachers who had attended the summer workshop played a key role in these meetings.

Community orientation. As the project developed, the superintendent and other administrative officers took full advantage of every opportunity to explain the television project to parents and patrons in simple, direct, honest ways. A full report was given by the superintendent at an early PTA council meeting. While the council was kept informed of all subsequent developments, talks were given at the PTA meetings held in the individual schools. A letter explaining the redeployment plan, and the changes that were to be made, was sent to the parents of students who were to be involved. This letter invited the parents to attend a special meeting, held at each participating school, where the plan and the use of television were to be carefully explained. Attendance at these meetings was excellent.

Since the inception of the project in the fall of 1959, parents and all other patrons of the district have been encouraged to come to the schools, or to the studio building, to see for themselves how television is being used as part of the overall instructional program. Newspaper reporters have been encouraged to spend a day in the district viewing the project, and numerous guided tours have been arranged for interested community groups. Demonstrations of television teaching were presented for parents at all the schools during the district's annual parent-teacher group conferences in October, 1959, and again each succeeding year.

It has been the policy of the district to let the parents and citizens decide for themselves the value of the project. The simple adage that "Good teaching will sell itself, whether on television or in the classroom" has proved true repeatedly.

INSTRUCTIONAL TELEVISION: THE ANAHEIM APPROACH

From its beginnings, when the telecasts were limited to pupils in grades 4 and 5 at twelve schools, the project has grown each year

Anaheim city school district
ITV project telecast schedule
school year 1962–1963

Grade 3

Channel 3	Monday	Tuesday	Wednesday	Thursday	Friday
10:45	Social Studies	Science	Social Studies	Science	Social Studies
1:20	Music		Arithmetic		

Grade 4

Channel 3	Monday	Tuesday	Wednesday	Thursday	Friday
10:00		Music			
12:55	Spanish I	Spanish I	Spanish I	Arithmetic	Spanish I
2:10	Science	Social Studies	Science	Social Studies	Social Studies

Grade 5

Channel 6	Monday	Tuesday	Wednesday	Thursday	Friday
12:55	Science	Social Studies	Science	Social Studies	Social Studies
1:45			Music		
2:30	Spanish II	Spanish II		Spanish II	Spanish II

Grade 6

Channel 6	Monday	Tuesday	Wednesday	Thursday	Friday
9:15	Social Studies	Science	Social Studies	Science	Social Studies
10:00				Music	
11:15	Spanish III	Spanish III	Spanish III		Spanish III

and now provides televised instruction in a larger number of subject areas for all pupils in grades 3 to 6 at all of the district's twenty schools.

Related classroom and televised instruction is provided in a wide variety of subject areas for grades 3 to 6, as shown in the above table. The televised lesson presentations vary in length from about ten to twenty-five or sometimes as much as thirty minutes. Each telelesson is designed to serve as an integral part of the overall lesson and study for the school day in the particular subject involved, and to be preceded and followed by appropriate classroom instruction.

The good instructional telecast, we believe, takes full advantage of the unique audio-visual characteristics of the television medium, leaving to the classroom situation those things best taught and learned in the conventional classroom situation, and assigning to the television medium those parts of the total teaching-learning process that are appropriate to the television medium. Thus the good instructional telecast is audio-visual in nature. It features the use of audio-visual devices. Maps, charts, globes, pictures, graphs, film clips, slides, models and exhibits, dramatizations, demonstrations, resource visitors, and all other means that can be used to illustrate and demonstrate are characteristics of the good televised lesson presentation.

Each classroom teacher receives a telelesson guidesheet about two or three weeks prior to each telelesson presentation. The telelesson guidesheet is prepared by the studio teacher under the direction of the project director and is approved by the project director before being mimeographed. It contains a statement of the lesson purpose, suggestions for classroom preparation prior to the telecast, a brief description of the nature of the telelesson presentation, and suggestions for related follow-up classroom instruction.

From time to time classroom teachers are encouraged to complete a Telelesson Reaction Form and to send it to the project director and the studio teachers (see Appendix E). The Telelesson Reaction Form, or feedback sheet, is important in maintaining good two-way communications between the studio teachers and the classroom teachers.

During the first year of the project, instructional planning groups made up of principals and teachers were formed to evaluate the year-long effort and to make recommendations for the improvement of instruction in each of the televised subject areas for the coming school year. These groups have been established each subsequent year and, as a result of their recommendations, a number of changes have been made in the project and in the scope and sequence outlines upon which the telelesson guidesheets are based. Studio teachers as well as principals often serve as chairmen of these groups. Interested classroom teachers who volunteer for service are appointed as members of the instructional planning groups.

All telecasts are produced in the district's closed-circuit television studio building by a studio staff which now includes eight production workers and eleven television teachers. The majority of the members of the studio staff were formerly district classroom

(Opposite, above) The key member of the Anaheim teaching team is the classroom teacher, who must prepare the students for television and then, at the completion of the televised lesson, review, provide enrichment, and do those things that can best be done when the teacher and the student work together. (Anaheim School District)

(Opposite, below) Often, during the telecast, students will be asked questions or requested to perform some activity under the direction of their classroom teacher. (Anaheim School District)

teachers. All, except for a general assistant and a graphic artist, hold teaching credentials and have a background of teaching experience. The district has continued to hold tryouts for all television teaching positions each year, selecting for studio teaching duties those who in every way seem to demonstrate the best available potentialities as television teachers.

The telelesson presentations during the 1962–1963 school year were received by some 2,150 third graders in 67 different conventionally organized self-contained classrooms; by 2,100 fourth graders in 62 such classrooms; by 1,404 fifth graders in 41 similarly organized classrooms; and by 1,271 sixth graders in 38 such classrooms. Two 24-inch television receivers are provided for each of these classrooms (see illustration, page 65). In this traditional self-contained classroom pattern for the organization of the elementary school, the same classroom teacher provides instruction in all subjects and works with the same assigned group throughout the school day. (Average class size in the district's third-, fourth-, fifth-, and sixth-grade self-contained classrooms is from 33 to 34 pupils per teacher at the present time.)

The same televised lessons received by fifth- and sixth-grade pupils in the self-contained classrooms were also received in the large audio-visual resource room by some 669 additional fifth-grade pupils and 687 additional sixth-grade pupils in groups of from 64 to 86.

STRETCHING THE SCHOOL DOLLAR

To maintain the traditional self-contained organization pattern and reduce average class size to 25 pupils each for the district's 3,700 fifth and sixth graders would require the use of 148 regular-sized classrooms and the assignment of 148 classroom teachers. By the use of television and our redeployment plan we can establish 25-student classes for all these students in the basic subjects, where small classes are most needed, by using only 126 regular-sized classrooms, 123 classroom and 6 television teachers. The differences in the two plans, in terms of required annual expenditures for salaries of teachers and in terms of additional classroom construction costs, are considerable (see table, page 67).

At one of the schools where the redeployment plan was established in 1959, a largely unused school auditorium has been put into use as an audio-visual resource room, thus gaining additional housing for pupils equal to that which would be provided by building at least two additional regular-sized self-contained classrooms. This represents an outright saving to the district of at least $36,000, estimating the present cost of building a permanent regular-sized classroom at $18,000.

Stretching the school dollar at Anaheim (some examples)

Objective: 25 students per classroom in the basic subjects (3,700 students, grades 5 and 6)

Needed	Standard techniques	Redeployment	Saving	Dollar saving
Classrooms	148	126	22	$396,000*
Teachers	148	129	19	115,000
		Total		$511,000

Objective: Better plant utilization

As television project expands to additional 5 schools with existing cafetoriums or auditoriums these plants will be able to house, in addition to their present enrollment, enough students to fill a new 12-classroom school (plant and site saving $435,000).

Objective: A comprehensive conversational Spanish program (6,000 students, grades 4, 5, and 6)

Needed	Standard techniques	Television	Saving	Dollar saving
Teachers	20 (impossible to locate)	3	17	$102,000

Objective: Music instruction for over 8,200 students, one period per week

Needed	Standard techniques	Television	Saving	Dollar saving
Teachers	10	1	9	$54,000 (plus travel expenses)

PLUS: **ALL THE ADVANTAGES THAT ARE INHERENT WITH HIGH-QUALITY TELEVISION INSTRUCTION.**

* Not including the cost of an additional school site which would also be needed.

At four other schools where minor remodeling work was done in 1959 to provide resource rooms and establish the redeployment plan, twenty-four groups of fifth and sixth graders are receiving instruction in the basic elementary school subjects in groups of twenty-five each. To accomplish this by conventional means would have required twenty-four regular-sized classrooms. With the establishment of the redeployment plan at these four schools, this is being accomplished in the equivalent of twenty regular classroom spaces (each of the remodeled audio-visual resource rooms being the size of two regular classrooms). By utilizing five available cafetoriums and auditoriums not now being used as instructional spaces at five of the district's schools where the redeployment plan has not yet been established, the Anaheim district can realize additional housing for pupils equal to that which would be provided by building a new twelve-classroom school on an additional elementary school site. To do this will provide an outright dollar saving in school plant and school site costs of at least $435,000. In terms of sound, businesslike school management, this seems worthy of serious consideration, provided the overall quality of the educational program is maintained and even strengthened by so doing.

Through the use of the closed-circuit television facilities, systematic instruction in conversational Spanish is being made available to more than 6,000 pupils in the fourth, fifth, and sixth grades of the Anaheim district. Three highly talented, truly bilingual teachers are providing the basic instruction via television at a salary cost to the district of approximately $18,000 annually. Not only would it be impossible to locate the large number of language teachers necessary to provide the same instruction by conventional means, but the cost of the instruction in terms of salaries and transportation expenses for such teachers (who would be required to travel around the district to do this teaching) would be practically prohibitive. By conventional means it would take at least twenty teachers to provide equal instruction at a cost of $120,000 per year.

Systematic, specialized instruction in elementary school science is also currently being provided in the Anaheim district for all pupils in grades 3 to 6 by two highly trained television teachers. In addition, classroom music instruction for more than 8,200 pupils is provided for one period each week, utilizing the services of one highly skilled music teacher. On the basis of present enrollment figures it would require ten such teachers to provide the same instruction by conventional traveling teacher means and, once again, provision would need to be made in the budget for the salaries and traveling expenses of the nine additional music teachers. One competent specialist in elementary school arithmetic provides special instruction in this subject for all third- and fourth-grade pupils to strengthen, supplement, and enrich the basic arithmetic instruction in the classrooms of these pupils.

COSTS OF THE PROJECT

Total expenditures for the instructional television project from the district's 1959–1960, 1960–1961, and 1961–1962 general fund budgets amounted to $586,069, or about 4½ per cent of all expenditures from the general fund during these three fiscal years. Of this amount, a total of $144,000 represented $94,000 in grants from the Ford Foundation and $50,000 in matching funds received from the Federal government for purchase of television equipment under the terms of Title III of the National Defense Education Act. Thus the net general fund expenditures for the project from the district's regular sources of funds during these three fiscal years amounted to $442,069, or about 3½ per cent of total general fund expenditures during these years (see table, page 72).

Total expenditures for television and other project-related equipment, studio facilities, and conduit installation, along with other capital outlay expenditures for the project from the district's building fund in these same fiscal years, amounted to $555,079, not including additional matching funds which were received, allotted to the building fund in 1960–1961 and 1961–1962, and expended to a total of $79,852 under the continuing terms of Title III of the National Defense Education Act (see table, page 73).

Since the project began in 1959, the district's yearly cost per pupil in average daily attendance has remained below the similar average cost per pupil for all elementary districts in booming Orange County, where the district is located, and it is substantially below the statewide average for California elementary districts (see table, page 74). The district's assessed valuation per pupil in average daily attendance is roughly at the midpoint for elementary districts in California.

EVALUATION

Procedures. Under the direction of Dr. Welty Lefever of the School of Education of the University of Southern California, plans were carefully developed to carry on a district-wide testing program and to conduct a continuous evaluation of the success of the television project. To allow for evaluation, students were divided by teaching-learning situations into three groups:

1. In regular-sized, conventionally organized classes by means of *related classroom and televised instruction* (regular TV classes)
2. In the redeployment plan large-sized classes by means of *related classroom and televised instruction* (redeployment TV classes)
3. In regular-sized, conventionally organized classes that *did not receive* the televised instruction (non-TV classes or "control classes")

The telelesson guidesheets prepared for each lesson were made available to *all* fourth- and fifth-grade teachers, including the teachers of the nontelevision classes.

During the first year of the project the effectiveness of the instruction in the three kinds of teaching-learning situations for grades 4 and 5 was measured and compared by means of specially constructed objective tests covering the basic curriculum content as outlined for instruction in science, social studies, Spanish, and arithmetic enrichment; the gains in achievement made by the pupils during the school year were measured from standardized

69

tests of the basic elementary school subjects: reading, arithmetic, spelling, and mechanics of English. The California Tests of Achievement were used for this purpose.

The specially constructed, or district-developed, objective tests therefore provided the data used to make direct comparisons between pupil achievement in those subjects taught conventionally, without televised instruction, and those taught with the aid of televised instruction. The data obtained by giving all pupils the California Tests of Achievement (standardized tests) were used to assess achievement in subject-matter areas in which no group received instruction by television (except for the arithmetic enrichment televised teaching, which was received in the regular TV and the redeployment TV classes).

Differences in the scholastic abilities of pupils were determined by giving all the pupils the California Tests of Mental Maturity, and these differences were equated by setting up trios of pupils,

The studio facility at Anaheim is designed to make maximum use of space and equipment. A single control serves two studios, making it possible to have a live production in one while rehearsals are being held in the other. (Anaheim School District)

one for each type of teaching-learning situation, matched as to IQs, reading achievement scores, and sex.

During the second year of the instructional project (1960–1961), it was expanded to provide related classroom and televised instruction for pupils in grades 3 to 6. Televised instruction was provided in science, social studies, and music for these four grade levels. Televised instruction in Spanish was provided for pupils in grades 4 to 6. The televised instruction in arithmetic enrichment was moved to the third- and fourth-grade levels. The redeployment plan was expanded to include eight schools and was moved up to the fifth- and sixth-grade levels.

Nontelevision classes were again established. These were selected by drawing the names of the schools at random from a box. Classes at randomly selected grade levels in randomly selected schools throughout the district received instruction therefore in the basic curriculum content, but without the aid of any televised instruction in social studies, science, and arithmetic enrichment.

A teaching studio in the Anaheim center. Usually one of the cameras being used will be remotely controlled from the control room. (Anaheim School District)

Anaheim city school district

Summary of general fund expenditures for ITV
for school years 1959–1960, 1960–1961, 1961–1962

ITV project budget item	Project expenses 1959–1960	Project expenses 1960–1961	Project expenses 1961–1962
Salaries:			
ITV project director	$ 11,500	$ 12,300	$ 13,100
Studio teachers	38,140	62,490	81,015
Redeployment plan consultant			7,365
Studio production manager	7,320	8,860	9,590
Studio producer-director		7,843	8,916
Studio controls operators		12,395	13,423
ITV summer workshop salaries	4,995	3,636	1,000
Resource rooms teacher aides		11,824	12,103
Studio floorman		10,860	5,544
Studio graphic artist		3,416	4,188
Studio assistant producer-director			6,781
Extra help (aides, artist)	8,048		
Other expenses:			
Studio supplies	4,376	5,762	6,889
Testing and evaluation program (contract with Univ. So. Calif.)	15,000	15,000	11,000
Cabling charges	19,322	24,585	30,060
Direct district maintenance	1	13	00
Capital outlay:			
Equipment, studio and schools	77,315	7,402	2,692
Totals (including grants and apportionments)	186,017	186,386	213,666
Ford Foundation grants	25,000	40,000	29,000
Title III NDEA apportionments	50,000		
All district expenditures from general fund, totals	3,901,742	4,171,279	4,723,686
Net district costs for ITV	$ 111,017	$ 146,386	$ 184,666
Per cent of total district costs (from general fund budgets)	2.85%	3.51%	3.91%

The IBM computer at the Western Data Processing Center in Los Angeles was used to analyze the test data for this second year of the project. The analysis involved comparing the achievement of pupils in the three different kinds of teaching-learning situations by sex and level of intelligence. The computer matched the pupils in the three different kinds of situations for any differences in intelligence by the use of the mathematical formulas for analysis of covariance.

A special effort was made to analyze the interactions between methods, sex of the pupil, and level of intelligence. (By interactions is meant any particular combination of factors or conditions. For example, it *might be possible* that high-IQ boys do better in the large classes than in the regular-sized classes, or that girls do better in classes not receiving televised instruction, etc.)

During the third year (1961–1962) the project was continued in very much the same manner as during the 1960–1961 school year, except that the nontelevision classes were no longer maintained for comparison purposes. All pupils throughout the district received the *related classroom and televised instruction* in science, social studies, and music in grade levels 3 to 6. The televised instruction in Spanish was continued in grades 4, 5, and 6, and the televised instruction in arithmetic was continued at the third- and fourth-grade levels. The redeployment plan was continued at the fifth-

---

Anaheim city school district

**Summary of building fund expenditures for ITV
for school years 1959–1960, 1960–1961, 1961–1962**

Building fund expenditures for ITV project	1959–1960	1960–1961	1961–1962
ITV teaching studios building			
Construction contract	$152,387		
Architect's fees	12,191		
Minor remodeling and conduit			
Contract (½ total)	44,763		
Architect's fees (½ total)	1,809		
Conduit contract (1960–1961)			
Streech electric contract		$ 10,930	
Fees (electrical engineers)		1,338	
Hallamore Electronics Company, Inc.			
Original contract	17,565	48,982	$ 48,982
1960–1961 & 1961–1962 contracts		189,862	76,659
Audio-visual equipment			
For studio and schools	4,012	930	2,908
Resource rooms audio systems	981		
Draperies	3,234	4,871	2,517
TV receiver stands	10,010		
Total costs	246,952	256,913	131,066
NDEA title III funds received (and allotted to building fund in 1960–1961 and 1961–1962)		64,802	15,050
Net district costs	$246,952	$192,111	$116,016

Current expenditures per pupil 1959–1960, 1960–1961, and 1961–1962			
	Anaheim elementary district	*Average, all elementary districts in same county*	*Average statewide in California*
1959–1960	$296	312	341
1960–1961	306	327	359
1961–1962	329	340	

and sixth-grade levels at the eight schools where it had already been established.

Both the standardized tests and a number of the district-developed objective tests were again given as a means of continuing to evaluate the achievement of pupils, and as a means of comparing pupil progress in learning in the redeployment plan situation and in the regular-sized classroom situation.

Results. The statistically significant differences obtained during the first year definitely favored the concept of *related classroom and televised instruction.* There were seven such statistically significant differences favoring the redeployment plan with television or the regular television classes, as compared with two such differences favoring the nontelevision, or control, classes. Again, it should perhaps be pointed out that *related classroom and televised instruction* was a feature of both the redeployment plan and the regular television classes.

A summary of the comparisons made on the basis of the test data obtained during the 1959–1960, 1960–1961, and 1961–1962 school years will be found in the table on page 75.

Results for the second year, in general, confirmed the findings for the first year. A surprising turn of events, however, was the finding that fifth- and sixth-grade pupils were doing less well in arithmetic reasoning and fundamentals in the redeployment plan small-group skills classes. Since no televised instruction in arithmetic enrichment was provided during this year at these two grade levels, and since these pupils were receiving all of their instruction in arithmetic in these unusually small groups, the contributing factors are not readily apparent. A special effort has subsequently been made to upgrade the quality of the arithmetic instruction in these small-group classes.

The computer analysis revealed that the three groups would have been sufficiently well matched for intelligence without the aid of the computer. The more complex form of analysis was needed, however, to determine this fact.

Summary of ITV project test findings
for the school years 1959-1960, 1960-1961, 1961-1962

Statistically significant comparisons

District-developed tests (subjects involving televised instruction)

1. Redeployment TV compared with regular TV classes:

Number of comparisons	Favors redeployment	Favors regular TV	No difference
28	39%	14%	47%

2. Redeployment TV compared with non-TV classes:

Number of comparisons	Favors redeployment	Favors non-TV	No difference
19	37%	11%	52%

3. Regular TV classes compared with non-TV classes:

Number of comparisons	Favors regular TV	Favors non-TV	No difference
23	48%	0%	52%

Standardized tests (subjects *not involving* televised instruction)

1. Redeployment plan compared with regular-sized classes:

Number of comparisons	Favors redeployment	Favors regular-sized	No difference
32	9%	25%	66%

2. Redeployment plan compared with the non-TV (control) classes:

Number of comparisons	Favors redeployment	Favors control classes	No difference
20	20%	20%	60%

3. Regular-sized classes compared with non-TV (control) classes:

Number of comparisons	Favors regular-sized	Favors control classes	No difference
32	19%	13%	68%

The computer analysis also demonstrated that there were no significant interactions between IQ, sex, and method of instruction. When a given method was superior, it was more effective for both sexes at all IQ levels. If a particular method was advantageous for the rapid learners, it also proved to be advantageous for the average and the slow learners.

In comparing the data obtained during this third year from the administering of the district-developed tests, a number of statistically significant differences were found to favor the redeployment plan large-class situation. On the other hand, results from the standardized tests again indicated that pupils in the redeployment plan skills classes were doing less well in arithmetic reasoning and arithmetic fundamentals.

75

On the whole the results of the full three years of the testing program indicate that the classes receiving televised instruction generally did better in the subject-matter areas involving the *related classroom and televised instruction* than did the nontelevision classes.

In concluding his report to the board of education regarding the findings resulting from the first three years of the program, Dr. Lefever commented:

> ... we are evaluating a "package,"—a complex pattern of factors influencing the learning experiences of children, rather than the effect of instructional television as a separate, isolated entity. Television instruction is but one element in the total combination of influences impinging upon the child, even though we limit our observations to what the child is learning while in the classroom.
>
> ... the evaluations indicate that television is a decidedly useful tool in the hands of this instructional staff ... [and] the redeployment system with its teams of resource room teachers and skills teachers appears especially promising.
>
> The results of this evaluation may be interpreted as distinctly favorable to the continuation of the instructional television program.

IN SUMMARY

We believe that the instructional television project has definitely, and to a marked degree, improved the quality of the educational program in the Anaheim school district. It has provided many kinds of improved learning opportunities (many of which could not otherwise have been provided) for the thousands of boys and girls who attend the district's twenty elementary schools. When capable teachers are relieved of regular classroom teaching duties, when they are helped to become competent television teachers and are given sufficient time to plan for and prepare each telecast presentation, when they are encouraged to meet regularly and to plan with capable classroom teachers for the continuing improvement of *related classroom and televised instruction,* when classroom teachers are involved as coworkers in the planning and evaluative processes and the primary importance of the classroom teacher's role in the total teaching-learning situation is recognized and emphasized, and when televised teaching is carefully planned to provide for the pupils a new and different kind of learning opportunity rather than a substitute for classroom learning opportunities—then the total teaching-learning situation is improved, and pupils benefit.

Television is only the tool. It is neutral. It is inanimate. It comes to life only when people start doing things with it. Whether or not it adds to classroom learning opportunities—the extent to which it motivates pupils toward further study and discovery and promotes learning—depends upon how imaginatively and how well it is used by those employing it.

It is not just the central office help, the television teacher, or the project director who employ television as an instructional medium. The classroom teacher is (or should be) using it as an aid to better teaching whenever good televised instruction is brought into the classroom; her importance in determining the worthwhileness and success of instructional television cannot be overestimated. If the televised teaching takes full advantage of the audio-visual potentialities of the medium, then the pupils in the classroom are very likely to receive a kind of learning experience which the classroom teacher alone could not readily provide, but upon which she can build, extend, and provide a much enriched learning situation for her pupils.

We have found that the introduction of television, particularly closed-circuit television, on a large-scale basis in a school system forces thoughtful and continuing reexamination of teaching methods, curriculum offerings, and curriculum content. It promotes improved curriculum planning and increases evaluation of total teaching efforts. It stimulates—it even demands—renewed thought and inquiry regarding the basic nature of the learning process. Staff growth is promoted as these things are pondered and considered. Decisions must be made regarding the proper role of television in the total educational process. What can televised teaching do that cannot be done as effectively in the classroom? What are its limitations? For what should it not be used? What kinds of teaching activities belong strictly in the classroom? How can television, with its unique audio-visual and powerful communicative characteristics, expand the child's opportunities for learning?

Some of the gains resulting from the Anaheim district's television project are quite obvious. Others are less obvious, but also important. In part, improvements are the result of televised teaching. But, to a considerable extent, and in varying degrees, they result from other contributing factors.

1. A three-year program of carefully planned instruction in conversational Spanish is being provided for all pupils in grades 4, 5, and 6. The program is spearheaded by the excellent teaching of three well-qualified, bilingual television teachers. Semester-length in-service training classes taught by these teachers are being provided for classroom teachers. Classroom teachers in growing numbers are learning to speak the language fluently. Every conversational Spanish telecast lesson for the pupils is providing a built-in training program for classroom teachers.
2. A district-wide curriculum in science has been established, and all pupils in grades 3 to 6 are receiving regularly scheduled *related televised and classroom* instruction in this subject.
3. The district's social studies program has been clearly defined, and all pupils in grades 3 to 6 are receiving closely related instruction, via tele-

vision and in the classroom, in this subject-matter area. Here, again, the televised instruction provides a kind of teaching that cannot readily be provided in the classroom.

4. A district-wide music curriculum has been developed, and all pupils in grades 3 to 6 are receiving one carefully planned televised music lesson each week, taught by an outstanding specialist in this field, with related classroom instruction and musical experiences being provided by classroom teachers.

5. Arithmetic enrichment telecasts are being provided for all pupils in grades 3 and 4, with a series of related in-service telecasts for teachers of these two grade levels being presented by the television arithmetic teacher on the basis of plans made in cooperation with the arithmetic instructional planning group.

6. The instructional television project has promoted more and better staff planning; it has brought more teacher involvement in planning for instructional improvement.

7. It has increased the amount and improved the quality of the district's in-service training activities—now better coordinated to achieve school district goals and purposes. (A series of in-service telecasts is planned for and presented each year. Here, as with the televised instruction for pupils, the concept of *relatedness* is basic: an in-service telecast guide-sheet is prepared in advance—the telecast portion of the in-service training period is used to present basic ideas, demonstrations, and illustrations —a related follow-up period is used for faculty discussion and activities after the screen goes dark, the principal or teacher serving as discussion leader.)

8. The district's television facilities have been used to improve staff communications. (Each week, on Wednesdays at noontime, a special program entitled "Staff Chats" is presented. News of district activities, parent-teacher association events, visiting celebrities, and board of education actions are regular features.)

9. The project gives every evidence of having brought improved staff morale, promoting a growing feeling of accomplishment, enthusiasm, and pride in the district's local pioneering efforts with a new instructional medium.

10. The work load of many classroom teachers has been reduced. They have fewer subjects to teach and prepare for, thus more time for planning and preparation for teaching those subjects which remain as their responsibilities.

11. The advantages of the redeployment plan have been realized: small-group instruction in the three R's; certain apparent learning advantages in the the large-class situation with two teachers, assisted by the noncertificated teacher aide; better plant utilization has helped to maintain an adequate school housing situation for all pupils; improved use is made of a variety of visual aids, equipment, and teaching materials.

12. Full recognition of the need for a district-wide testing program has been developed and its continuance ensured.

13. The district's television facilities have proved helpful in a number of ways in maintaining and improving home–school and community relationships.

Each year a televised program has been beamed to all schools for parents of pupils of each grade level during a series of back-to-school nights. Thus the superintendent and other staff members, including many of the district's teachers, have been able to speak directly to all parents to show and tell about the district's instructional program. (Recently this means was used to present an explanation of the newly developed report cards for primary grades.)

In addition, the district's facilities have been used from time to time by various civic groups to present televised evening programs in the interests of civic betterment. Assistance in the planning and presentation of these telecasts is provided by the district's studio production staff. (In 1960 the city council used this means to explain to interested citizens its request for approval of a 12-point bond issue.)

Finally, experiences with television in the Anaheim district provide evidence that closed-circuit television facilities and televised lesson presentations, when of high quality and when blended and fitted appropriately into (and used as an integral part of) the total instructional process, offer to a large and growing school district such as the Anaheim district a useful means of improving its educational program within a framework of limited additional school dollars. As a vehicle for bringing about instructional improvements, closed-circuit television holds forth unusual promise. Excitement permeates the district; our program of instruction has improved and the content has been expanded. Television deserves prolonged and serious consideration as an educational medium in many school district situations.

chapter 6

Statewide closed-circuit television:
the South Carolina program

George E. Bair

While a majority of the chapters in this book are concerned with a limited number of schools and school districts, this one is an exception. Dr. Bair describes how, faced with limited funds, a high proportion of school-aged children, and an immediate lack of highly skilled teachers, South Carolina has used television in an attempt to raise the level of its entire secondary school program by the use of a statewide closed-circuit network.

In 1962 the state of South Carolina had a median family income of $3,821, far below the national norm of $5,657. Nearly one-third of its population attends school on a regular basis and although 48 per cent of the state's tax dollar is spent on education, the amount spent per student is still the second lowest in the nation. The average teacher's salary of under $3,500 is also far below the national average of over $5,100 and this relationship cannot be expected to change in the immediate future.

The question, therefore, is a basic one: How can South Carolina, faced with these problems, give its children an education comparable to that given children in other states?

TURNING TO TELEVISION

While this particular complex may be peculiar to South Carolina, other problems plaguing education are not: too few well-qualified teachers; too many students; too transient a population; too little money, time, and talent to do the job we all know needs doing. As a possible solution, South Carolina turned to television.

Planners, including industrialists, legislators, and educators, sought a method or combination of methods by which television

Dr. Bair is Educational Director for the South Carolina Educational Television Center.

could be used to bring to a large number of schools the benefits of wide curriculum and superior teaching—at a cost which could be borne.

A survey of metropolitan junior and senior high schools showed that thirty-six different courses were already available. The planning group sought through television means to make all of these courses available in schools where they were lacking. In addition, they hoped to enrich the teaching of art, music, mathematics, science, history, and reading on the elementary level.

The widening of curriculum was not the planners' only problem. A further look at resources revealed that the number of well-qualified teachers of mathematics, science, and foreign languages in the state was distressingly small. There was abundant evidence that what the system needed along with cultural enrichment was systematic, first-rate direct teaching in the schools.

The goal of the planners, then, was to widen, deepen, and strengthen the curriculum throughout the entire state. That goal led to the first basic decision by the planning group: we had to have multichannel potential to do the job.

WHY CLOSED-CIRCUIT

In 1958, when educational television channels were being allocated, South Carolina had received only four channels, and these were of such a nature that had they been activated, their signals would have reached a maximum of only one out of three schools—and then only with a single channel. To extend the existing ETV setup to cover the state would have entailed the granting of many additional allocations, the construction of transmitters, and, in addition, either the operation of a variety of production centers or the linking of all transmitters by a closed-circuit system. Under either alternative, we would still have been limited largely to one channel.

Our present solution was made possible when the telephone companies in the state quoted us the first noncommercial tariff in the United States, enabling us to combine microwave and coaxial cable. The result? By September, 1962, we had developed our present closed-circuit network, which reached into all forty-six counties of South Carolina, linking 130 high schools to a central production center in the state capital, Columbia[1] (see map, page 83).

[1] At the time of writing this system reached 155 public secondary schools, 36 elementary schools, 4 state-supported colleges, 5 university extension centers, 5 private colleges, 2 private high schools, and 8 hospitals.

THE PROGRAM

From the production center the high schools are being fed the following courses: Algebra I, Algebra II, Geometry, French I, French II, Physical Science, and South Carolina history. Each course consists of 160 lessons of one half-hour's duration. Also available are one-semester, 80-lesson courses in college algebra and trigonometry and a basic electronics course consisting of 120 lessons.

Not all the teaching, by any means, is done by television. Students have two teachers for each television course; one in the studio and one in the classroom. The classroom teachers assist in the curriculum planning, attend summer workshops in educational television utilization, are provided with lesson plans well in advance of the showing of lessons, and in other ways are kept as close as possible to television developments. The statewide nature of the program makes such liaison less perfect than it might be otherwise, but has not made the program appreciably weaker. Every effort is devoted toward reaching the teachers in the classroom through the medium itself instead of asking them to travel to the production center.

In addition to an early commitment to multichannel transmission, two other decisions have affected our operation: every lesson we offer is video-taped in advance, and all phases of the production—art, direction, and engineering—are of the highest quality. Actually, these two commitments overlap, since video taping is conducive to a quality, achieved by editing, which is not otherwise possible.

Television production gobbles talent. For example, our five-man art department produced 2,000 visuals for the geometry courses alone. To provide production talent commensurate with instruction talent, it is imperative that we stick with one production center. South Carolina does not yet have artists, directors, cameramen, video tape machine operators and other television engineers in enough supply to support more than one first-rate production center.

To ensure quality, all our major staff positions are filled by persons who are full-time employees of the center. This is true of the teachers. They are paid a salary which is twice the state's average, and they work at television teaching full-time for eleven months to produce their course material. We are hoping to extend this time in cases where production is particularly complex.

RESULTS

We have been in statewide operation for only two years, so that our results are still tentative. Objectively, we have been able to test students taught with the aid of television on nationally standardized examinations in our algebra and geometry courses. We find from such testing that the mean results for TV-taught students in our rural schools are consistently equal to or above the means in the metropolitan systems whose test results are available for our use. We know that we can bring a high level of instruction to all our schools that has not always been available to them. We know that with an expenditure per pupil per annum which is well below national average, we can produce children who score at the national average or above in sufficient numbers to show that through educational television, South Carolinians are getting a great deal for their educational dollar.

Those are results which have been objectively demonstrated. But there are further results of which we are certain, although we cannot provide objective proof. We know, for example, that more students are learning to concentrate and to take notes at an earlier age than in the past. We know that there are classroom teachers in the state who are learning subject matter and teaching technique from watching telecasts with their students. We know that we enrich the whole curriculum through pouring into our productions pictures, film, slides, guests, equipment, time, talent, and

With its production center in Columbia, the South Carolina closed-circuit television project reaches 155 public secondary schools, 36 elementary schools, 4 state-supported colleges, 5 university extension centers, 5 private colleges, 2 private high schools, and 8 hospitals.

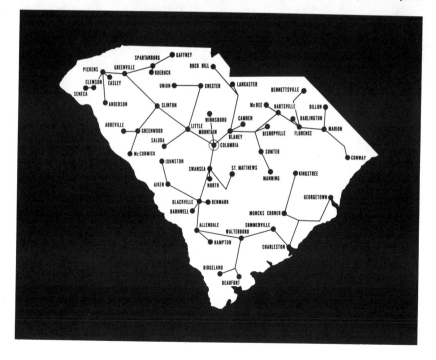

energy which could not possibly be mustered in any classroom in the state day in and day out.

We also are convinced that a multichannel operation can serve many educational needs other than in-school instruction. We have already produced an electronics series and a series on landscaping for adults; three in-service courses for teachers;[2] a group of programs for the postgraduate education of doctors for the Medical College of South Carolina; a series on new techniques for nurses; and—at the request of the school board association—the nation's first training program for school trustees.

[2] For an account of in-service education by TV, see Chapter 13, "Television, Kinescopes, and In-service Education."—Ed.

To assure quality instruction, the graphic artist, television teacher, and director combine their talents to produce each lesson. (South Carolina Educational Television Center)

COST

Obviously, this kind of project costs money. To get under way in South Carolina, we have spent about 3 million dollars, the major expenditures being made for equipping the center and for transmission costs. Yet, according to our present estimates, we can offer thirty-six courses to all 413 high schools in the state at an annual cost of only $12 to $14 per pupil. Since the state's annual budget for education is now about 120 million dollars, the use of television is not adding significantly to the total cost; nevertheless, we have already added considerably to the general quality of education in the state.

THE FUTURE

Like everyone else in educational television, we are still feeling our way. We shall, of course, extend our programming considerably so that we may serve as many educational needs as possible, from kindergarten through adult education. We shall also activate open-circuit outlets to our system to reach persons in homes as well as students in classrooms. We shall experiment with the whole spectrum of educational television from pure enrichment through supplementation to total teaching by television.

Educational television has been described as the giant eggbeater which stirs the educational mix. It has already done so in South Carolina. We have had to ponder changes in school design, the length of a class period, the length of the school day. Television has also reawakened us to the old idea of the school as a community center open at all hours and throughout the year.

TEACHER REACTIONS

Even more provocative are some of the implications I see stemming from our initial efforts in South Carolina. For the individual classroom teacher, for example:

1. Television has a way of exposing weaknesses in teaching which have heretofore been unknown, hidden, or explained away.
2. The creative teacher finds ETV a uniquely rich resource to complement her talents.
3. The use of the medium may lead to many redefinitions of certain aspects of education, such as the apprentice system in teacher education, the functions of certification, and the role of the classroom teacher. Beginning teachers can now teach behind a superior teacher on television; whole segments of instructional material can be certified as valid instruction; and classroom teachers can now become specialists in adaptation, rein-

forcement, and evaluation without being asked to be specialists in preparation and presentation as well.

PROBLEMS

We have found, too, that television raises a whole new area of problems directly concerning the television teacher:

1. The determination of teachers' rights. These include the right to participate in curriculum planning, the right to be responsible for the preparation and presentation of lessons, and the right to negotiate in the case of reuse of taped material.
2. The clarification of teachers' responsibilities. These include learning from those who know the medium of television, accepting criticism from all segments of society, and assisting in the development of ETV as a profession.

LONG-RANGE IMPLICATIONS

Finally, I see also some long-term implications for the teaching profession as a whole:

1. We have a unique opportunity to show the general public what great teaching is.
2. Through the medium of television, we have a chance to give the profession a new status, to convince taxpayers it is worth their support, and to attract to it young people of high caliber.
3. I believe that we can draw to teaching talents never before available. We can capture on tape teachers who never knew they were teachers and can offer an opportunity for a career in TV teaching to persons who, while superb teachers, do not want to be tied down to the classroom.

Always striving to use television as a means, where possible, to attack educational problems which have not been solved in any other way, and dedicated to the highest available quality in all phases of the ETV job, we hope in South Carolina to prove the proposition that through educational television and the mustering of all other resources, we *can* provide for our children an education comparable, if not superior, to that available to students in any other state in the country.

chapter 7

"Shoestring" television

T. H. Bell

A financially distressed school district turned to television as the only possible means of providing the classroom teacher with assistance and improving and expanding the curriculum. It found that this could be done within its severe budget limitations.

The Weber County (Utah) School District was faced with a need to provide instructional specialists in the areas of art, music, science, and foreign languages on the elementary school level. One cannot expect all teachers on the elementary school level to have background in the subject areas listed above in addition to competency in the other areas of the curriculum. The choice must be made either to provide instruction in art, music, science, and foreign language only to the extent that each classroom teacher is trained in these fields, or to employ rotating subject-matter specialists. The former choice promises a badly undernourished curriculum in many classrooms; the latter is costly.

THE RATIONALE

Since our school system, containing twenty-three schools and 14,000 students, is one of the poorest districts in Utah from the standpoint of taxable wealth per child, the funds available for employment of subject-area specialists are very limited. We therefore turned to television as an alternative solution—as an economy measure, in other words, for a poor district that could supplement and enrich its curriculum only through some means of extending the instructional influence of the most capable teachers.

After observing its attention-holding capacity in the home, it is hard to deny that television is a very powerful means of communication. A study of the geographical location of the various schools and the terrain in this particular area of Utah determined that a

Dr. Bell is Superintendent of Schools for Weber County School District, Ogden, Utah.

low-power television transmitter could easily reach all units of the school system.

It was also decided that television would be the most effective and economical means of providing special help to elementary school classrooms in the subject areas of art, music, foreign languages, and science. Although we could not afford a large staff of specialists, we were able to find the money to employ four full-time television teachers with special training and unusual ability.

THE PROJECT

A central studio and transmitting station were located adjacent to the district's administration building, broadcasts being made over a 1,000-watt ultrahigh-frequency channel (UHF Channel 18). The signal proved to be effective in reaching the twenty-three schools of the district.

An electronics teacher was selected as engineer. After considerable study, this regular member of our teaching staff secured his first-class engineer's license and has continued to serve up to the present time.

Student participation. Students from nearby Weber County High School serve as technical assistants and cameramen under the supervision of the teacher-engineer; time spent in the studio constitutes part of their study in a regular work experience class. Camera crews are changed each period of the high school day, since student crew members must not spend more than one class period in the television studio. With a high degree of selectivity for student technicians, talented students who can learn quickly and adapt readily have been available to handle the actual operation of studio equipment. While the changing of crews from period to period has created some problems, it has at the same time saved thousands of dollars for the district and has provided very unusual and valuable learning experiences for students who are planning a career in communications electronics.

The television teachers, subject-area supervisors, and regular classroom teachers spent an entire summer planning ways and means of making television instruction effective in enriching and supplementing the regular instructional offerings. Study guides and schedules were prepared. Special areas of emphasis peculiar to television application were outlined and plans made to gain the most from the medium.

Cost. A used UHF transmitter, tower, and antenna were purchased for $29,700—a figure greatly below cost. The relatively low price to us was made possible because the transmitter had originally been purchased by a firm which had failed financially; the manufacturers had had the equipment in stock for a number of years and were anxious to dispose of it. Another $23,000 was spent on a minimal internal facility which included cameras, camera control units, film projection equipment, and related items.

One television set was purchased for every two classrooms. Old electrical wire conduits were used to make a movable stand on wheels for each set. It was then a simple matter for two teachers to exchange the receiver across a corridor.

Assistance under the National Defense Education Act (NDEA) was available for purchase of the receiving sets and for a distribution in each school building in the district. This saved a huge sum of money, 65 per cent of the cost being paid under NDEA support.

The National Educational Television network (NET) has also been of great assistance, both in a financial way and in providing excellent films and video tapes. The video tape machine used by the district came as a grant through NET.

With our salaried personnel performing dual functions and our camera crews student-staffed, with the purchase of used equipment and, wherever possible, war surplus electronic components, and with careful use of vidicon cameras rather than the expensive image orthicon units, we have been able to operate at a very low cost. We estimate that the operational costs of our educational television program amount to approximately 1.2 per cent of the total operational fund budget of the district.

Program.   In October, 1960, all preparations were completed and the county school system was receiving television instruction in all elementary school classrooms. Conversational French, special music and art instruction, and special lectures and demonstrations in science came into the classrooms on a regular schedule.

Results.   Most of the teachers in the district received the special help of television instruction with enthusiasm. Academic achievement in science, based upon nationally utilized standardized tests, was increased 17 per cent. Students received a systematically planned program of music instruction for the first time, and teachers in the regular classroom situation welcomed the help of an art specialist. The response given the music instruction was equally favorable.

The reaction of students and teachers to offerings in conversational French was especially gratifying. The teacher learned with her students, and French was being spoken with varying degrees of fluency by the end of the first semester.

Science was very enthusiastically received. Experiments were projected clearly and with outstanding success. The impetus of space-age rocket travel, nuclear power, and other recent scientific developments was used by the science teleteacher with excellent results.

Classrooms throughout the district reflect the influence of television instruction. This visible influence ranges from the attaching of French words to various objects in elementary school classrooms to an intensified interest shown in the works of the old masters in art and music.

We found that teachers responded in varying ways to the impact of educational television. A small number had status problems, since their role was changed from being the focal point of instruction for 100 per cent of the classroom time to sharing the spotlight with the television teachers. Some teachers were skilled at teaching one or more of the special subject areas and resented the intrusion of the teleteacher. A very few teachers reacted in a way that indicated an awareness that teaching competence as demonstrated on television was being compared with methods and procedures carried out in the regular program. A few teachers felt that they were somehow in competition with the television instructors.

Careful orientation of all teachers whose students will receive television instruction is a necessity. Although we attempted to be thorough in this, we find that a more intensified program in this area would have been valuable.

Some presentations in art, music, and science were not wholly successful. The lack of color, for example, places a serious limitation on certain kinds of art instruction. Some details in science and music sometimes were not received in the classrooms as clearly as anticipated.

Television is in no sense "in competition" with the classroom teacher. An electronic tube obviously cannot stop to repeat when a child raises a hand to ask a question. Individualization of instruction must come in the follow-up by the regular teacher.

In spite of such limitations, however, television is a very powerful tool that educators should use to give more breadth and depth to the curriculum. With telecasts spanning continents, the entire world will soon be available to the classroom teacher as he teaches social, cultural, and scientific phenomena.

Our total experience with educational television has been very fruitful. We have learned a great deal about the use of the medium that will be of tremendous value in the years to come. We have improved our total teaching staff by presenting examples of the finest type of instruction every day. We have brought new dimensions of enrichment into the classroom—not only in the presentation of special subjects, but in the regular curriculum as well. For example, all students in the school system watched the Chief Justice of the Supreme Court adminster the oath of office to President Kennedy. Most students also observed Colonel Glenn's history-making orbits of the earth.

Educational television can, of course, be very expensive. Yet it can be had on a minimal basis if care is taken to shop for bargains, use NDEA funds, and cut corners wherever the opportunity presents itself. Since Weber County is one of the districts at the absolute bottom in taxable wealth per child in Utah, television instruction has, of necessity, been purchased and operated by a dollar-conscious staff. Our conclusion is that educational television does indeed provide an inexpensive means for poor school systems to offer an enriched curricular program, since one expert can reach all classrooms through this means of instructional communication. Thus we have come to look upon television instruction not as a luxury for a rich district but as a necessity for the poor district that cannot afford large numbers of subject-area specialists.

chapter 8

The Schenectady approach: using the educational station

Robert Murray

The Schenectady public school system was one of the first to explore the potential of both open- and closed-circuit television in education. In this chapter Dr. Murray reviews their experiences and results, presenting the rationale for that district's emphasis on open-circuit television.

Television, acknowledged to be the most significant force in modern communication, is having an unprecedented influence on the peoples of the world. Educators can ill afford to ignore television's dynamic potential for motivating and strengthening the learning process. For many, however, the how, what, and when remain an enigma. In spite of extensive experimentation in the use of educational television and the availability of an abundance of written material on the subject, there is little agreement about the role of television in the school program, the type of programming most desired, or the most effective means of utilizing existing programs. With ever-ascending school costs, local school boards have difficulty stretching budgets to provide adequate funds for equipment, personnel, and materials essential for making optimum use of television as an educational tool. The popular theory concerned with the potential savings realized by pooling board area resources for outstanding television instruction has yet to be satisfactorily substantiated by fact. State and Federal interest in support of educational television is publicized; yet grants are limited and many appeals go unheard. Foundations have been generous in sponsoring educational television experimentation, but educators are often expected to yield beyond a tolerable compromise with professional interests and standards in order to gain approval for such projects.

Dr. Murray is Superintendent of the Schenectady Public Schools and has been president of the Mohawk-Hudson Council on Educational Television.

The Schenectady school system was among the very first pioneers in the field, with early exploration of the possibilities of producing and using educational television to enrich and improve the curriculum on all levels—kindergarten through adult education.

Our community furnishes a natural setting for experimentation with this medium, since the General Electric Company's radio and television studios are located in Schenectady. From 1940 to 1948, there were only five television stations in the country, WRGB, Schenectady, being the second oldest. Schenectadians, therefore, needed no orientation to the value of experimentation with this mass medium, since many of our citizens were actively engaged in the process.

PREPARING FOR TELEVISION

Because the formulation of acceptable programming standards was recognized as essential to the future planning of television programs, local programmers consulted members of the State Legislature, the Federal Communications Commission, topflight producers, and other agencies in policy formation. Schenectady schools participated by utilizing the public service time donated by the local station for educational programs. During 1952–1953, our schools had full responsibility for a fifteen-minute per week public relations program interpreting school policy and program to the public, and at the same time one hour per week was allotted to the adult education department for public service–type programs. Local school staff members were released from regular duties for short periods to serve as coordinators for such programs, and worked closely with the television station director to develop content and to produce the programs. These test programs were viewed with enthusiasm by the school administrators, teachers, and various civic groups. School personnel regarded these initial attempts as an opportunity to get off the ground with this new medium.

These early and successful experiences with radio and spot television programs made us aware of the value of the mass medium as an educational tool. The trial and error of our initial attempts with education via television developed a readiness for more intensive exploration in this field. Television's superiority was immediately discernible—the added stimulus of visual presentation accompanied by the more familiar audible presentation served to catch and hold the attention of the pupils.

As a direct result of these early experiences, it was decided that the district would explore the potential of both open- and closed-circuit television.

CLOSED-CIRCUIT TELEVISION

In September, 1956, a Ford grant of $10,000 made possible a pilot project using rented closed-circuit television equipment in one of our high schools. Local teachers using television instructed students in such areas as science, mathematics, and French. A former supervisor of television and radio at the University of Connecticut was brought here to coordinate the program and to work with local administrators in preparing the final report, which was distributed on request to others interested in similar programs. This experiment led to the installation of closed-circuit conduits in the new Linton High School. It also identified the types of programs most appropriate for the secondary level.

When our new high school was completed in May, 1958, another experiment in closed-circuit television was initiated and successfully accomplished, using local staff for all aspects of programming. Equipment was lent to carry on the new equipment. Insufficient funds prevented this program from continuing.

Still another experiment with closed-circuit was tried on the elementary level, using a portable television camera—again with borrowed equipment. If and when funds become available, Schenectady schools have the "know-how" and personnel to take full advantage of closed-circuit programming. Other cities have used our findings and counsel when exploring possibilities in this field.

OPEN-CIRCUIT TELEVISION

Several years before our first experience with closed-circuit television, the district had expanded its support for open-circuit programming. This interest was stimulated when in early 1953 the local station offered more time, one hour per day, to organizations interested in education and willing to work on the extension of educational opportunities through television. In addition, the station gave $2,500 toward the salary of a program director.

In May, 1953, many organizations had responded, and the Mohawk-Hudson Council on Educational Television was formed with a seventeen-member governing board representing some one hundred civic, cultural, and educational groups in the area. Member organizations were assessed $25 per year. School systems paid a membership fee of $100, plus 10 cents per pupil. Groups such as parent-teacher associations and the American Association of University Women, associated with the council but not involved with programming, were encouraged to donate a $25 fee, and individual $5 memberships were solicited. The New York State Board of Regents granted the council the first New York State charter as a nonprofit educational group in June, 1953.

The Schenectady approach: using the educational station

As the Mohawk-Hudson Council on Educational Television explored the potential of the medium in education, it had the active support of area school districts, colleges, museums, and the community at large.

"Natural Science," with Martin Davis, Board of Cooperative Services, Gloversville, N.Y. (WMHT)

"Our Trip to the Museum," with students from St. Casmir's School, Albany; one in the series, "Friendly People and Places" (WMHT)

(Opposite, above) "Aspects of Modern Art," presented by the Schenectady Museum (WMHT)

(Opposite, below) The Suburban Symphony Orchestra, composed of local high school students (WMHT)

Miss Pat Peterson, a local dance teacher, demonstrates modern dance techniques. (WMHT)

"Exploring Your Community" highlights the role of the blacksmith in early Schenectady history. (WMHT)

(Opposite, above) "Experiments with Art," presented by the Rensselaer County Junior Museum (WMHT)

(Opposite, below) Elizabethan music, art, and literature, with Prof. Sven Peterson of Union College and Miss Meg Larkin (WMHT)

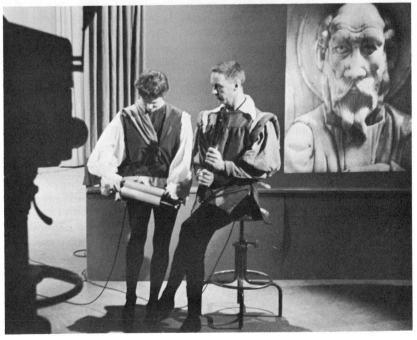

In 1953 Ann Slack presents "Fun with French" for the first time on television. (WMHT)

With scarcely one month remaining to prepare telecasts to begin in September, the council, nevertheless, was able to attain a wide variety of programs. Grouped under the general title "TV School-time," the time was equally divided between school-aged children and adults. Schenectady schools were given responsibility for half of the program time during the first period of the "TV Schooltime" telecasts, since our staff now included a school coordinator for programs who could be assigned the additional responsibility.

Preprogram materials were distributed and follow-ups were supervised by the coordinator, who visited classrooms to assist the classroom teacher and to view programs from within the classroom. Student reaction was thus incorporated into planning of policies and procedures for future programs.

"Fun with French" was one of the school-sponsored programs at this time. The city elementary schools had long been interested in introducing a second language to the young child. Mrs. Ann Slack, a native of France, was employed by the school system to organize a program for the eighteen elementary schools using a television series as the basis for classroom instruction. Merely to state that we were fortunate in our choice of Mrs. Slack would be an under-statement. The enthusiasm, vitality, and charm which she brought to the program made her a "television natural." Teacher education relative to utilization of the "Fun with French" series was arranged with the cooperation of the Union College Extension Division. Mrs. Slack assisted with classroom follow-up and teacher training. The teaching of French to elementary school children via the televised series received both national and international attention. The development and expansion of the local Foreign Language in the Elementary School program (FLES) emerged, and, although Mrs. Slack now works with the Boston area TV, the tapes and kinescopes produced there are available not only to Schenectady's station, but across the nation.

Science, music, art, language arts, elementary industrial arts, and mathematics were other areas of program experimentation in the early days of educational television. Evaluative techniques were developed, and school committees were formed to make recommendations to the council. The Audio-Visual Department of the school system allocated part of its budget each year for the purchase of television sets for schools and maintained facilities for installation service and repair of equipment. A television handbook including recommendations for utilization was prepared and distributed. Television teachers were regular teachers receiving no extra compensation and with only a minimum of time provided for preparation and production of programs. Some professional help was given in preparation of scripts and guides but never enough for the tremendous burden. It has always been a source of amazement to me that staff interest remained high when personal sacrifice was, unfortunately, so great.

At the present time, our energies are being expended in all-out support for the Mohawk-Hudson Council's new educational UHF television station, WMHT.

THE LOCAL EDUCATION STATION: OUR BEST APPROACH

After reviewing our experiences with television, it has become apparent that, for the present, the only practical type of television for our entire district is via the community educational station. The reasons for reaching this decision are as follows:

1. *Economy.* The cost of connecting our schools by cable or microwave is prohibitive. Furthermore, with open-circuit television, the cost of operation is shared by the entire viewing area.
2. *Quality.* With an educational station, higher-quality programs are possible with a wider choice of talent and a greater accessibility of tapes and films than would be available to our district working alone.
3. *Shared responsibilities.* A larger coverage offers more resource personnel for program planning and presentations, reduces the burden on any one school system, and shares the specific abilities of the personnel.
4. *Flexibility.* Round-the-clock viewing reaches more students and reduces

the need for rigid scheduling. A longer program day than is possible with most closed-circuit operations offers more choice of curriculum areas and thus a greater variety in a specific area (e.g., three programs on mathematics, one experimental, one remedial, and one on fundamentals).

5. *Quantity.* Open-circuit television reaches the home and can continue after school hours and throughout vacations.

6. *Adult education.* Open-circuit television opens up an entirely new approach for adult education, an area in which the Schenectady school district has been extremely active.

PROBLEMS

Our early problems with the use of television were numerous and varied. The lack of receiving sets in the schools was critical. Often as many as two or three classes had to view a single receiver when, in reality, we have found that under certain conditions, several sets are needed within a single classroom to assure proper viewing.

The problem of identifying, recruiting, and orienting staff members with special aptitudes and abilities to assist in the development of the programs themselves was immediately apparent. How to utilize a telecast effectively, what was the proper time for telecasting a specific program, what preprogram materials were needed by the teacher—all these were questions that had to be solved during our period of exploration. It should also be mentioned that an important matter of concern was the fact that no established criteria for objective evaluation of the programs themselves existed. It has only been in the last few years that we have actually been able to measure, even partially, the effects of television in our classrooms.

RESULTS

We have found that television has been worthwhile to our district in many subject areas and in many ways. It has proved to be a boon in improving the teaching within our schools, as teachers have been kept up to date with new developments in content and teaching techniques. Subject-area enrichment has been available in many fields. The French series brought a master teacher to every third- and fourth-grade classroom in eighteen elementary schools, and has made possible a comprehensive foreign language program for grades 3 to 12.

Television has offered our schools a series of current events presentations geared to the child viewer's level of understanding. It has strengthened the district immeasurably by developing a common interest and improving the cooperation between our schools.

It has also served as a dynamic public relations tool, communicating school policies, procedures, and program to area viewers.

In those areas where the school program was weakened by insufficient equipment or "know-how" (e.g., elementary school industrial arts and science), there has been a rewarding improvement throughout the curriculum. There have been few areas, if any, where the effects of television have not been noticeable.

SOME INSIGHTS

Instructional television will not fail when carefully integrated with the existing curriculum. The limitations or failures obviously rest with the implementation of the medium.

Television on the secondary level poses more complexities due to the period scheduling of classes. It has been difficult to take full advantage of programs that are shown only once. With the new educational station and the expanded use of video tape, it is anticipated that this problem will be reduced, since programs can be repeated several times per day or per week as appropriate.

The success of television in Schenectady has been the result of much effort on the part of many individuals. The number of television sets has been increased as the budget has permitted. We have found that portable sets are especially useful when few sets are available in a particular school. Effort has been made to assure the early preparation and distribution of preprogram materials in time to aid the teacher in program selection and use. Our special teachers (i.e., art, music, physical education) have been especially cooperative in rearranging their schedules so as not to conflict with daily or weekly viewing of television.

The station has adjusted the viewing times to reach the widest audience. Where small-group viewing has been most desirable, teaching teams have worked together. While one teacher was with the students viewing the program, the other worked with the remainder of the class on another facet of the subject or in another subject area.

Many groups assisted the Mohawk-Hudson Council in activating its UHF station. Area stations donated equipment estimated to be worth well over a quarter of a million dollars.

Last year the state paid $25,000 for programs produced by the station, and the council anticipates that this amount will be substantially increased as the new station is able to do more programming. The council assessment to schools was raised to $1 per child. The Schenectady Board of Education was the first agency to arrange this budget allocation. In addition, contributions from individuals on the school staff added another $3,000.

Once the goal for 1962 was reached, a survey of program interests was made, and fifteen committees were established to develop program recommendations. Educational television station WGBH in Boston agreed to make its daily five-hour schedule of programs available to Schenectady's new station, WMHT, at no cost. These were received by microwave relay with the cooperation of a local station. The council continues to telecast over WRGB, General Electric's commercial station, and sends out programs for fourteen hours a day over the new station. Boston programs as well as selected programs on WRGB are taped and repeated at different times on WMHT. New WMHT programs are also taped for repetition as needed.

LOOKING AHEAD

The future of educational television looks bright, in spite of the increasing need for more personnel to give talent and time. The Schenectady school system furnishes space for the educational television studio. Already incalculable hours have been generously contributed to program planning by Schenectady's teachers and administrators, as well as by personnel of the area's public and private schools and other community representatives.

Within the present framework of council activities, a school system faces many problems related to the development and use of programs. Since each school district in New York State is autonomous with respect to developing specific philosophy, curricula, and methodology, a program geared to one school system may not conform to the policies and procedures of another. Television's impact at the grass-roots level of instruction—that is, on the child in the classroom—requires that educational leaders in various school systems develop flexibility and receptiveness to change and that they work cooperatively toward compatibility of purpose.

Education by television cannot come of age until the "frill" or extracurricular misconcept is eliminated by demonstrable results that justify its cost and ensure television's rightful status as a bona fide classroom tool of our times. The team approach is a basic prerequisite for each program, with the individuals concerned contributing their best talents and skills toward the common goal.

School systems must take a new look at organizational patterns in order to provide time for viewing on a carefully selective basis. Teacher training in the full use of televised programs will require in-service education with background courses in teacher training colleges—a foreseeable requirement.

It is evident that momentum for the use of television in our schools has been of the self-propelling type, stemming from an ever-continuing conviction of its worth. Trial and error have not proved a deterrent to progress but a stimulant to growth. Schenectady's example should illustrate that much can be accomplished with very little when community, school board, and school staff cooperate with common understanding and purpose. I think, given a choice, I would not have changed the process through which we have lived. It has been well worth the cost—both financial and personal.

chapter 9

The Des Moines approach:
the district-owned station

John A. Montgomery

This chapter illustrates an example of a district-owned and district-operated television station. In it Mr. Montgomery highlights the program itself with an emphasis on the procedures that have evolved to assure quality programming and effective utilization.

In April, 1959, Station KDPS-TV went on the air as the fortieth educational television station in the country, the first in Iowa, and one of the few owned and operated by a single school system. The station was the result of an extensive eight-year investigation and campaign conducted by the school administration, the board of education, teachers, county school officials, and an active citizens' committee composed of representatives from various educational and cultural groups within the community.

The decision to strive for a district-operated station was based on several factors:

1. The Des Moines school district had been using its own FM radio station regularly as a means of instruction in the public schools, so that facilities already constructed for the radio operation could easily be adapted for television at a minimum cost. The school district had available the most scientifically constructed and best-adapted studio in the city. The sound equipment required for television was already in operation as part of the FM station.
2. The Des Moines Technical School offered a full two-year course in radio and television, and many of the operating positions in the station could be filled by students in that program.
3. Although many educators were convinced that a statewide network would be the most economical, efficient, and effective means of extending Iowa's educational resources to all citizens, legislation for a statewide network could not be obtained. In Polk County and in Des Moines especially, however, interest among laymen and educators remained strong enough to break through on a local basis.

Mr. Montgomery is Director of the Educational Television Station KDPS, Des Moines, Iowa.

The reasons for choosing open- rather than closed-circuit television were these:

1. A VHF open-circuit channel was available for use and was considered a choice allocation.
2. Some of the major items of expensive equipment, such as a transmitter and video tape recorder, were given to the school district.
3. The schools within the district were widespread, and the cost of the co-axial cable necessary for closed-circuit operation seemed prohibitive.
4. The interest lay as much in adult-level evening broadcasting as in instructional broadcasting.
5. Original thinking focused on a statewide network, and scattered rural areas could be reached only by means of open-circuit programs.

EQUIPMENT AND STAFF

Early in the summer of 1957, the Cowles Broadcasting Company presented the school board with a 5-kilowatt transmitter which had been in use at one of its commercial stations. In the fall of 1958, a 300-foot tower was erected on the Technical High School, at a total cost of more than $50,000. Studio equipment, including one image orthicon and two vidicon cameras, was purchased for approximately $43,000 plus installation costs. Since that time, an image orthicon camera has been added, as well as a video tape recorder, rear screen projection equipment, and 16-millimeter sound photographic equipment. The station is operated by a staff which includes manager, educational director, program director, four engineers, three producer-directors, one film director, three clerk-stenographers, ten teachers, one classroom consultant, and a serviceman.

FINANCIAL BASE

The station reaches an increasing number of school systems beyond the Polk County borders as these districts install antenna systems. This will, in time, provide a financial base which would render any ideas of UHF or closed-circuit broadcasting impractical. In 1962 two entire counties, with a combined school population of 10,000 pupils, were already subscribing as total units at the token fee of 50 cents per pupil enrolled. A growing number of individual school districts in other counties are also participating at from $1 to $3 per course for each pupil viewing.

From the start, most of the cost of the station's operation has been borne by Polk County taxpayers. A county board of education property tax levy of about ½ mill provides the station with $161,000 for the major portion of the 1962–1963 budget. The Ford

Foundation's Fund for the Advancement of Education helped during the first three years, but now the remaining $30,491 of the $191,491 budget comes from the Des Moines school district. Besides the $100,000 worth of donated equipment already mentioned, the school district originally invested about $112,000 in getting the station on the air.

INSTRUCTIONAL OBJECTIVES

A county-wide advisory committee was set up to recommend policies relating to expansion, curtailment, or changes in program and operation. Later, to make this committee more functional, elementary, secondary, and adult subcommittees were also organized under it. The initial programs, in secondary school history and physics and in elementary school science, began in the spring of 1959 and continued through the remaining five weeks of the school year. Since then a full schedule of educational programs has been offered.

The advisory committee from the start advocated that in-school telecasts be direct instruction which would:

1. Pace the development of the course of study throughout the year.
2. Focus the emphasis on very important concepts and skills needed by each child.
3. Enrich and supplement the child's experiences beyond what could be done efficiently and economically by the classroom teachers alone.

This philosophy has governed most courses since. Twenty-two different subjects, ranging from kindergarten to grade 12, are being televised during the 1962–1963 school year. For the 1962–1963 offerings see the table on page 111.

Since KDPS-TV serves 45,000 pupils of the Des Moines district, 15,000 in other school systems of the county, and hopes eventually to reach 100,000 beyond county borders, some difficult curriculum problems are evident. The following policies represent our efforts to meet this problem:

1. No program series is taught on KDPS-TV without previous recommendation to the advisory committee by the appropriate subcommittee.
2. Courses of study receive approval of the total membership of the appropriate subcommittee before that committee can recommend the inclusion of the said courses on TV.
3. No single textbook is used as a guideline for determining the courses of study to be followed by studio teachers of KDPS-TV, although many textbooks should be usable with any TV series.
4. TV subcommittees have the responsibility of determining the overall scope and sequence of any TV series without domination by the curricu-

lum department of any one school system. However, generous representation of the various systems is a feature of both elementary and secondary subcommittees.

KDPS-TV subject offerings
1962–1963 school year

Names of courses	Grade level	Minutes in each TV lesson	Number of video lessons in telecourse	Number of times in week
Elementary				
Fun with Sounds	K	15	18	1
Fun with Sounds	1	15	17	1
Music	1	15	35	1
Arithmetic	2	15	70	2
Music	2	15	35	1
Social Studies	3	15	40	2
Science	3	15	30	2
Music	3	15	35	1
Social Studies	4	20	93	4
Science	4	20	46	4
Music	4	15	35	1
Social Studies	5	20	93	4
Science	5	20	48	4
Music	5–6	15	35	1
Social Studies	6	20	92	4
Science	6	20	48	4
Spanish	6	10	170	5
Secondary				
World Geography	7	20	140	4
World History	10	30	128	4
American Literature	11	20	140	4
Driver Education	10–12	30	30	

The subcommittee gives due consideration to as many school systems as possible in establishing courses of study selected for TV. When a subject is chosen to be presented on television, a curriculum committee blocks out the scope and sequence of the course to be presented on camera. A study guide is prepared for the television course and distributed to each teacher. Periodic meetings of these curriculum committees are scheduled to evaluate, revamp, and update each unit. The television studio teachers, selected from the ranks of the classroom teachers, lead these committees in the development of printed materials. This "team teaching" is a step forward in terms of well-organized, large-school system teaching.

LARGE-CLASS INSTRUCTION

By June, 1962, KDPS-TV had completed three years of participation in the National Program for the Use of Television in the Public Schools sponsored by the Ford Foundation's Fund for the Advancement of Education. The initial plans for the project were made in cooperation with Dr. Alexander J. Stoddard of the Ford Foundation. City and county schools joined the extensive experimentation being conducted in other major cities utilizing television instruction with large classes and at the same time attempted to improve the quality of instruction.

Under these conditions, the large experimental TV classes showed as much and in some cases more measured growth in the subjects televised than the control (normal-sized) classes. There were also a number of unmeasured factors in favor of large-class instruction using TV as a major resource.

We found that there was better utilization of school plant and an improvement in instruction; hurdles such as foreign language instruction in the elementary schools were overcome. In addition, we found that large-group instruction decreased the pupil-teacher ratio in basic skills instruction, increased the amount of planning time in the teacher's day, increased the amount of time for instruction in some basic skills subjects, allowed for more teacher specialization, provided opportunities for more flexible scheduling, and made possible better and more economical use of other audiovisual aids.

By the third year (1961–1962) evidence was sufficiently significant to justify elimination of the testing program and the inclusion of nearly 6,000 pupils in large-class organizations. This represented a 97 per cent increase over the previous year.

VALUES

While there is much further exploration needed in some areas, the use of television itself in Des Moines is no longer an experiment. Thus the question no longer is "Can television be used as a successful means of direct instruction?" but rather "How can we improve the quality of educational TV in terms of both production and utilization?" We do not look upon TV as a panacea for all the traditional school ills. The medium itself is not a virtue. Those things which can be said in its favor are directly dependent upon the wisdom and imagination of the "teaching team." This team (production staff, studio teacher, and classroom teacher) determines whether the experiences provided have scope and quality beyond that of the conventional classroom. The emphasis now is upon the necessity for excellence in the total scope of the program.

Television's possible role in the stimulation of mental, emotional, and physical activity, which results in learning, makes the quality of curricula, methods, and materials of great significance. A higher degree of efficiency can be realized in the learning process if content, composition, visual acuity, sound fidelity, and classroom utilization are what they should be for each lesson taught. All concerned with the project are working together diligently toward these ends. Television is taking advantage of special equipment and resources not generally accessible to individual classrooms. Lessons are presented more effectively because the television teacher has only one daily presentation, averaging twenty minutes in length.

TEACHER REACTION

Twice during the last school year, surveys were made of classroom teachers' reactions. Each teacher using the programs was asked to check points which characterized her evaluation of the program series utilized. The teachers also made specific written criticisms and commendations. While results varied from program to program, the overall impact was impressive, with teachers responding mainly favorably to the television instruction. The change in attitude evident when comparing the fall and spring reaction sheets was also clearly a favorable one. (A summary of the spring educational television checksheets is found in the table on page 114.)

STUDENT TRAINING

One of the most rewarding things about KDPS-TV is that all operating positions are manned by students studying in the related high school core areas, with adult staff supervision. Offering this training program to high school students in the Des Moines Technical High School and similar training to other high schools in Des Moines and Polk County is an important function of the station. Students may receive training in radio and television production or in broadcast engineering. Some of the areas of training are announcing, camera operating, staging and design, video switching, filming, photography, writing, audio and video control, producing, directing, and acting in the theater. Each year more than twenty students learn the background in broadcasting and receive many hours of practical experience comparable to that given by many colleges and universities. Workshops with high school credit are held during the summer for students from other schools throughout the county.

A summary of teacher reactions to educational television conducted in the Des Moines-Polk County area spring 1962

	Number reporting
A. *TV presentation*	
1. Central purpose	
a. Clear	687
b. Not clear	6
2. Development	
a. Step by step	654
b. Lacks organization	17
3. Content of telecast	
a. Just right	511
b. Too much	103
c. Too little	38
4. Pacing of unit	
a. About right	473
b. Too fast	172
c. Too slow	20
5. Vocabulary	
a. Adequate	624
b. Too difficult	50
c. Too simple	15
6. Teaching technique	
a. Effective	608
b. Mediocre	47
c. Ineffective	8
B. *Student reaction*	
1. Attention	
a. Good	430
b. Poor	26
c. Varies	253
2. Interest	
a. Enthusiastic	196
b. Interested	498
c. Indifferent	72
d. Rebellious	4
e. Varies	6
C. *Lesson plans*	
1. Too voluminous	24
2. Too brief	45
3. Practical	549
4. Superfluous	5
5. On time	408
6. Late	7

ADULT PROGRAMS

During the evening hours, KDPS-TV offers programs of information and education to both children and adults. The broadcast schedule is made up of college credit and noncredit courses; public service, including a "Know Your Schools" series; programs in the areas of the humanities, sciences, and arts; and programs of international scope. Other programming each week is obtained through affiliation with NET (National Educational Television) and through MET (Midwestern Educational Television).

INSIGHTS

What then can we say has been learned during these first few years that will condition our activities in the immediate future? What benefits have resulted which make us so certain that educational television is actually here to stay and will continue to make its mark in the public education of central Iowa? From a purely mercenary standpoint, it is quite obvious that there is now better utilization of the entire school plant than ever before. Auditoriums and lunchrooms which were formerly idle for the major part of the school day are now used extensively as instructional areas. Special rooms for physical education, music, and art are now utilized by students in the primary grades as well as by older youngsters. Buildings which were crowded to the limit on the basis of one teacher for every thirty students are now able to accommodate a significantly larger number, and provide better instruction in the more specialized areas at all grade levels.

This improvement of instruction should be the most important consideration, and fortunately from every aspect it appears that this factor does take priority in our continued use of TV. By sharing good teachers in specialized areas with all children, by constantly reevaluating curricula, by increasing the amount of information presented, and by presenting highly organized, systematic, visual instruction, more learning is taking place. In some areas instructional hurdles have been overcome. For example, all elementary children can now have the benefit of a native Spanish-speaking teacher in foreign language study. In-service telecasts for teachers, as well as the daily lessons for children, have proved a significant means of classroom teacher self-improvement.

THE TELEVISION TEACHER

Another very important factor is the improvement of the studio-classroom coordination. Each studio teacher must constantly exchange ideas with the viewing classrooms. To facilitate this, he is required to visit some classes each week.

Responsibilities in classroom visitation include the following:

1. To observe and therefore better understand the reception and utilization aspects of educational TV.

115

2. To maintain some direct contact with children.
3. To sense the reaction of classroom teachers toward the utilization of TV.
4. To seek to clarify purposes of specific lessons.
5. To evaluate the studio teaching and its accompanying lesson plans.
6. To gather ideas regarding good related activities for distribution with the lesson plans.
7. To locate visual materials worthy of utilization on future telecasts.
8. To foster good public relations between the television station, the classroom, and the home.

Occasionally these visits are made by teacher and producer-director together. Usually this is done when the program has been prerecorded and they can view their own production while it is actually being received in the schools.

Studio teachers and their directors also need opportunities for self-improvement. While much can come through daily practice and self-analysis, this is not enough. Visits to other production centers and studios, careful study of instructional kinescopes produced elsewhere, and local workshops are all effective means which have been used.

ADMINISTRATORS AND CLASSROOM TEACHERS

Equally essential is the involvement of administrators, curriculum supervisors, and classroom teachers in planning the total scope and sequence of any given course. This is done most effectively during summer workshops, when participants receive financial reimbursement. Such paid sessions are supplemented by frequent committee planning meetings during after-school hours throughout the year. This means of ensuring flexibility for TV courses should not be overlooked.

In addition to curriculum and production workshops, orientation must be provided which familiarizes teachers with the theory and method of utilization. It is hoped that more college courses on television teaching techniques will be made available in the near future. If TV is to be used as a major instructional tool, such concepts as team teaching and large-class instruction should be understood by the receiving teacher. One of the major problems will be his need for a complete reevaluation and redefinition of the teaching role. Perhaps the use of TV, even more than the use of texts and films, demands that the classroom teacher be both a manager of learning situations and an individual counselor, rather than a mere teller and tester. A little effort on the part of the classroom teachers can result in such greatly improved skills for the learner as note-taking, listening, organizing of ideas, and critical thinking. Most classroom teachers will find themselves spending more time in preparation to keep up with the pace of TV and the high motivation of their students. Furthermore, teacher attitude is all-important. Children respond and learn in a manner directly related to the responsiveness of their classroom teacher.

THE STUDENT

However, children must *learn* to listen and respond to the TV screen. Years of indiscriminate practice at home viewing commercial channels leave something to be desired as far as good viewing habits are concerned. At every age, children in an educational TV class must learn the lesson of responsibility—responsibilty for listening, seeing, and retaining the essentials of the telecast in its entirety.

THE FUTURE

As we look into the future, fewer than four telecasts per week in any given area may be offered without detracting from the direct instructional approach. This will allow more time for related classroom activities and more time within the broadcast day for other programming. The length of the most instructional programs will continue to range from fifteen to twenty minutes. Pacing with flexibility will remain an important factor. Increased efforts are being made toward correlating FM radio programs with certain TV series to improve instruction further. This will serve as a means of effectively revitalizing the use of radio as well as conserving television time.

Great possibilities are foreseen through continued association with NAEB (National Association of Educational Broadcasters), MPATI (Midwest Program on Airborne Television Instruction), NETRC (National Educational Television and Radio Center), MET (Midwestern Educational Television), and GPRITL (Great Plains Regional Instructional Television Library).

I can only conclude that instructional television is making great strides in the Des Moines area. Who can tell what the ultimate will be? Certainly we can anticipate continued progress in the quantity and quality of educational TV usage.

Credit for the progress thus far and the optimistic outlook for the future goes to the outstanding team of national leaders, Iowa laymen, local administrators, board members, committeemen, staff members, and teachers whose vision has made present accomplishments possible and paved the way for even greater things ahead.

chapter 10

Guidance and television

Catherine L. Beachley

This chapter describes a practical and successful application of television within a comprehensive district-wide guidance program; the approach discussed here has interesting implications for both open- and closed-circuit television.

If students are to make wise educational and vocational choices and solve in a reasonably satisfactory way their more urgent personal problems, there is a basic need for more and better-trained school counselors. The lack of qualified guidance personnel, the limitations of budget, and a rapidly increasing school population have caused the counseling load in many school districts to become exorbitant. How to relieve the tremendous pressure on counselors is perhaps the main problem of most guidance departments. Outside consultants (e.g., college representatives and vocational specialists) contribute to counseling programs, but their contribution is limited by the fact that most consultants cannot take the time to cover more than one or two schools in a district.

TURNING TO TELEVISION

Dr. William M. Brish, Superintendent of the Hagerstown, Maryland, schools, was faced with these and related problems when in 1956, under his direction, the district began to explore in a county educational workshop the use of closed-circuit television as a tool for improving instruction in a variety of subjects, on levels ranging from grades 1 to 12.

The experimental project was to be conducted over a period of five years under the sponsorship of the Fund for the Advancement of Education of the Ford Foundation. Each member of the supervisory staff of the board of education in Washington County was asked to assist in devising ways to utilize the new educational medium.

Catherine Beachley is Supervisor of Guidance for the Board of Education of Washington County, Hagerstown, Md.

To those in high school guidance work, the use of closed-circuit television appeared to offer at least a partial solution to several major problems. It seemed likely, for example, that television could be employed to keep students informed on the latest guidance information, to utilize efficiently the time of educational or vocational specialists in disseminating information, to bring large numbers of students together with specialists, and finally, to provide more adequate means of follow-up with students who received the guidance information disseminated.

PLANNING FOR TELEVISION

Accordingly, one of the groups in the 1956 summer workshop devoted itself to the utilization of the Washington County closed-circuit facilities for guidance. A team consisting of guidance supervisors, counselors, classroom teachers, and secretarial help planned a series of guidance telecasts that could fulfill the needs of students by providing the necessary guidance information in such areas as personal and social relationships, curriculum course selection, college information, career choice, military guidance, and general orientation to junior high school.

Many special-resource personnel donated their time and effort to appear on the telecasts. Guests ranged from high-ranking national government officials to several individuals who had not even completed a high school education. Virtually no limitations were placed on choosing guests for appearance in the guidance series. If a person had some valuable knowledge to contribute, he was utilized to the best possible advantage for the viewing students.

Important in the developmental and experimental stages of the guidance telecasts was the use of varied techniques of presentation to enhance audience interest. Consultants on camera transmitted their message by such diversified methods as demonstrations, discussions, cartoons, silhouettes, question boxes, skits, student panels, movies, film clips, interviews, style shows, songs, and dances. A rich variety of visual representations accompanied and strengthened the productions.

As a result of the summer preplanning, weekly half-hour guidance telecasts began in 1956 and have continued into the present.

During the developmental period, the guidance supervisor worked closely with the school counselors to ensure the success of the programs. The importance of preplanning sessions with school personnel, students, and community leaders, and of the follow-up activity by counselors in their individual schools, cannot be overemphasized.

119

RESULTS

After five years of experimentation with guidance telecasts, students, counselors and program participants generally agree that the quantity and quality of guidance information, as well as the interest of students in planning for the future, have markedly increased as a result of closed-circuit television. The success of the guidance series has been indicated in many ways:

1. Voluntary reading of materials on the telecast topics is regularly done in the guidance office by members of the student audience.
2. Requests by counselors for additional telecasts to supplement telecast areas previously offered have been common.
3. Voluntary requests by students for interviews with counselors and other qualified personnel on topics previously shown have become the rule rather than the exception.
4. Letters and telephone calls from parents and teachers have been favorable and numerous.
5. Over the years there has been a steady increase in the number of students viewing the optional telecasts.
6. Students are known to have based decisions regarding college or career upon what they have learned from the closed-circuit telecasts.
7. There has been an increase in enrollments from the district in those colleges represented in the series.
8. Telecast information concerning the availability of financial assistance has led to an increase in the number of scholarships earned by Hagerstown graduates.
9. There is indication that as a result of the telecasts pupils have learned to choose subjects and courses more nearly in line with their vocational interests and achievements than previously.
10. High school principals have requested the video taping of each telecast to allow for reruns, thus accommodating students who could not attend the regularly scheduled telecast.

Over the years we have learned a great deal about televising guidance programs. There were, of course, minor problems that arose daily and had to be solved as they came up. Others, requiring more study and consultation, provided the kind of knowledge of guidance telecasting which can be of use to potential experimenters in the field.

SOME INSIGHTS

On our first college information telecasts, for example, two colleges divided a half-hour program equally. This occasionally caused some tension, since one guest was obliged to wait until the other had finished his presentation. Moreover, under this procedure both college representatives had to be from the same type of educational institution, since the viewing student was "there" because a certain type of school interested him. This early difficulty was quickly overcome by limiting the thirty-minute telecast to a presentation by a single college.

Our early telecasts often ran overtime, causing many faculty complaints. This problem pointed up the fact that definite criteria concerning format must be adhered to. Today, without exception, the major portion of the telecast is limited to an absolute maximum of twenty minutes, allowing approximately five minutes each for the moderator's introduction and his summary.

A few participants were found to be extremely ill at ease in front of the television camera. It became a definite necessity that the guests be individuals who could project personality without the distraction of nervous facial expressions or gestures, and who had the ability to enunciate clearly and pleasantly. On the other hand, it became our responsibility to ensure a guest's understanding of the television environment—how to use a microphone, movements of the camera, the meaning of hand signals, etc. Even when a participant assured us that he had been on television before, these instructions were repeated. We found that when these steps were followed, the guests were far more relaxed and much more effective.

During the first two years of experimentation, the college representatives were often invited to two of the local high schools immediately following the telecast. This proved unnecessary. Questions asked by the students usually duplicated what had been covered on television, and this use of the consultants' time and effort negated a primary reason for using television in the first place. As one consultant said, "It is important for the student to hear information about several different colleges. Then, when he has decided upon the one or ones which really interest him, he is ready to talk to the college admissions officer—on the campus itself."

COST

Since guidance forms an integral part of the total school program, it would be a difficult matter to express even a tentative opinion as to how much this trail-blazing television project in guidance has cost financially. The expense of the coaxial cable is based on an annual rental, regardless of the amount of time it is used. Personnel such as directors, artists, and others were also available on a full-time basis for regular and special programs, so that no additional costs were involved. The primary expense entailed by the presentation of guidance telecasts, therefore, was that of the $1.25 hourly wage rate paid to the television crew, including cameramen, floor managers, and others. This personnel was

Attractive displays are prepared in the individual schools to focus attention on the guidance telecasts. (Board of Education, Hagerstown)

composed of students from the communications class at the local junior college, part of whose laboratory period consisted in time spent working in the closed-circuit studios. There were a few additional minor costs for supplies. The twenty-five copies of each weekly script, for example, consumed about fifteen reams of paper annually. Estimated cost for the yellow or black visual and super cards probably totaled only ten dollars.

Expenses for the special guests have been at a minimum. Every invited participant and consultant has cheerfully and graciously donated his time, talent, and energy, neither asking for nor receiving an honorarium.

Greater than the monetary costs were the large amounts of time and energy expended by the supervisor, the director, and the production teams. Constant attention is required from the first planning of a guidance script through the securing of participants, the completion of arrangements in minute detail (including, at times, the writing of a script), the rehearsal and video taping of the program, and the final evaluative work so necessary to the success of the experiment.

Nevertheless, in view of the results achieved, the money, time, and talent expended were at the barest minimum. No additional investment was required by the district. The guidance personnel were permanent employees before the project began, and the guidance programs were but a small part of the total television project.

CARE IN PLANNING: A NECESSITY

Much of the success of the guidance series and of the entire Hagerstown project is a direct result of the care taken in the introduction of television into the district. During the five-year experiment in instructional television, summer workshops continued and were supplemented during the regular school terms with additional consultant service as well as with field trips. During this period there was no lack of emphasis on the fact that the teacher in the classroom, who followed up the instructional telecasts, was the key person in the teaching team. Teams of teachers met monthly to discuss the weaknesses and the strengths of the television lessons.

In advance of the telecast related materials are distributed to the schools. (Board of Education, Hagerstown)

A similar technique was pursued in connection with the guidance telecasts. Topics for presentation were selected in consultation with counselors, principals, and teachers. Detailed information about the programs—who was to appear, date and hour of presentation, etc.—was provided for the counselors, who in turn took responsibility for publicity within the schools. Counselors worked to secure the cooperation of classroom teachers, monitored the telecasts along with students, and, of course, conducted both immediate and delayed follow-ups of the telecasts with the students concerned. The counselors also provided the essential evaluative information to the supervisor by recording on a "feedback card" the number of students in attendance, the reaction of the students to the content of and personalities appearing on the telecast, and comments on the pacing and audio-visual reception of each program. Such weekly evaluations keep the series practical and functional.

Counselors on the receiving end also shared directly at some time in the production of guidance telecasts—securing talent, or serving as moderator, floor manager, director, or producer. In order that guidance telecasts be most effective, such direct participation is almost obligatory. Firsthand knowledge of production activities facilitates better understanding and utilization of television in guidance services.

The importance of keeping continual records of student attendance and reactions cannot be overemphasized. The evaluation process plays a large role in planning future programs.

Were changes to be made in our guidance series, we would probably choose first to increase emphasis on the area of the personal problems of the junior high school student. Telecasts covering that phase of guidance have proved overwhelmingly popular. Staff and budget limitations, however, make an expansion of the program impossible at this time.

Television can certainly assist school districts in improving their guidance programs. To assure success, telecasts must:

- Form an integral part of the total educational television program.
- Be carefully preplanned by a team.
- Encourage further desirable learning experiences, appropriate research, discussion, and planning before and after each program.
- Feature up-to-date, reliable materials and counsel from expert resource personnel drawn from education, the professions, government, armed forces, labor, business, and industry.
- Offer in-service training along the lines of educational, vocational, and personal problems for new and present counselors.

The Hagerstown experiment, operating along these lines, has convinced us of the value of television guidance programs. Expert consultants have been able to reach a far wider audience than under standard methods; guidance personnel have been able to increase their effectiveness; and parents, students, and teachers alike have responded with enthusiasm to the entire program.

chapter 11

Television in the secondary school

Martha Gable

Today the greatest percentage of all instructional television programs are designed for use within the elementary classroom. Faced with complex scheduling problems and a wide variety of courses, we have tended to overlook the potential of television in the secondary schools. This chapter highlights how one school district has used open-circuit television in its junior and senior high schools.

Any school administrator contemplating the use of open-circuit television must first answer several basic questions:

1. How can the medium be used in a given situation with maximum results in improved learning?
2. What modifications of school organization are possible and desirable?
3. Will the returns justify the financial investment?

Obviously there are no pat answers. The many studies conducted throughout the country on instructional television indicate that the greatest successes are being achieved where the use of television has been planned to meet specific needs. A wide variety of patterns has emerged as educators have studied the medium and adapted it to serve their particular situations.

A secondary school principal has a combination of alternatives from which to evolve a useful type of service for his school. Like administrators on all grade levels, he must consider faculty and parent orientation, receiver placement, and equipment maintenance. There is, however, one problem that is unique to the secondary school: how to schedule programs for a particular course when that subject is taught concurrently by several teachers and is scheduled during many periods of the day. The scheduling problem is further complicated by the fact that secondary schools offer a greater variety of separate courses than do elementary schools; moreover, teaching problems arising under these circumstances tend to be more restricted, more individualized, and they must be dealt with accordingly.

125

Miss Gable is Director of Radio and Television for the Philadelphia Public Schools.

These points may seem obvious, but unfortunately there seems to be a tendency to concentrate time and money on transmission facilities and on the preparation of television lessons, with less attention being given to plans for good reception, effective utilization, and the creation of a climate of receptivity in the school community.

The Philadelphia public schools have used open-circuit television successfully in a number of ways in the secondary schools.

Programs are telecast over local educational and commercial stations. The television teachers assisted by curriculum experts plan the lessons, which are then produced under the direction of a director supplied by the station.

AS A SUPPLEMENTARY TEACHING AID

(Where lessons related to the course of study are presented once or twice a week by an expert to augment classroom offerings.)

This is probably the most widely used pattern of television teaching on all grade levels.

In ninth-grade English, for example, an outstanding scholar of contemporary and classic literature discussed books, plays, and poems included on the reading list. At first the television presentations were in the form of readings and dialogue; later they included dramatized excerpts presented by college and semiprofessional dramatic groups.

These programs relieved the classroom teacher of repeated exhaustive preparation of material; they permitted the sharing of the special talents of scholars and gifted teachers with a large number of pupils and teachers, who recognized and appreciated the talent —yet such sharing could have been achieved by no other technique. Most important, an evaluation of the series showed that the telecasts aroused interest in reading on the part of pupils who did not respond to a standard "reading" approach.

Television was used in another instance to supplement a twelfth-grade social studies course. In this case, a series on the Constitution and the law was presented at the request of social studies teachers who desired to stimulate interest in this part of the course. The lessons were prepared by a teacher, with the cooperation of the Philadelphia Bar Association and the Radio-TV Staff, for presentation at such times as they fitted appropriately into the course. During the twelve telecasts in the series, short scenes were enacted raising points of law, after which pupils in the studio asked questions of the guest lawyers and judges.

DIRECT TEACHING BY TELEVISION

(When the major part of a course of study is presented by the television teacher. This configuration has been variously described as "major resource," "basic," or "direct" teaching by television.)

A review of reports from secondary schools across the country reveals a wide variety of subjects taught and many combinations of television and classroom procedures. The final plan has depended upon the type and placement of equipment and the organization of classes needed to achieve the desired results.

In Philadelphia, one secondary school scheduled seven classes in the auditorium three days a week for seventh-grade science. The telecasts occupied twenty-five of the forty-two-minute periods. One teacher, selected for experience and competence, conducted the preparation and follow-up activities; the other six teachers assisted with individual questions, the distribution of materials, and homework assignments.

On the other two days of the week, the classes were scheduled in regular-sized classrooms for testing, conferences, and laboratory experience. This particular organizational form was used to maximize the effectiveness of the television and follow-up teachers.

In another school, the same programs were used, but a different type of organization was selected. Whereas in the first example all the teachers viewed the television series within the auditorium, only two teachers in the second school were assigned to meet with the seven classes in the auditorium. A schedule was arranged so that the seven classes met with one or the other of these two teachers in regular classrooms for the nontelevision periods.

This pattern freed five teachers for three periods every week. Since eighth-grade mathematics was also taught by television under the same plan of organization, ten teachers were released for three periods a week in just this one school. Their free time was used to increase the program of special small-group work with the gifted and the slow pupils.

In the third secondary school, a multipurpose room with adequate desk facilities for 240 pupils replaced the auditorium. Our newer schools have sets of rooms with movable walls, so that three classrooms can be converted into one. This permits six classes to receive telecasts simultaneously, in two groups of three classes each. One teacher is assigned to each large group; the principal is able thereby to release the remaining teachers for increased work with small groups or with individual students.

One principal assigned an experienced teacher to conduct the preparation and follow-up activities for the large group while leaving the other two teachers in the room, to assist when needed, but mainly to observe the telecasts and the techniques of the follow-up teacher. The obvious emphasis here was upon in-service training for newer teachers rather than upon deployment of personnel.

Evaluation showed achievement by both television and nontelevision students to be almost the same in the science program. The use of television, however, has produced two positive results: it has allowed the schools to increase the amount of individual attention for our exceptional children, and it has permitted an excellent program of teacher education with minimal expense to the district.

Another television experiment proved highly successful in terms of student achievement. In this instance, two high schools used a sixth-grade language arts television course for two periods a week in the "common learning" groups (courses are not identified on the air by grade level). The pupils in these groups were slow learners, with special reading and writing problems. The results were excellent. In fact, a teacher in one high school reported that "common learning" pupils in the television class improved sufficiently to return to regular classes, not only in greater numbers, but more rapidly than pupils in the nontelevision classes.

TELEVISION AS ENRICHMENT

(Programs designed to capture outstanding local resources, or talent which may become available to the classroom for a short period of time.)

A fine example of this type of television is the series entitled "Exploring the Fine Arts," which has been presented over a commercial station in Philadelphia for the past fifteen years. The programs in this series, while not directly related to any particular course of study, are used by many of our teachers because of the excellent presentations in art, dance, music, and drama.

TELEVISION AS TOTAL TEACHING

(Where an entire course is taught over television, without assistance from classroom teachers.)

While courses of this type are not presently used in the Philadelphia district, a number of high schools in the country have used television lessons for subjects in which no local teachers have been available. For instance, "Continental Classroom" courses in both physics and chemistry were received for credit through local rebroadcasting services in areas where it was not economically feasible to hire a teacher for the few pupils who required these subjects.

The scheduling problems which arise as a result of the use of open-circuit instructional television must, of course, be solved. Our Philadelphia experience has shown us that the solution lies in advance planning with teacher cooperation. We have found that when the various television series are requested by the teachers and when the cooperative planning takes place far enough in advance, no major difficulties arise from the adjustment of bell schedules to TV lessons. At the present time, our fall television schedule is completed by March 1 of the previous school year. In addition, for greater flexibility, we limit our telecasts to a maximum of twenty-five minutes for use within the regular forty-five-minute period.

Change of bell schedules necessitated by long assemblies, special testing programs, and the like, have occasionally created additional scheduling problems. However, since all television subjects are presented on the same three days of the week, we avoid the difficulty by making every effort to schedule assemblies, etc., on one of the other two days. This illustrates again the fundamental requirement which must be met if instructional television programs are to succeed: that is, the requirement that the principal and the faculty agree in advance on procedures to be followed.

What, then, have been the reactions of teachers and students to our applications of television in the Philadelphia secondary schools?

Secondary school teachers are usually the most reluctant to use television in the classroom. Probably their resistance is due in large part to the fact that they are specialists in their respective subject areas and therefore do not feel the immediate need for the TV lessons.

However, reports indicate that negative attitudes usually disappear as both teacher and pupils understand the purposes and values of television.

These are typical reactions of Philadelphia teachers:

"At first I thought that I had to reteach everything that the TV teacher presented. I realize now this is not necessary, and I am able to concentrate on applications and other follow-up activities."

"The TV teacher has time to use resources and prepare lessons in a way that is impossible with my schedule. The TV materials are excellent."

"The visual-verbal TV lessons in science have helped those pupils to learn who have reading and writing difficulties. I find that pupils who cannot read questions with comprehension, or write the answers, can go to the blackboard and draw and explain difficult concepts. TV teaching has underlined a need for more adequate testing of these pupils."

"TV prods us into viewing all the units in the course of study. Too often, important units have been omitted because of lack of time."

"We expected discipline problems in large classes. There have been none. There seems to be a compulsion about TV which is different."

The reaction of our pupils has been fascinating. A few of the more significant comments:

"I must listen and get it the first time."

"The TV teacher seems to be talking directly to me."

"We can't get the teacher off the point in a discussion—we learn more."

"We aren't held up by so many unimportant questions."

Those who have been involved with instructional television realize that it is, and must be, in effect, a form of team teaching. The television teacher presents, challenges, demonstrates with many resources; the classroom teacher extends and reinforces, helps pupils with understanding and application, assigns outside projects and research, and provides for individual differences. A skilled partnership exists.

A word should be included about the use of television on commercial and educational stations during out-of-school hours. Excellent drama, public affairs programs, fine music, documentaries are used as a resource in increasing numbers of secondary schools. For example, cooperative ventures to stimulate reading are now under way between commercial television stations and public libraries. Several commercially produced series in the field of social studies have excellent study guides which are available without cost to interested teachers.

Television is a powerful device when used wisely; it is too expensive for casual trial-and-error approaches. Each principal and school administrator must determine whether the returns to be gained are commensurate with the investment.

part III

Administrative uses of television

IN REVIEWING instructional television there is often a tendency to overlook the many applications outside the regular teaching situation. Television has been successfully used for in-service education, student orientation, and testing programs, and in furthering school-community relations. It cannot be anticipated that a school district will enter into the use of television for these applications alone, as they are rarely used enough to warrant any large expenditure of funds. However, once an open- or closed-circuit project is under way, many additional administrative applications are possible for a minimum additional expense. Programs of this type are rarely scheduled on a regular basis but are employed only at those times when the need exists.

One practical application has been in student orientation programs. Districts have used television at the beginning of the term to explain school procedures and policies and to introduce administrative officers. Such programs, televised into the homerooms, have eliminated the need for assemblies and the related schedule changes and confusion.

Of all traditional orientation programs, that of the library is perhaps the most time-consuming and inefficient. Under normal procedures one class at a time visits the library to receive orientation from the library staff. In many schools this operation takes several weeks, during which period the normal library program is greatly curtailed. One combination junior-senior high school moved its portable camera units into the library and televised the orientation program into the regularly scheduled English or social studies classes. The twenty-minute presentation explained library procedures, highlighted the materials available and the services provided, and introduced the library staff. By repeating the presentation several times over a two-day period, it was possible to reach 2,500 students with a minimum of strain upon the library staff and the classroom teacher. The librarians found that the students were able to utilize the library as well after orientation by television as they could with the traditional orientation procedures.

The first example in this part, "Standardized Testing by Television," is concerned with an area that has been receiving increased emphasis over the past decade. In this chapter Dr. Woodward describes a practical use of television that can effectively reduce administrative expense while actually improving a school- or district-wide program of standardized testing.

Administrators have found television to be an excellent means for reaching both teachers and parents. Dr. Shanks, in his chapter on the Anaheim project, mentions the practicality of weekly "Staff Chats" (see page 78), informing teachers of various district policies and new educational developments. The use of television to facilitate district-planned in-service education is highlighted in the final two chapters in this part: "Television, Kinescopes, and In-service Education" and "Television and Classroom Observation." Both chapters describe methods by which the in-service program has been able to offer more for less.

Other related applications should be mentioned at this time. Several chapter writers have referred to the positive effect that instructional television is having upon their school-community relations. This is particularly true of open-circuit programming, where a surprisingly large number of parents regularly view those programs used in their children's classes. Many find that by viewing the lessons they can be of greater assistance to the children and their teachers. Television has proved itself as an excellent means by which the school district can reach the community. Programs have highlighted curriculum changes and explained the need for the passage of a school bond issue. As a result many administrators have found it practical actually to design informational programs for the community at large.

Any school district using television has the opportunity of using the medium for administrative purposes outside the regular teaching program. These techniques are valuable, effective, and possible at a minimum of additional expense. Possible administrative applications of open- and closed-circuit television should be thoughtfully explored.

chapter 12

Standardized testing by television

John C. Woodward

In the last decade, standardized testing has become an integral part of our educational guidance and evaluation programs. In this chapter Dr. Woodward highlights the applications of television toward the achievement of standardization, efficiency, and an ideal environment for school testing procedures.

The administration of standardized psychological tests in the areas of academic aptitude and achievement in school situations has become an accepted practice. Statewide testing programs in California, New York, Iowa, and other states attest to this fact.

As a student progresses through the school system from kindergarten to high school and college, he will almost certainly have been subjected to much standardized testing. Many students will spend forty-five hours taking as many as ten separate batteries of standardized tests.

At the elementary level the student will take general intelligence or scholastic aptitude tests, reading-readiness tests, and achievement tests in content subjects. At the secondary level, in addition to the foregoing, the student may have administered to him interest inventories, special aptitude tests, and prognostic tests in special subject fields.

If the secondary student is college-bound he will usually take one or more of the national standardized batteries in his junior or senior year, one or more of the national scholarship test batteries, and perhaps another battery of tests when he arrives at the specific college of his choice.

PROBLEMS

The problem facing school boards, school administrators, teachers, and college test officers is how to carry out the accepted testing in an efficient and economical way with the best use of professional

Dr. Woodward was Associate Professor of Education at San Jose State College, where for two years, as College Test Officer, he administered various tests over television. He is presently Director of Evaluation, University College, University of Miami.

time while still adhering to the accepted practices of a good standardized testing program.

A major problem in test administration has to do with procedures used in testing large groups.

In most schools it is usually necessary to test large groups at one time. National programs such as the College Entrance Examination Board, National Merit Scholarship, American College Testing Program, and others with uniform national dates demand this. In a majority of cases the school adminstrator sets aside certain periods for testing so as not to disrupt schedules any more than necessary.

In testing large groups of students, most test administrators are faced with two alternatives: one, to use auditoriums or other large facilities with a small number of competent examiners and a large number of proctors; or, two, to use many small rooms with a large number both of competent examiners and proctors.

The first method involves scheduling in gymnasiums, theaters, coliseums, auditoriums, and other large facilities not ordinarily used or well suited for these activities. Lighting is usually inadequate, folding chairs in gymnasiums are not designed for long periods of sitting, and even with the more comfortable auditorium seats, lap boards are necessary for writing purposes. Ventilation in these large facilities is normally not up to par for long periods; distribution of materials to large groups is usually complicated and time-consuming; and proctoring is, at best, inadequate.

The second method (i.e., testing in well-lighted, well-ventilated, comfortable classrooms) seems to leave little to be desired. The main disadvantage is the need for a large number of competent examiners, which is seldom available. To detain a professional person for long periods of time to test a small number of individuals is obviously expensive, inefficient use of staff time.

USING TELEVISION

Administration of standardized tests by closed-circuit television appears to offer the advantages of both alternatives without the concomitant disadvantages. Administering the instruction for the examinations over closed-circuit television to students seated in many well-lighted, well-ventilated, comfortable classrooms that are well-distributed throughout the school eliminates the need for large numbers of test administrators.

Procedures. In schools where this method has been used, the test administrator is stationed in the television studio. Regular standard classrooms with seating capacities ranging from thirty to fifty are used for the examinees. Proctors are stationed in each room.

One or two are used, depending on the size of the room. The rooms are equipped with television receivers and two-way communication telephones. Often this may be accomplished by using the school's existing intercom system. The examiner in the television studio directs the students and the proctors via television; the proctors, in turn, communicate with the examiner over the two-way communication system.

A necessity in any program of this nature is pretest program instruction and coordination of the system. Proctors must be given complete and preferably individual briefing concerning their duties. Instruction in the use of the two-way communication system is obviously important.

Besides the reduction in the required number of professional examiners, closed-circuit television offers the advantages of the use of visual materials.

Enlarged copies of answer sheets can be televised to show students how the sheets are to be marked. This technique has markedly reduced the number of student errors in completing the test forms—errors that often necessitate time-consuming hand scoring by the testing staff.

A large elapsed-timing clock, available at most photography stores, can be used with excellent results. This clock is set for the total time of the examination and appears on all television receivers during the examinations. In this way examinees and proctors can tell throughout the testing how much time remains.

Signs are used to announce breaks and the time that testing will resume. In cases where students may leave if they finish early, further instructions, such as when to return after the lunch break and where test results may be obtained, may be superimposed over the clock.

If the person administering the examinations desires visual feedback from the rooms, and equipment is available, a television camera can be set up in one of the testing rooms to enable the examiner to see the examinees and to get a sense of what is going on in the testing rooms. However, such visual feedback has not usually been found necessary.

Results. The closed-circuit system of testing has been used extensively at San Jose State College since May, 1959. As many as 1,700 students in separate classrooms have been tested simultaneously by this method. The system has resulted in great savings of time and money and in a more accurate and standardized system of testing. Errors in instruction and in the marking of answer sheets by students have been virtually eliminated. At one time it could be anticipated that 5 per cent of the students would record some information incorrectly. Experience has shown that each paper incorrectly completed meant at least five minutes of addi-

137

Television permits a single competent examiner to serve an unlimited number of students. With this technique the students, in an ideal testing environment, receive completely standardized instructions.

tional work for the testing staff. Furthermore, it has become possible for one professional test officer helped by graduate assistants to administer the standardized examinations to an unlimited number of students. No significant problems have resulted from the use of television in testing.

In the elementary school, teachers may act as proctors. In the primary grades, this is especially desirable because of the difficulties encountered in having primary students mark answers. Television testing relieves the primary teacher of administrative responsibilities, allowing the teacher to work carefully with the students, making sure that the test booklets are marked correctly.

In the upper elementary grades, teachers may be relieved of proctoring by parents, especially room mothers or individuals from parent organizations such as the home-school club, PTA, and other groups. The teacher can then spend his time in other professional activities.

In conclusion, television testing offers a very real solution to the problems of testing large groups with standardized examinations. Problems usually associated with large-group testing are virtually eliminated. Fewer directions are misinterpreted by the students; complete standardization is achieved; a smaller additional profes-

An enlarged testing form is televised during the initial period of instruction. As a result, student errors in completing the necessary information are virtually eliminated.

A portion of the testing form as seen by the students in the various testing rooms

A large clock on the television screen keeps the students informed of the remaining time. The proctor, in the front of the room, is in direct contact with the testing officer in the television studio.

sional staff is required for testing. For schools with closed-circuit television installation, the method offers a substantial saving in professional time and in school funds. This approach has, within limits, been applied to open-circuit television as well.

chapter 13

Television, kinescopes,
and in-service education

William Hansen

*Faced with constant changes in curriculum and methodology, and
handicapped by a limited budget, the Union Elementary School District
joined forces with other districts and a local college to explore the potential
of television as an economical and efficient means for expanding its
in-service program.*

The Union Elementary School District is a rapidly growing elementary district in the southwest foothills of Santa Clara Valley. Although one of the older school districts in the state of California,
its growth from a one-school rural community to the present ten-
school "bedroom" community has taken place in the past twelve
years. The quality of instruction has been maintained at a high
level in spite of the many changes that have come with growth.
The superintendent and board of trustees have developed a written set of policies which provide a framework within which to
operate. The policy statement on professional growth stipulates
that a high priority be given to in-service education. The duties of
the coordinator of instruction include the providing of "a program
to efficiently orient the personnel new to the district" and a com-
panion program of "in-service activities to maintain teacher
competency."

THE DISTRICT IN-SERVICE PROGRAM

There are three distinct facets of in-service training which must be
considered when planning a district program: first, the need to
orient teachers new to the district to current policies and practices;
second, the necessity to develop stimulating and valuable activities
which will maintain teacher competency; and third, the more
recent problem of communicating to our teachers the continual
changes in curriculum and methodology.

William Hansen is Coordinator of Instruction for the Union School District, Cambrian
Park, Calif.

Until recently, the planning for the first two aspects of the program was not difficult. We scheduled the typical subject-matter or grade-level meetings for discussion. When techniques or methodology were of concern, we held demonstration lessons. However, in the past four years, we have had to assimilate over seventy new teachers into the district, and sheer numbers have caused us to take another look at our approach. It has become difficult to reach all the teachers with a quality program, and our expenses for in-service activities have risen sharply.

The problem of communicating change to the staff has become a real challenge to the district. Our teachers must be informed of new methodology in team teaching, programmed instruction, and instructional television. Experienced instructors must be found to demonstrate new techniques and equipment. The cost of retaining qualified consultants is prohibitive. We must also face the pressure of new curriculum changes in the fields of foreign language, science, and mathematics. Again, the need for qualified people has created a demand for their service, and costs are beyond the means of a district our size. Even when we have set aside funds for outside consultants, we have often found it difficult, if not impossible, to find someone available with the necessary talent and experience.

APPLYING TELEVISION

The Union school district approached open-circuit television as a possible solution to its in-service problems for three basic reasons: first, a higher percentage of teachers within the district could be reached than by other procedures; second, the most qualified consultants would become available; and third, the district would be able to receive more actual value for its in-service dollar.

We were extremely fortunate in our timing, for San Jose State College, which serves the area and is the largest teacher training institution in California, had simultaneously expressed an interest in exploring the potential of televised in-service education.

One fact became immediately apparent. Although the college had expressed a willingness to cover production costs as a service to the area's school districts, instructors' salaries and the cost of related printed materials could not be covered by the college and certainly could not be carried by our district alone. These additional expenses could be met only if several districts could and would share the responsibility.

The Santa Clara County School Department was interested in the possibilities of the project, and since this type of activity came within its role as a coordinating body, it offered to organize a meeting of interested parties.

Television brings to the district-sponsored in-service workshop outstanding consultants, who have the assistance of a talented production team and the use of the many techiques and materials that are possible with television teaching.

COORDINATING THE PROGRAM

The first meeting brought together representatives of nine school districts, two adjoining-county school officials, and a representative from the college. The local television station, KNTV San Jose, had been contacted by the college and had volunteered to donate time for the series. The college offered the services of its Instructional Television Center, which had the equipment, personnel, and experience to develop and produce the programs. For the first year of operation, the station also donated the cost of a closed-circuit connection between the center and its transmitter, a cost which was later absorbed by the college.

The group, under the title of Television Coordinators, met monthly. While the college would produce the program, it was left to our group to decide program direction, objectives, and general content. The group also suggested the television instructor and evaluated the telecasts. Once the purposes for the programs were spelled out by the districts, responsibility for final content and production was left to the television instructor and the college production staff.

143

With television, over 2,300 teachers from school districts in six counties were able to have the services of a specialist in the field of elementary school science teaching.

This pattern, begun three years ago as an experiment, has proved to be effective. The group continues today in a similar capacity, with one slight modification. After the district coordinators have selected general topics to be covered, the television instructor meets with a subject-matter specialist from each of the participating districts. At this meeting specific areas to be covered are discussed, and follow-up activities are planned which will be carried on by the specialist within his own district after the telecast.

The first series of nine programs was experimental, covering various subjects at many grade levels and exploring their practicality. While it was felt that the approach was generally correct, it was also thought that the programs should be subject-centered, and that, for the present, the emphasis should be placed on in-service education for the elementary teacher. The latter decision was reached for three fundamental reasons: first, the majority of the teachers taught all subject areas and, as a result, needed assistance; second, there was more unanimity as to what should be taught at the elementary level than on higher levels; third, there were simply more teachers with common problems at the elementary level.

A second series was planned with an entirely different approach. It was to be a televised college course for credit in the teaching of

144

elementary school science, with the costs to be covered by the enrollment fees. For an additional unit of credit, the teachers were offered a fifteen-hour laboratory course which was designed in conjunction with the television series and was taught by the television instructors. In spite of Sunday morning scheduling, the course had an enrollment of 231, with fifty-nine of the teachers enrolling in the several laboratory sections that were offered. We had five teachers from our own district enrolled in the course for credit, and an additional fifty or so auditing.

While the total number of teachers enrolled in the course was excellent, we still found that a credit course of this type did not reach enough of our teachers. For this reason, it was decided by the coordinators that the districts should go one step further. For an additional cost of less than $300 per program, a kinescope could be made. The kinescope—a regular 16-millimeter sound film of the program—could then be made available to the participating districts at their request.

COST

By this time, the Television Coordinators group had expanded to include twenty-two school districts and three county school offices. While a single district certainly could not finance the twelve-program series, now costing approximately $1,000 per program (kine-

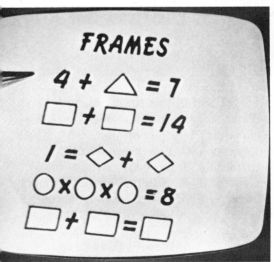
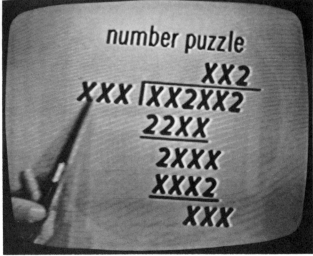

By the use of graphic materials, illustrations can be clearly seen by the viewing teachers. Two charts used within a series of in-service telecasts in the field of elementary mathematics showed framing and a number puzzle.

A new California law states that geography will be taught as a separate subject in its schools. At the request of the school districts a series of telecasts in geography were planned and produced by the San Jose State Instructional Television Center, presenting the concepts, tools, and techniques of geography for elementary and secondary school teachers.

scope included), costs came well within our limits when divided among the districts. Each district agreed to finance the series according to the number of elementary teachers on its faculty. A fee of $2.50 per teacher was agreed upon. Our district paid $427.50 for the twelve telecasts. Approximately 40 per cent of the total cost was covered by the college. It has been anticipated that as more districts participate, our cost may be reduced to approximately 12 cents per program per teacher.

UTILIZING KINESCOPES

The decision to kinescope the series was a major step forward. By having the programs on film, it became possible for KQED, the educational station in San Francisco, to repeat the telecasts on

Thursday afternoons at 3:30, an ideal time for maximum viewing. But the most important advantage was that whereas Sunday morning had previously been the only time the program could be viewed, we could, with the kinescope, schedule the films for use within our districts at our own convenience.

The value of the kinescopes was immediately apparent when our district began to explore the area of mathematics. The principals of the district had been taking part in a two-day mathematics workshop under the direction of a specialist from a nearby college. During this period, three of the televised programs were devoted to this subject area. These programs, presented by a teacher from another school district, were excellent in the way in which they covered the practicality of some of the recent mathematical concepts. The principals, as a group, saw the kinescopes, after which arrangements were made for them to show the films to their own faculties. Thus we were able to capitalize upon the immediate interest in the subject, precisely because we had available the kinescopes and the excellent, comprehensive teacher guides that were prepared in conjunction with each telecast and supplied to every teacher in our district as part of the $2.50 package. The kinescoping of the in-service series has been an investment with residual benefits to us. The kinescopes will be available to us as long as they are applicable, and it is anticipated that the number of films available and the number of subject areas covered will expand each year as the project continues.

In retrospect, over the past three years we have learned much about using television for our in-service program. We have found that it can be used economically and with excellent results. The programs themselves are becoming more and more specific; they are aiming at one or two grade levels instead of the entire elementary school curriculum, and now emphasize specific teaching techniques that can be used by the teacher.

The telecasts have provided excellent focal points for our curriculum meetings, and the kinescopes have overcome the rather inflexible viewing schedule associated with open-circuit television. We have found that using kinescopes as a follow-up to a consultant's presentation is also successful. This is especially true when the workshop can be held under the direction of a specialist on the district staff.

The cost has not been as great as we originally estimated, largely because of the role of the college and the large number of participating school districts. While they have not been kinescoped, the televised courses have paid their own way with registration fees; as mentioned earlier, however, with this approach they do not reach the majority of our teachers.

Looking toward the future, we are more enthusiastic about the potential of in-service education by television than we were when the project began. The district is setting aside one third of its total in-service budget for television. The care taken with the planning and production is certainly an integral part of our success. The wide use we are finding for the kinescopes alone justifies the cost. We are planning to publish a series of newsletters to keep our teachers informed of the in-service series.

Television is playing an increasingly important role in our in-service program. Its ultimate success depends upon how we use the materials and resource personnel available in our district. We are convinced that television, properly used, will bring the most talented instructors and the highest quality of instruction to 100 per cent of our faculty at a cost well within our budget.

chapter 14

Television and classroom observation

John M. Hofstrand

In this chapter Dr. Hofstrand describes a practical use of television within a district-sponsored in-service observation program. Through the use of closed-circuit television, an unlimited number of individuals can observe a classroom without the confusion and unnatural conditions associated with standard techniques.

For many years, school administrators have found value in providing staff members with opportunities to see other members of the profession in action. Many school districts encourage organized visits to observe teachers who are particularly skilled in specific teaching techniques or who have developed stimulating programs. Responsible school officials have felt justified in making time available and in providing substitutes for those teachers scheduled to observe. The logic behind such action is evident: by watching how others use materials or solve common problems, teachers often see ways of improving their own techniques or programs.

Preservice programs in teacher training institutions use observation to provide students with a general picture of the roles of the teacher, along with an understanding of children, their learning problems, and the use of materials in teaching and learning. The oft-heard statement, "We teach the way we were taught," is not without supporting evidence.

Indeed, Bricknell, for example, points out that "the most persuasive experience a school person can have is to visit a successful new program and see it in action."[1] Furthermore,

> Teacher education programs...do not attempt to equip the prospective teacher with specific instructional techniques, but concentrate on developing a general professional wisdom out of which he can develop the specific techniques he needs for any given task. Actual instruction in specific techniques is said to be the responsibility of the schools which employ the college graduates.[2]

Dr. Hofstrand is Associate Professor of Elementary Education at San Jose State College and for several years has actively used television as an observation technique within his classes at the college.

[1] Henry M. Bricknell, *Organizing New York State for Educational Change*. Albany: University of the State of New York, State Education Department, 1961, p. 27.
[2] *Ibid.,* p. 47.

If one accepts, even partially, such statements as these, the necessity of observation programs for in-service education seems obvious. On the other hand, the difficulties of organizing extensive observation programs are numerous. In addition to the problems of providing substitute personnel, of scheduling, and of the considerable expense of anything more than a very limited observation program, the administrator has to meet complex problems of a physical and psychological nature. These include the following:

1. It is physically impossible to have more than a few teachers observe in a particular classroom at one time.
2. Children tend to react unnaturally to visitors—especially if a visitor is attempting to see what a particular child is doing.
3. If visitors are placed in an out-of-the-way location so as not to interfere with the classroom activity, their observation is limited to the immediate vicinity.
4. Visitors must usually observe all happenings from one point in the room rather than from several.
5. Discussion of what is happening is impossible without disturbing the teaching-learning situation.

ONE POSSIBLE SOLUTION: OBSERVATION BY TELEVISION

Results of studies and experimental programs suggest the use of closed-circuit television as a possible solution to these problems.

First, there is no limitation upon the number of observers who can watch a classroom at one time.

Second, it has been found that students, after a short orientation period, are not normally distracted by the equipment in the room; cameras are impersonal and as much a part of the environment as the chairs or desks.

Third, television provides a means of seeing children up close or from a distance, as desired, without interfering with either the classroom activity or the normal response of any one child (see illustration). With multiple cameras it is possible to watch any element of the room from several viewpoints.

Finally, common experiences are offered to the large group of observers, and discussion or analysis is possible at the time of observation. Information regarding the students being observed can be used before, during, or following the observation without movement of the observers or students. Such use may be particularly important to the understanding of specific situations in the classroom or techniques the teacher uses.

Limitations. Two possible limitations of observation by television should be mentioned at this time. First, by not being in the classroom, viewers may lose some of the naturalness and "feel" of what

Views of the classroom as seen on the television screen during a classroom observation (Fontana Unified School District)

While an overhead transparency charts the student's IQ or reading ability, two views of the classroom can be seen. One monitor, second from the right, presents an overview of the entire classroom, while the others highlight a particular scene. Views to be highlighted are selected by the college instructor, who is in direct contact with the engineers in the trailer control room located outside the public school building.

is happening, or have a distorted understanding of the environment in which the teaching is actually taking place. This limitation seems more important when the observation is done by preservice teacher trainees; regular teachers are often unaware of any loss, for they have a general empathy for the televised teacher and a general understanding of classroom environment.

Second, limitations may be imposed because of possible legal problems. Observation does invade the privacy of the individual to some extent, especially when the dissemination of confidential information is involved. Usually there is little or no difficulty in ob-

In order to minimize interference, the television cameras are mounted on pedestals above head level. Additional lighting is supplied by very-high-output fluorescent fixtures.

taining clearances from teachers and parents when they are fully informed of the purposes behind the program, and are assured that control over the viewing audience will be exercised. Control over the audience is impossible over open-circuit television, and for this reason most, if not all, observation programs require the use of closed-circuit systems.

THE EQUIPMENT

The main difference between studio equipment and that needed for observation of a classroom is in the cameras. Classroom work calls for remotely controlled cameras so that cameramen or other tech-

153

A direct-line phone connection between the observing room on the college campus and the public school classroom allows the students at the college to talk directly with the classroom teacher at the completion of the observation.

nical or professional personnel may be eliminated from the lesson. Several experiments have attempted to use cameramen in the classroom during the lesson, but invariably the cameramen and the larger studio equipment created major distractions. Simple remote-control cameras operated by a teacher or technician located outside the classroom have solved most problems associated with viewing equipment. By using a pan/tilt head and two or three cameras with zoom lenses, it is possible to focus on any part of the room with a minimum of disturbance. Recent developments have eliminated the noise usually associated with camera and lens movement, and children seem to adjust more quickly to this equipment than to that used previously.[3]

Experience has indicated value in using two channels for the observation (one for the action and close-up work, the other for an overview of the whole room). It is suggested that one stationary camera be used to present the overview over one channel, and that the other cameras show close-up views over a second channel. Cameras are best located in inconspicuous spots above the general eye level of the children and teacher, so that blocking of views by moving individuals are rare (see illustration, page 153).

[3] For a more detailed description of equipment see pp. 236–237.

Remote-observation technique being used during an aeronautics class. The lower screen shows the "link trainer" cabin dials, while the upper monitor is focused on the flight plan.

One of the major problems in all observations has been to discover adequate ways in which to bring usable sound into the viewing room. Microphones tend to pick up all extraneous noises in the lesson environment—shuffling of feet, rattling of paper, outside traffic, and many others—while missing the soft voices of children. For some time a regular studio microphone was worn by the teachers during our experience at San Jose State College, but the problem of moving freely while dragging the microphone wire was often insurmountable. This difficulty was virtually eliminated with the invention of the wireless microphone, which allowed the teacher complete freedom of movement. With a little practice the televised teacher will automatically locate himself near reciting children. Standard microphones may be placed in the middle of small-group work areas for committee or small-group assignments; when whole classes are being observed, several standard microphones located in front of the seating arrangement will pick up most voices.

Normal classroom lighting has usually proved adequate; occasionally, inexpensive portable lighting units have been used which, when mounted near the ceiling, provide enough light without causing student distraction or discomfort.

If television exists or is being installed in a school district, the

155

addition of observation programming adds tremendous potential for in-service education with relatively little additional expense. On the other hand, television is probably too expensive to warrant installation for observation alone, except in situations calling for major programs similar to those of teacher training institutions.

THE APPLICATIONS

Many successful observation programs have been carried out with relatively small amounts of equipment in a variety of study areas and for a variety of purposes. The Fontana School District in southern California explored remote-control observation under a one-year grant from the United States Office of Education.[4] Observation programs were held for parent groups and visiting administrators as well as for teachers. Television observation proved an effective method for improving school-community relations. At the same time, teachers, administrators, counselors, and specialists used the system for in-service observation of such activities as classroom teaching, testing administration and techniques, interview techniques, and the use of new teaching techniques and materials.

A very different use of remote-control observation was illustrated by the use of closed-circuit television to provide a learning experience for San Jose State College students which would otherwise have been unavailable owing to lack of facilities. In this instance, an entire aeronautics class watched, simultaneously, the flight diagram and instrument panel of a link trainer (see illustration). The use of remote-control cameras, then, need not be limited to in-service education programs.

San Jose State College also used closed-circuit television in an extensive observation study with their elementary teacher trainees.[5] This project indicated that the more planning that goes into an observation, the more successful it is (see illustration, page 152). It is imperative that all those connected with the observation—those planning, directing, and viewing—have the specific objectives of the observation well in mind. This knowledge assists the person directing the cameras to pick up the events which support these objectives, and helps the observer to direct himself to the important elements of the observation. Many techniques have been developed to provide observers with backgrounds necessary for understanding of the individual students, groups, or classes, and

[4] Fontana Unified School District, *The Use of Closed Circuit Television to Improve Teacher Effectiveness.* Fontana, Calif., 1961.

[5] San Jose State College, *Television Utilization in the Observation Program for Teacher Education.* San Jose, Calif., 1962.

for intelligent interpretation of what is observed. Graphs, slides, or overlay materials for projection by the overhead projector can show sociograms, IQ and ability charts, groupings, home environments, and many other things simultaneously, prior to, or just following the viewing. Lesson plans and chart materials prepared in advance may be distributed prior to the lesson. All materials which can provide broader understandings about those being observed help to achieve the objectives.

The experiences of San Jose State College, the Fontana School District, and many other institutions and school districts have demonstrated that television has a definite place in the observation program.

part IV

The perspectives for instructional television

THE FOLLOWING four chapters are primarily designed to place instructional television into perspective. The opening chapter reviews the present status of research in the field and offers some concrete suggestions for those teachers and administrators wishing to evaluate their own projects.

In Chapter 16 an administrator who has been involved in the development and operation of a comprehensive television project reviews many of the fundamental problems that were faced and the role of the administrator in solving them.

Throughout this book an effort has been made to reinforce the basic assumption that television is but one of many alternatives available to the teacher or administrator wishing to improve his educational program. Under certain conditions television offers the most practical solution, while under some circumstances it will be an unwarranted expense. In Chapter 17 a communications and media specialist discusses some of these alternatives, relating them directly to the learning situation and to television.

In the concluding chapter the editor relates instructional television to education in the United States and then goes out on a limb to foretell the future of the medium in our schools. The chapter concludes with a discussion of the major problems that must be overcome if television is ever to gain its proper role in the instructional process.

Perhaps, more than any other section of this book, Part IV reiterates the conclusion that instructional television is, and must be, many things to many people.

chapter 15

Evaluation of instructional television

Roscoe C. Brown, Jr.

Evaluation must play an important role whenever a new educational technique is introduced. The lack of proper research and follow-up investigation has been a major concern of those involved with instructional television. In this chapter Dr. Brown reviews what we already know and offers some suggestions for those administrators and teachers who are planning to explore the potential of the medium.

The effectiveness of an educational activity can best be determined by proper evaluation. The purpose of evaluation is to find out the extent to which the goals or objectives of an educational activity are being achieved. Too frequently, the judgment of the effectiveness of instructional television is based on general impressions, isolated praise or criticisms, and even personal "hunches." It is vital for those concerned with the medium to be aware of the importance of evaluation and to become familiar with the skills of evaluation. When planning instructional television activities, specific budgetary allocations must be provided for the evaluation function.

We are fortunate in having the early studies by Kumata[1] and later Holmes[2] summarizing educational television research up to the time of their writing. Some of the more important findings may be listed as follows:

The overwhelming majority (almost 90%) of gross comparisons between television and conventional communication conditions show no substantial difference in achievement or information gain.

The relatively few comparisons which have indicated differences in achievement and information gain show that: (1) small-discussion type classes are slightly favored over one-way television, (2) one-way television

Dr. Brown is Professor of Education at the New York University School of Education. He specializes in educational research and has had experience in evaluating instructional television projects in the New York metropolitan area.

[1] Hideya Kumata, *An Inventory of Instructional Television Research.* Ann Arbor, Mich.: Educational Television and Radio Center, 1956. 152 pp.

[2] Presley D. Holmes, Jr., *Television Research in the Teaching-Learning Process.* Detroit: Wayne State University, 1959. 152 pp.

is slightly favored over large-lecture type classes, (3) small-discussion type classes are greatly favored over television with audio feedback, (4) small-discussion type originating room is about equal to television with audio feedback, (5) small-discussion type favored over small-discussion type originating room, and (6) one-way television is slightly favored over printed material.

For the presentation of information, the straight talk or lecture produces greater information gain than does a discussion, in which students do not actively participate but merely observe.

An equivalent or greater gain in information can be effected in a shorter period of time when the content is presented by means of television, compared to conventional conditions.

There are no significant differences in information gain attributed to the size of the receiving room, when the total of students per receiver approximately equals in number the screen size in inches.

There are no significant differences in achievement among students placed in the front, middle, or rear of a television receiving room, when the minimum distance from the screen is approximately twice screen size, and the maximum distance is approximately screen size expressed in feet.

There is insufficient data on information gain concerning the lack of color with television.

Greater achievement is shown on information tests by students who receive "simple" television presentations, as compared to "highly visualized" presentations.

There is a suggestion that visual material attracts the attention of the student to such an extent that the learning of the verbal material is interfered with.

No significant differences were evidenced between males and females due to receiving information under television or conventional conditions.

There is a significantly greater gain in critical thinking and problem-solving under conventional conditions than there is under one-way television particularly for high intelligence students.

Face-to-face interaction produces more positive changes in group structure, attitudes, and socialization than does one-way television, but television can stimulate and enhance the process.

Television students develop psychomotor skills as well as conventionally taught students, providing they have equal access to any equipment which is to be manipulated.

The intelligence of the student is a greater predictor of information gain than are the Communication conditions.

There is conflicting information regarding the high and low intelligence groups, as to which fares better under certain Communication conditions.[3]

Kumata, in his presentation at the International Seminar on Instructional Television, made some interesting comments concerning the research that has been done to the present.

In the United States, we have put most of our bets on the discovery of some effect which is directly attributable to the means of message transmission and hundreds of similar studies have been conducted. Almost all

[3] *Ibid.*

of them say that it makes no difference whether TV is present or absent. They say that if you ignore audience variables, the nature of the student; if you ignore the nature of the source, those who put on the program; and if you look just at the media of transmission, you will get rather ambiguous results.

We have been insisting that perhaps we should look at television instruction as part of a general communication process and that we may get some valuable hints from other research which has been done in the communications field.

If we were to characterize the research done, I think four points would stand out. First, no particular theoretical framework has been apparent in most of the studies. Almost all of the studies have been of an applied nature and, in Dr. Becker's[4] terms researchers have tried "to mend punctured tires." Further there has been very little dependence on prior research. Second, the overwhelming majority of these studies have been what we call "comparability" studies, and almost all of these have been comparisons of television versus face-to-face instruction. Very few studies have been done as comparisons of radio, film, and television. Third, almost all of the main dependent variables in these investigations have been some measure of students' information gain. Perhaps I could state this another way. We have been trying to find out primarily whether students can reproduce items which they heard or saw over the medium, so most examinations have been in the nature of requests for students to reproduce information previously supplied by the instructor. Fourth, most research in instructional television has been done in the classroom situation, with regularly enrolled students. In other words, research has concentrated upon the captive audience aspect of educational television.[5]

WHAT TO EVALUATE

To initiate the evaluation process, we must first know what we want to evaluate. It is possible to investigate many areas: technical matters surrounding a television lesson or series, the competency of the personnel conducting the instructional activity, both in the classroom and on television, or pupil behavior and attitudes as a result of being exposed to a particular television lesson or series of lessons.

Each of these examples might be only part of the evaluation process in any given situation. The direction of the evaluation must depend on the questions you are trying to answer. As Kumata stated,[6] the majority of the investigations up to this time

---

[4] Dr. Samuel L. Becker, Director, Radio-Television-Film, State University of Iowa, Iowa City.

[5] Report presented at the International Seminar on Instructional Television, Oct. 8 to 18, 1961, at Purdue University, Lafayette, Ind. These are quotes from *History and Progress of Instructional Television Research in the United States* by Hideya Kumata, Communications Research Center, Michigan State University, East Lansing, Mich.

[6] *Ibid.*

have, unfortunately, been of one type, comparing television with "face-to-face" instruction.

When considering pupil outcomes, it is essential to consider the question of objectives, namely, what do we expect to happen to a student's behavior, attitudes, or interests as a result of a given educational activity?

A major problem facing instructional television research, and all educational research in general, is the lack of clearly stated, measurable objectives. Without them it is impossible to measure whether or not a particular approach is a success or failure.

Mager[7] highlights the frequent use of terms such as "understanding" and "appreciation." He points out that understanding is composed of many elements, and that a statement which does not delineate the specific nature of an understanding is almost useless when it comes to planning or evaluating instructional activities.

The lack of specifically stated objectives makes evaluation of pupil behavior extremely difficult. For example, if the objective of a series in art education is "to increase the student's appreciation of fifteenth-century art," the evaluation would have to be based on certain identifiable behavioral aspects of appreciation. This might involve the student's being able to describe the particular elements of an art work that lead to its being considered a classic. Since there were many art works in that particular century, the objective must then indicate which are to be appreciated.

This need for prestated objectives virtually eliminates the practicality of conducting an investigation in an ex post facto situation, with the project being completed before any concern is given to the evaluation. When this is done, the unstated objectives are often so vague or unclear as to make any specific evaluation extremely difficult. Therefore, any evaluation process should begin with specifically stated objectives of the televised instruction.

THE TECHNIQUES OF EVALUATION

Many techniques can be used to evaluate instructional television. Among the techniques are checklists, pupil attitude scales, laboratory exercises, written tests, oral examinations, group discussion, group projects, and standardized tests. In too many instances, a comparison of the scores on written tests achieved by pupils who have received certain instruction via television, and those who received identical instruction without television, is used as the major technique for evaluating televised instruction. Practically all these comparisons, as mentioned previously, show no statistically

[7] Robert Mager, *Preparing Objectives for Programmed Instruction.* San Francisco: Fearon Publishers, Inc., 1961.

significant differences between the televised and nontelevised instruction, as any fairly knowledgeable person in education would
predict. Other techniques are more helpful in evaluating the effect
of instructional television on behavioral outcomes.

Checklists.   Checklists are helpful in determining opinions about
such factual matters as the adequacy of coverage of a program, the
clarity of the picture, the number of new ideas presented, or the
length of the presentation. Most items can be rated yes/no, or
good/fair/poor, or on some similar pattern.

Pupil attitude scales.   The measurement of attitudes is difficult because of the subjective nature of attitudes. Scales can be developed
where students respond to questions such as:

I would prefer to study General Psychology I on instructional television.

Strongly agree   Agree   Undecided   Disagree   Strongly disagree

A list of similar items would help assess the general direction of
pupils' attitudes. We often find that a student's attitude will directly affect his achievement under *any* teaching technique, and
that it may be wise to test for attitude toward the course itself as
well as toward televised instruction.

Laboratory exercises.   Where a specific experiment or skill is stressed
on a television program, students' performance on a similar exercise in class can easily be used for evaluation.

Written tests and oral examinations.   Well-prepared objective tests,
essay questions, and questions for oral discussion are helpful in
evaluation. It is important to be sure that the questions reflect the
areas of instruction covered on television, for otherwise the findings will be misleading. This makes it imperative that the evaluation material be prepared *after* the actual contents of the program
have been decided upon.

Group discussion and group projects.   Often the topics presented on instructional television suggest group activities that can be used for
evaluation purposes. Presentations on social issues are examples of
these topics. Class debates, preparation of related materials, and
development of assembly programs, while difficult to measure,
could be used for evaluation purposes.

Standardized tests.   In cases where an entire unit of study in an area
such as arithmetic, general science, or English is being evaluated,
standardized tests can be used in addition to some of the techniques described above. But again it is important to take care that

167

these tests do measure the material covered in the television presentations.

When there is no standardized instrument to measure the behavior or attitude with which we are concerned, it is necessary to develop the evaluation instruments for the particular situation. The reliability and validity of these instruments should be determined before using them. Reliability refers to the ability of an instrument to obtain consistent results under similar conditions. Validity is concerned with whether the instrument is truly measuring the variables that we are studying. The items on the evaluation instrument or scale should be reviewed by a specialist in the particular content field in order to establish its validity. Also, a pretest should be made before using the instrument in the actual evaluation situation. Reliability should be determined by administering the instrument to a specific group of students. The test-retest method can be used, or the scores on the odd and even questions can be compared. These comparisons should be made by using one of the simpler correlation techniques which will be found in any book on educational testing.[8] One of the major weaknesses of "homemade" evaluation instruments is the lack of validity and reliability, which can easily be determined beforehand. Thus, the procedures described above should be used whenever possible.

ANALYSIS OF RESULTS

The analysis of the data from the evaluation instruments or techniques is the next step in the process. Where the evaluation involves the comparison of groups, the usual tests of statistical significance should be applied, to determine if any differences are due to chance. In most cases, however, the evaluation will not be a comparison of two groups. Sometimes the comparison may involve a pretest and a posttest, thus simply determining what change, if any, has taken place. It is often desirable to make an item analysis, or to study groups of questions or items, to determine specific strengths and weaknesses of the lesson. The question of what is a

---

[8] For further information on any of the techniques mentioned, the following references are suggested:

Anne Anastasi, *Psychological Testing,* 2d ed., New York: The Macmillan Company, 1961.

John W. Best, *Research in Education.* Englewood Cliffs, N.J.: Prentice-Hall, Inc., 1959.

Allen L. Edwards, *Experimental Design in Psychological Research,* rev. ed. New York: Holt, Rinehart and Winston, Inc., 1960.

James Wert, Charles Neidt, and J. Ahmahn, *Statistical Methods in Educational and Psychological Research.* New York: Appleton-Century-Crofts, Inc., 1954.

Dorothy A. Wood, *Test Construction: Development and Interpretation of Achievement Test.* Englewood Cliffs, N.J.: Charles E. Merrill, Inc., 1960.

strength or a weakness must be determined from standards established by the specialists in each instructional area. For example, a score of 60 per cent on an evaluation instrument in one area may be considered adequate, while a score of 80 per cent in another area may be considered inadequate. The interpretation of the results of evaluation involves cooperative effort on the part of the evaluation specialist, instructional television specialist, and the educational specialists who actually conduct the televised instruction.[9] Evaluation by its very nature is a process that requires the involvement of many kinds of specialists from the initiation of the evaluation to its completion.

It is also helpful to obtain other kinds of information about televised instruction. The comments or impressions of students or teachers should not be overlooked, as they may be helpful in determining why a given instructional activity was effective or ineffective. A list of questions, interviews with selected students and teachers, or an open-ended inquiry, are techniques that can be used to collect this collateral information.[10] Students may indicate that a given subject was not easily understood because of visual problems, or that a given instructor talked too fast. Responses may indicate that too much or too little time was given to a particular topic. While this type of information does not tell you whether you are achieving the objectives of the televised instruction, it might give clues concerning the reasons for success or failure of a lesson.

THE PERSONNEL

What kind of personnel are necessary to carry out the evaluation? An evaluator should have had some training in measurement, evaluation, and statistics. In addition, it is desirable for him to have had some teaching experience and an understanding of instructional television. The problem of finding skilled investigators to work with television is mentioned by Kumata:

> In academic circles, research in instructional television is not a highly regarded activity. I say this even though some researchers are sitting here before me. To speak further, most academic researchers in the social sciences feel that instructional television research is not worthwhile. It is not worthwhile because one cannot find respectable outlets for his publications. If you cannot find such outlets, your chances for university promotion decrease. Second, researchers have an inability to talk at the level of the common man. They have an esoteric language which may not even be understandable among themselves. When they face television producers, those who work in the art, they find an almost unbridgeable chasm, a

[9] A worksheet for planning an evaluation can be seen in the table on p. 170.
[10] Examples can be seen in Appendix E.

chasm of language, even though both parties speak English. Third, researchers frequently do not know the television medium. They are very ignorant of the medium and, as a matter of fact, they may be more ignorant than the layman who spends about 30 hours a week watching television. As a result, this gap is widening and few people have dedicated themselves to closing the gap. Perhaps one solution is to attempt to train people who know both the medium and research methods. These people will be coming along, but so far we haven't had many of them, so their impact has not been felt in instructional television.[11]

Worksheet for planning evaluation			
Course _____ Instructor _____ Evaluation _____ Date _____			
Televised activity	Objective	Evaluation technique	Time administered

[11] Hideya Kumata, *History and Progress of Instructional Television Research in the United States*. Communications Research Center, Michigan State University, East Lansing, Mich.

Familiarity with the process of selecting objectives and teaching to achieve them is valuable experience for planning an evaluation. Where the evaluation is conducted using available staff personnel, and promising leads are found, it would be wise to engage a professional evaluation consultant to assist in the comprehensive follow-up evaluation.

SUMMARY

Evaluation is a necessity if you are to learn about the effectiveness of instructional television. The specific objectives of televised instruction must be known if the evaluation is to have any real value. Appropriate instruments or techniques should be used to collect and evaluate the information obtained. Evaluation must be a cooperative process involving the television staff, the teaching staff, and the evaluation staff. If done properly, it leads to increased knowledge about the contribution of instructional television to teaching and learning.

chapter 16

The administrator, educational problems, and instructional television

Clifford G. Erickson

The administrator is the key to any successful application of instructional television. In this chapter Dr. Erickson clearly defines many of the problems that will be faced and offers some specific suggestions as to how these might be minimized for effective application.

From the administrator's viewpoint, the rapid growth of instructional television has brought as by-product a series of needs that demand immediate attention. There is, first, a need for a new kind of educational statesmanship and leadership; second, there is a need for an increase in inventiveness and flexibility; finally, there is a need for new methods of safeguarding our educational standards. Some of our administrative experiences with instructional television at the Chicago Junior College may prove valuable to school administrators considering the use of instructional television. Instructional TV makes stern demands: it requires that we not only face squarely many of the old problems of education, but also that at the same time we deal with new problems arising from the introduction of the medium.

The technological aspects of the use of television are indeed minor when compared with the basic educational questions raised. This is not intended to minimize the contributions of the engineers, technicians, and all the specialized personnel whose assistance we must have. Rather, it is to assert that introducing television into an educational jurisdiction, be it a single school, a school system, a region, a nation, or an international cooperative, places upon us a clear and urgent need for a sound definition of program objectives. What serious educational goals are we seeking to pursue? Who shall be

Dr. Erickson, former Dean of Television Instruction for the Chicago Junior College, is now Executive Dean of the Chicago City Junior College. Since 1956 the college has televised over fifty different college courses and has had over 27,000 individuals take these courses for credit toward their Associate of Arts degree. This chapter is a modification of a presentation before the International Seminar on Instructional Television, held at Purdue University, Oct. 8 to 18, 1961.

educated? What are their educational needs? What are the most appropriate means of achieving these objectives in the given situation? If television is an appropriate medium, what relationship will television have to the other learning media—the classroom, the library, the audio-visual center, and so on? These are searching questions to which there are no easy answers.

THE NEED FOR A NEW EDUCATIONAL LEADERSHIP AND STATESMANSHIP

It is in the area of supplying answers to these fundamental questions that we must develop a new strength in educational leadership. One of the most important contributions that educational leadership can make is in the formulation of educational objectives. Educational objectives must be defined in behavioral terms, in terms of the kinds of things we want students to do and the ways we want them to react. And these objectives must be defined for an entire program, for a given course, for an individual lesson. Moreover, attention must be given to the educational climate of the learner. An example of the importance of this awareness is found in a literacy project in Memphis where it was found that those who needed the instruction had a fear of involving themselves in the instruction. A very careful procedure had to be set up whereby those who needed the instruction could be placed in groups and given the comfort that would make it possible for them to learn.

Furthermore, educational leaders must attempt to answer such questions as these: Will the novelty of the situation enhance or impair the feasibility or acceptability of this learning experience? Will communication through the electronic medium lend an aura of authority to the presentation beyond that intended? Will the learner be able to make a transition from televised learning to books, classroom teaching, and other kinds of learning experiences? What is his educational background, his language skill level, his rate of comprehension?

Educational statesmanship enters the picture when we consider the problem posed by the classroom teacher. We know, from our Chicago experience, the key role played by the classroom teacher. On some occasions, when we have used direct TV instruction for classroom groups, we have found that a classroom teacher not properly oriented to the whole program can, by raising an eyebrow or making a casual derogatory remark, destroy the effectiveness of the television lesson. As a matter of fact, the negative attitude of the classroom teacher can destroy the effectiveness of a whole course of television instruction.

Let me illustrate what I am saying about the framing of objectives by citing a couple of examples of procedural error in our Chicago project. We began in fall, 1956, to give direct instruction to adults in their homes or wherever they could watch sets. Great care was taken to prepare and present courses for the home viewers. Study guides were prepared. Face-to-face conferences, telephone conferences, correspondence channels for assignments and examinations were set up. But in our enthusiasm to get maximum use of the television medium, we decided not to employ such elaborate methods for classroom groups. And so, in a rather offhanded manner, we organized some instruction for college-age groups in classrooms. It can quickly be said that this classroom instruction was less than successful.

Although the end objective was a worthy one, it was not enough simply to envision a worthy goal. We must allow time to study and to plan limited objectives, each leading, in turn, to a further objective. Full utilization of available techniques is not of itself an adequately formulated goal. Instructional television demands analytic planning at every stage. The reason for our failure was that we had not taken the time to orient the classroom teachers to their role, to involve them in shaping the objectives of the course or in accepting the established objectives. We had to withdraw quickly and conclude that we could not assume that a classroom teacher, who by training and experience thinks of himself in a one-to-one relationship with his students, can suddenly work successfully as one member of a teaching team. The preparation of the classroom teacher is a step that is important and we needed to prepare for it. As a result of this experience, we decided to remove ourselves from the area of this kind of classroom involvement. For several years we concentrated on our main objective. Only in recent years have we come back to the use of classroom groups. We are now careful to schedule telecourses within the on-campus time pattern so that we do not disrupt teacher and student schedules. Experience has taught us, too, that two forty-minute telecasts per week, rather than three half-hour sessions, lend themselves well to classroom instruction, especially since comparisons of the performance of adult at-home viewers with that of teen-age classroom viewers reveal that the latter require weekly supplemental classroom discussion led by a classroom teacher.

Another miscalculation resulting from our enthusiasm to use the medium came from our seeking ways to help in the education of gifted high school students. Every high school principal in Chicago was trying to identify the gifted 100 in his high school, and was trying desperately to provide a program on enrichment for these students. We suggested, "Let us enroll them in college courses via television and let them earn advanced standing credits." Although the program was well conceived, we did not enroll many students. Why did we fail? Simply because we did not have time to work our way up through the branches of the administrative "tree," that is, to establish acceptance of this program in the right circles, to get to the district superintendents, the principals of the high schools, the students' counselors, and the teachers of these gifted students. Our problem was one of winning people to our side.

At present we are enrolling gifted high school students in a mathematics course. Patient explanation and low-keyed persuasion have helped us "sell" this service. We have invited only a limited number of high schools to participate, believing that success on a modest scale will put us in a better position to invite others to participate. In addition, we are making every effort to ensure the satisfactory performance of these bright young people by setting up an hour's supplemental instruction each week under the supervision of our video teacher.

After all this has been said about developing a program, still another important question that leadership must face arises. This is the problem of evaluating instructional television. We must not become so enamored of the gadgetry that we assume that because we have our gadgets, we will improve our instruction. Cold-blooded and eagle-eyed, we must evaluate the situation, examine our defined objectives, and then measure the success and effectiveness of our instruction against these objectives. Only thus can we learn whether we are succeeding or falling short of success.

THE NEED FOR AN INCREASE IN INVENTIVENESS AND FLEXIBILITY

Inventiveness and flexibility are essential to the success of instructional television. The former is needed not only by the television teacher, but also by school administrators, program directors, and all involved in instructional TV. Television offers us many new ways to reorganize our entire educational program—if we are inventive enough to exploit them.

TV gives us new ways to organize pupils and teachers. In a real sense, the television teacher and the student become a learning team. As for the adult teacher, our experience in Chicago demonstrates that he can and will accept a new and high order of responsibility. As for the classroom student, our experience proves that we may now choose to organize groups of larger size than we did formerly with conventional groups. We teach hundreds of students at one time by TV, and then break these groups into small groups for face-to-face instruction.

Instructional TV makes it possible for us to vary and enrich the teaching role. For the sake of variety and enrichment, we can place at the disposal of the television teacher a number of specialists. We increase the value of the TV teacher's contribution by allowing him seven times as much time to teach a course as we did to teach

175

the same course in the classroom. To achieve the kind of creativity that will give good television instruction, a liberal allocation of released time is essential. None of this can be achieved without administrators who are willing to make decisions which break the crust of old practices. The need for this kind of flexibility has bearing on the kind of buildings we build, the way we select our faculty, and the way we organize our entire educational program.

Inventiveness and adminstrative flexibility can cut the admittedly high cost of TV instruction. The costs may now be spread out over several teachers in a given department, or over departments within a school, or over schools cooperating with another, or over one region cooperating with another, or over nations. In Chicago we found that when we began, in 1956, the cost of televised instruction was high as compared with classroom costs. We found that the unit cost of teaching one student for one year was about one-third higher than the cost of teaching a classroom student for a year. But with growth in enrollment, increased knowledge of the medium, and administrative adjustments, we are now able to offer credit instruction at a cost well below classroom cost—as a matter of fact, *about $100 less than classroom instruction.* How can we do this, even though we are using what is supposedly a high-cost medium? We spend one-third of a million dollars each year on television instruction. Yet we have enough students enrolled (an average of 700 to 800 full-time students per course) to bring our unit cost below classroom cost.

In addition, we earn a tremendous "bonus." This bonus, or extra dividend, warrants discussion. Regularly we attract about 5,000 students who do not enroll for credit. Besides, we have many other students—we cannot obtain an accurate head count—who follow these programs. Proprietors of local bookstores tell us that they purchase the books prescribed. For each telecast, our audience-measuring people tell us, there are as many as 200,000 viewers.

What we are getting is, we think, higher-quality instruction at a cost significantly below classroom costs. Also, we are offering this to a metropolitan area of six million people. This consideration is a factor to be reckoned with when, as administrators or teachers, we boggle at the thought of the high cost of equipment. How much is too much to pay for increasing the educational service to the community many times over?

THE NEED FOR NEW METHODS FOR SAFEGUARDING EDUCATIONAL STANDARDS

The administrator cannot long avoid dealing with the problem of agreement on educational objectives. This is a key problem. As soon as we decide to use television in more than one classroom, we presuppose that cooperating teachers or supervisors in the receiving rooms are willing to accept the objectives of the television teacher. Where the television instruction is of essentially an enrichment nature—as in programs for gifted high school seniors—the circle of influence is even wider. Indeed, the more television instruction moves in the direction of total instruction, the more grievous is the problem of agreement between the television teacher and his receiving teachers on the primary objectives of the course.

There is also what can be thought of as the "institutional problem." Institutions, and departments within institutions, cling to cherished institutional images of themselves. These images make it difficult for members of an institution to admit the possibility of high levels of competence in the instruction of other institutions and departments. Autonomy for the college, in particular, and even sometimes for the lower schools, is a familiar aspect of the American educational scene. His training and experience make the teacher see himself as an independent leader of a group of students. The elements of bias in both the institution and the individual teacher may account for the snail's pace of enrollment growth in, say, "Continental Classroom," and the relatively slow development of interschool and regional cooperatives and interchanges of instruction.

Another problem of administrative statesmanship in instructional television, knotty in the extreme, arises from the problem of teachers' rights. In the entertainment arts, there has developed a culture that defines fairly precisely the role of the performer and his rights. In the field of education we do not have this practice to draw on as a precedent. When a teacher writes a book, it is true, he contracts with the publisher and receives royalties in the fashion agreed upon. Now that we have, by means of TV, the opportunity to put the services of a teacher beyond a group of 30 students to 3,000, 30,000, or even 3 million students, does the teacher have a right to share in the fruits of his productivity in the same sense that he shares in the fruits of his productivity as writer of a book? This problem of rights has held back the development of an interchange of high-quality instructional television films in this country. Over the years we in Chicago have received countless requests for permission to use excellent telecourses stored in our vaults. We have consistently turned down these requests because we have as yet no policy satisfactory to the Chicago Board of Education, the college administration, and the teachers involved. Needs for quality programming in certain instructional areas make it imperative that we solve this problem. Why, for example, should College A settle for a so-so course in physics or psychology taught by one of its own instructors when a course taught by a distinguished scholar of College B—a scholar perfectly at ease before a camera—is available in a film library? The pooling and exchange of taped courses

177

will effect what is one of the undeniable advantages of TV education, that is, the exposure of a first-rate teacher to a greater number of students than has ever before been possible. Is it too much to hope that in time to come future Alfred North Whiteheads and future Mark Van Dorens will inspire more than a mere handful of students privileged to attend a few outstanding seats of learning?

But the problem of pooling resources is only one of many. It is time to look at a problem of more immediate concern to schools with teachers directly involved in instructional TV: namely, the matter of building quality into TV courses. Any program of instructional television will stand or fall on the quality of the instruction. After a number of years of experience, we in Chicago have developed what a manufacturer calls "a system of quality control."

The first step in ensuring instructional quality is to achieve clarity in the definition of objectives. Before we select a television teacher from among our best teachers, and before the teacher selected is allowed to begin preparing his course, he must formulate a set of objectives for his course. This is often a distressing experience for a teacher. At first, he seems unable to do it. He will express objectives in terms of content alone, in terms of what he expects to do, rather than in terms of the reactions or behaviors he expects from students. After a period of development, during which he consults with a director skilled in curriculum matters, the teacher does succeed in developing a set of objectives. Once he has done this, he finds that he has a whole new concept of his course. He may choose different text materials; he may even choose a different approach. He proceeds through a series of steps in which he takes his objectives and translates them into an outline to guide him through the course, and into a study guide to direct the students in their activities. He devises materials which relate the students to the television instruction, selects reading materials, arranges conferences and assignments, and attends to any number of things. The teacher is now really getting ready for his debut as a television instructor.

The orientation to television instruction in our system always includes at least three, and sometimes more, direct studio experiences. Without much advance guidance the teacher presents whatever he likes—perhaps a portion of a lesson he enjoys doing—in a trial lesson before the television camera. As he sees himself on film, he makes a self-evaluation. It is our feeling that, after the first camera experience and the first painful self-evaluation, the teacher learns more of the uses of television than at any other point in his career.

The last phase of this quality control sees the teacher working with us in the development of evaluation instruments. These instruments grow out of the objectives for the course. As he brings in his materials, the consultants in evaluation ask questions of him:

"Which of these items permits you to evaluate progress toward objective one?" "Which of these items will evaluate progress toward objective two?"

The kind of experience through which we move our television teacher makes him a quite different person. When he gets back to his classroom teaching, he testifies that he has learned a new approach to education and to his own teaching. The study guides which he developed are requested by many of his colleagues. These new courses, these new curriculum materials which have evolved, are suddenly in great demand.

An educational revolution has, indeed, taken place in our institution. Television has been the catalyst. Our institution has undergone permanent change. We now have at hand much more competent evaluation of progress than ever before. As a result of our instructional TV program, fifty-five different courses have been rebuilt. Our teachers have had the opportunity to make self-evaluations of their work in ways not possible before. The opportunity has been a tremendous one.

chapter 17

Television: part of the answer

Jerrold E. Kemp

In this chapter Dr. Kemp brings into focus the fact that when we explore possible applications of television we must keep in mind other media that may offer sensible alternatives at a saving of both time and money.

There have been tendencies in education to look for that one solution that may hold the answer to most problems being faced in the total educational process. This was true with the extreme advocates of the progressive education movement, and it may be true for those who look to television as the salvation for all present-day problems—classroom shortages, teacher shortages, more information to be transmitted, more efficiency in teaching, and so forth.

But unfortunately (or fortunately!) television is too costly and complex a tool for us to accept in any bandwagon fashion. When should it be used? Are there times when other media can do an equal or even better job for instruction? These are important questions for anyone considering the installation and use of television equipment in a school program.

Television must be considered in perspective, within the range of all available instructional resources and instructional patterns. For certain purely mechanical uses, such as for magnifying small objects, or for administering tests to large numbers of students (see Chapters 1 to 4 and 12), we can immediately accept a form of television for its obvious efficiency. But for true teaching-learning situations, careful thought should be given before television is accepted as the primary solution.

Recent technological advances have made available for our use, in addition to television, such tools as electronic learning laboratories, self-threading and cartridge-loading motion-picture projectors, overhead projectors, synchronous sound-slide projectors, and self-instructional devices of many kinds. Some of these materials and devices are not really new; however, advances in production techniques have made them more compact and convenient or able

Dr. Kemp is Coordinator of Materials Preparation Services and Associate Professor of Education at San Jose State College, and is the author of *Planning and Producing Audiovisual Materials* (see Bibliography, p. 287).

to project brighter, more detailed images, so that they have become useful and effective for a variety of teaching-learning purposes. The administrator or teacher exploring the potential applications of television should, for proper perspective, have in mind the other media that are available as possible alternatives.

Electronic learning laboratories. These include recording, playback, and listening equipment which make it possible for a student to listen, speak, hear, and record his voice. The teacher may control listening and student participation through an electronic console, or choices may be available to students at each station. The electronic learning laboratory was originally designed to serve foreign language instruction. But alert teachers and supervisors are finding broader utilization possible on all grade levels for experiences in speech pronunciation, literature and music appreciation, mathematics drill, typing and shorthand dictation, and other subjects.

Motion-picture projectors and films. Sixteen-millimeter motion-picture projectors have been a familiar tool for teacher use for many years. Films are available in every subject and on most grade levels. Two recent and seemingly diametrically opposed developments have increased the effectiveness of films for instructional uses: first, the availability of complete courses on film (at present, principally in the sciences and mathematics), some of which originated as television productions; and second, short films that treat a single idea or concept in depth for a specific audience. In the latter category are such films as simple how-to-do-it designs, illustrations of a specific process, or demonstrations of an applied principle.

The developments and refinements in equipment, such as easy-to-operate self-threading projectors or projectors that accept cartridge units, now permit anyone to show films—to groups or for his own self-instruction. Also, with the advent of sound projectors for 8-millimeter film, new possibilities for inexpensive, locally prepared materials are opening. Eventually, less expensive prints of commercial films may be produced and deposited within an individual school as part of its instructional materials resources.

Overhead projectors and transparencies. These projectors offer tremendous potential for improving and increasing classroom communication—within a small group or before a large class. Because it is used from near the front of a room, with moderate lighting, and the instructor faces the class while pointing to features on large transparencies, the overhead projector is receiving increased attention. Difficult concepts may be presented through step-by-step disclosure or by the addition of overlay sheets to a base transparency. Three-dimensional transparent objects or silhouettes and even simulated motion can be shown. Although some sets of commercial

The perspectives for instructional television

An electronic learning laboratory, with a high school language teacher at the console dictating test material to all students

A high school student responding to a self-study question projected from film onto a rear screen in a teaching machine. The student, after selecting her response, pushes the indicated button which controls the advance mechanism, to reveal the selected answer.

transparencies are now available, a variety of simple techniques permits local preparation of many types of transparencies in black and white or in color.

Opaque projectors. These projectors, using the principle of reflected light, project many materials in their natural color and appearance —single sheets, mounted pictures, magazine and book illustrations, and small three-dimensional objects. Materials require little or no preparation before use. In addition to projecting materials for examination and discussion, the opaque projector can enlarge small drawings and pictures, which can then be traced for other uses. Opaque projectors are becoming more convenient as their size is reduced; however, complete room darkening is necessary for their use.

Recorders and recordings. Small, compact tape recorders permit the recording of voice and other sounds from many sources onto magnetic tape for repeated playback. Besides being an integral part of electronic laboratory equipment, recorders may serve as aids when preparing reports, conducting interviews, keeping records, self-evaluating presentations, and listening to dramatic and informational programs.

Slide projectors and tape recorder combinations. Filmstrips or 35-millimeter slides can be combined with tape recordings, and the two used concurrently. Electronic signaling devices permit automatic changes of slides or filmstrip frames in synchronization with a recording. This equipment permits student-prepared projects as well as carefully designed teacher-made materials to be presented satisfactorily to groups of all sizes, and for as many further showings as are necessary.

Aids to self-instruction. A recent development in the field of new educational media which involves carefully written or programmed materials for individual student study is the "teaching machine" or "programmed learning" device. Such a device, when used in any of its possible forms, presents small increments of information and requires active participation by a student in the learning process through overt responses. Immediately after a response the student finds out whether he was right or wrong. Programs may be of a variety of types, presented as printed materials in conventional book or workbook form, on film, or by means of various electromechanical devices.

Programmed materials are best developed for informational and skill-type subjects. Their value lies in the responsibility that is placed upon the student for learning phases of a subject or a skill by himself, at his own rate, without necessary teacher supervision.

A great deal of time goes into the design and preparation of programs in which careful, small-step sequencing will draw out learning responses with little or no error. Each response is built on the ones before until an entire concept to be learned has been presented and responded to in detail, with reinforcement to the point of retention.

These media comprise only a part of the total variety of aids available to the teacher. No mention has been made of printed materials or of such simple devices as flannel boards and bulletin boards, or the newer hook-and-loop or magnetic boards. Also, educational exhibits, displays, and community resources find definite applications in educational programs for certain instructional purposes. The important fact is that all are, or should be, available for instruction and may be used to supplement or take the place of television.

The availability for instruction of all these media, including television, is forcing educators to face honestly questions that formerly were given only lip service and a nod. "What are the objectives of an instructional unit?" Then, "How can each purpose best be accomplished?" If educators understand the unique qualities and teaching capacity of each medium at their disposal, judgments can be made about where each one best fits into a sound pattern of teaching and learning, or whether it is necessary in the particular instance.

This is perhaps what is called the "systems" approach to teaching and learning. Television is but one link or resource in this learning system. It therefore becomes necessary for the administrator or teacher to analyze each instructional situation objectively before decisions can be properly made. Thus, recognition of both the limitations and the unique teaching opportunities afforded by television is essential.

A number of related factors must affect these decisions. Let us examine the major ones and offer suggestions about when television might be preferable to some other medium.

THE AUDIENCE AND ITS LOCATION

A single classroom. If the audience is composed of a single class—small or large—capable of being instructed in one place at one time, then, except in those cases when simple image magnification is desired, appropriate media other than television are often preferable (see Chapters 1 to 4). By careful lesson planning and by making good use of necessary audio-visual materials and equipment within the classroom, effective instruction can take place. Many of the resources that are normally part of television production—careful planning and programming, remotely controlled projectors which ensure "right time" projection, and even rear-screen projection to permit room illumination at a reasonable level, can serve the group without the expense, remoteness, and problems of television transmission.

Simultaneous meetings in many rooms. On the other hand, if the audience consists of a number of classes (of any size) meeting simultaneously in different rooms, then the efficiency of instruction by television is undeniable. As mentioned on page 46, it does not usually make financial sense to put a lesson on television unless that lesson reaches a minimum of 200 to 250 students. With

Team teaching in a large group at San Jose State College, utilizing both the overhead projector and single-camera closed-circuit television

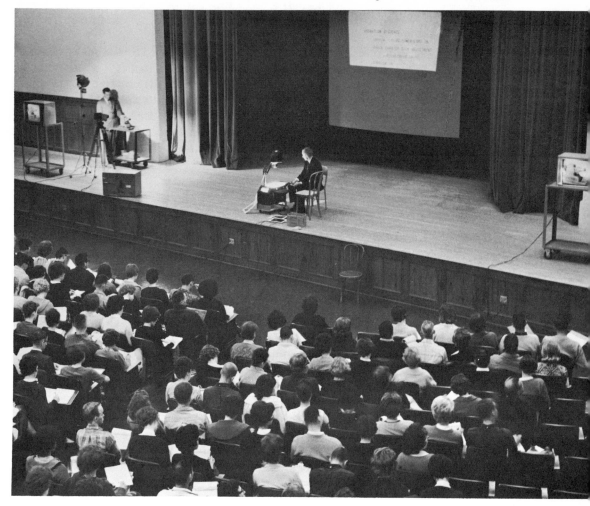

groups below this number it is more feasible to plan for use of audio-visual resources—motion pictures, slide series, recordings, overhead transparencies, and so forth.

For numbers greater than 200, where adequate transmission lines or broadcast facilities exist, a telecast can serve groups in two rooms or in twenty, or at individual home receivers, all at the same time. This is one of the best services of television—it reaches any number of receivers simultaneously.

Meetings at various times.   If groups will meet at different times, then the value of repeated telecasting must be balanced against repeated "in person" classroom presentations. The choice will depend upon the difficulties of scheduling personnel and facilities, and of setting up equipment, demonstrations, or other parts of the lesson. This problem will no doubt be resolved in favor of television when video tape recording and playback equipment is installed in a television facility. Then, at the time of the first telecast (or during final rehearsal) a recording can be made and replayed any number of times without requiring additional time from the instructor, staff, or studio.

Here again the interrelations among media become apparent, this time in connection with scheduling difficulties. If the number of distribution channels is limited, and multiple programs on tape must be replayed, it would be desirable to convert a tape-recorded program into a motion-picture film. By this means, expensive video tape would be released for reuse, and a film and projector in a classroom would provide the flexibility in use that television transmission lacks.

THE TEACHER AND THE STAFF

Limitations of the traditional classroom.   In the traditional teacher-and-thirty-student classroom concept, very little opportunity has been available for the teacher to develop specialties as a presenter of information, as an expert in some phase of his subject area, as a discussion leader, or in guiding skill development of individual students. Most teachers must be generalists, performing many jobs and filling many roles, some of which they may not be interested in or particularly qualified to perform. This may be especially true in an elementary school where the teacher spends all day with one class, instructing the students in all subjects as well as serving their many other needs.

New patterns and new roles.   With the emergence of new instructional patterns, teachers' roles are changing. Instruction to large groups, for the purposes of informing and providing background for discussion and further exploration, requires instructors with one set of skills. Directing small-size groups, which permit face-to-face discussion and teacher-student interaction, requires other qualified teachers. Finally, the new instructional patterns provide for individualized learning activities, during which students are directed and encouraged to progress as far as possible at their own rate. In the latter situation, teachers and other staff members again have important roles to play: witness the new programs utilizing the team teaching concepts or the reorganization and redeployment plans suggested by the National Association of Secondary School Principals.[1]

In such programs some teachers, specializing in certain subject matter and having the ability to communicate before large groups, serve as presenters. Other individuals, having strengths in leading discussions and working directly with groups of students, are assigned to the small groups, while another team may assist individual students or even work behind the scenes in planning and preparing instructional materials of many types. The special ability of each teacher is thus utilized to the fullest extent.

In addition, staff and technical positions are being filled to assist teachers with many classroom and extraclass routine duties. Teacher aides can relieve classroom teachers of up to the 40 per cent of their time reportedly spent on nonteaching responsibilities. Their duties may include record keeping, paper grading, cafeteria and playground assignments, and the routine preparation of instructional materials. Teachers can thus devote large amounts of their energies and talents to the more creative aspects of teaching, rather than to the mechanical or routine matters.

The place of television. Television fits into these new instructional patterns in a natural way. But now it must be considered more than just a one-way path for the transmission of information. True, the transmission phase may be similar to what we have indicated is common in all large-group instruction; nevertheless the success of television, in these new programs, is closely related to and very much dependent upon the concurrent activities in the viewing groups, and also on the follow-up activities—the small groups and the individual study assignments. It has been shown that television instruction alone, without appropriate follow-up by the classroom teacher, is largely ineffective.[2]

Now, the selection of television as an instructional method will

[1] J. Lloyd Trump and Dorsey Baynham, *Focus on Change: Guide to Better Schools.* Chicago: Rand McNally & Company, 1961.

[2] *Summary of Research on Parlons Français, Year Two,* Modern Language Project, 9 Newbury Street, Boston, Mass., as reported by Earle S. Randall, "What Have We Learned about Foreign Languages in the Elementary School?" *Audiovisual Instruction,* 7:628, November, 1962.

depend, in large part, on the availability of qualified personnel—those to work with student groups from the viewing end, those in charge of the small discussion groups, and those responsible for the individual study activities, as well as those who must plan and carry on in the television studio. Successful teachers and staff members on each of these levels must have special qualifications. One instructor, highly qualified in his subject field, who does a fine job in a classroom, may not be able to serve the same function before the television camera. In other situations the successful use of television may depend on the ability of individuals in a group to work together in the planning and operational phases of a program. If they cannot coordinate their efforts the success of a new program may be seriously affected. Uninspired television teachers and program directors, confined within the limitations of traditional classroom teaching—the textbook, talk, a blackboard, and a few simple visuals—can only be expected to produce unimaginative and mediocre lessons.

Therefore, when television is being considered, it is essential to locate within the school system or to employ from elsewhere those unusual teachers who can serve on television, and any others who are or can become qualified for the many other responsibilities that are part of an instructional system that includes television. Until qualified personnel are available, a school system may not be ready to make use of the medium.

INSTRUCTIONAL METHODS

The basic purpose of any education is to change people in desirable ways—to change the way they act or think by supplying them with information, building new skills, and creating or changing attitudes and appreciations.

In traditional methods of teaching, great emphasis is placed on verbal communication, and the average classroom is strongly dominated by the teacher. In such situations use is made of only a few instructional resources—textbooks, workbooks, the chalkboard, and maybe simple visual materials such as bulletin board displays and models.

The newer instructional patterns previously referred to are proving more successful in accomplishing basic educational purposes than are the traditional methods. Through more effective communication, utilizing a variety of audio-visual media such as pictures, slides, transparencies, motion pictures, and recordings, and through the more direct involvement of students in the instructional process, many gains are being realized.

Advantages and limitations of television. Television has certain qualities remarkably adaptable to educational purposes. These include the following:

1. Television can transmit both sounds and pictures—three-dimensional or two-dimensional, still or moving. The television teacher can make use of all audio-visual materials and can employ a variety of activities—all without losing the one-to-one relationship with the individual student.
2. Television can be viewed by an unlimited number of students in an unlimited number of classrooms.
3. With the use of kinescopes or video tape recordings, carefully prepared presentations may be repeated at the most effective times. This permits outstanding programs and outstanding personalities to be fully utilized.
4. Television has a tremendous range of possible uses. It may be a simple magnification device within the classroom, it may provide the teacher with supplementary materials, or it may form the basis for an entire course.

Unfortunately, the medium is frequently used to transmit no more than the picture of a person as he talks. True, a few people communicate effectively in this way, but for an instructional situation, if television is to be properly used, we must plan to make extensive use of all the aspects listed above. If not so planned, then television serves no better purpose than radio transmission, a tape recording, or a recording plus a few slides of the speaker.

Television is most often thought of as a medium for transmitting information. For this purpose it is generally very satisfactory. Also, through carefully planned programs, it can fulfill other basic educational purposes concerning attitudes and appreciations. But when independent learning or skills must be taught, can television be used?

For some skills, such as those taught in foreign language instruction, when students can join the television teacher in vocal drills or respond to general questions, studio television may be satisfactory. But if the main purpose is overt participation to learn a skill, then an instructional approach not using studio-produced lessons should be sought. One obvious solution is single-room television, where the instructor can work directly with the students, but along with this technique are many others that should be explored fully.

Finally, when discussion is important in a learning situation, the impersonal nature of television again makes it questionable for use except in simple image magnification applications. Telephone connections from viewing rooms to the studio teacher have somewhat overcome the absoluteness of one-way transmission, but this technique has often been found impractical. While new electronic devices are being explored that would provide the television teacher with immediate feedback, nothing as yet can substitute for face-to-face questioning and discussion. So again, if the exchange of ideas and the freedom to discuss is a key part of the learning situation, then television is not the sole or ideal medium. It is only part of the answer.

ANALYZING INSTRUCTIONAL SITUATIONS

We have examined some major instructional needs and have discussed class size and distribution, teacher and staff competencies, and instructional methods as factors to be considered before selecting television for school uses. We have pointed out the variety of other available media which must be considered in perspective with television. One final factor remains for consideration. How are instructional situations analyzed? Who makes the decision to use television or to use other resources?

Personnel involved. The analysis should not be done solely and superficially by a few administrators or by a school board. It should also involve those most concerned on the operational levels —curriculum supervisors, teacher committees, and communications specialists. Curriculum supervisors, working with teacher groups, have always been involved in the decisions or recommendations that effect change in educational programs. But with the new resources now available, from television to teaching machines, someone familiar with their selection, preparation, use, advantages, and limitations must help pass judgment and make decisions. This is the contribution of the "communications specialist" in the school system. This role may be filled by more than one person, so that we include not only a person with broad understanding of and enthusiasm for television, but also someone who understands the "systems approach" to the use of printed materials and other audio-visual teaching resources.

Analysis procedure. When committees made up of curriculum supervisors, communications specialists, and teachers consider the purposes or objectives of a course of study and state them clearly in meaningful terms, as related to the actual audience group, they are in a position to make recommendations concerning the use of television or of other media. It is only after establishing *what it is that is to be communicated* that we are able to recommend properly the channel or medium which will do the best job. Unfortunately the cart is often placed before the horse: television is selected for use and a search is made for a course or unit to use with it. With proper planning the best medium or combination of media to do the job can be selected, and those areas that can best be handled on television will be recognized.

Thus we have seen that television will be an important part of the answer as new methods are considered for new instructional programs. What part? Those parts of the total teaching-learning job which could be done better than by any other teaching medium—in the light of the many factors described and discussed here.

chapter 18

Instructional television:
its potential and its problems

Robert M. Diamond

In this concluding chapter the editor attempts to define the role of instructional television within the American educational system. This is followed by a look into the future at some of the problems that must be solved if television is to assume its proper place in our schools.

EDUCATION IN THE UNITED STATES

In a nation that has fathered the efficiency expert, been midwife to the production line, and prided itself on its sophisticated use of technology, it is somewhat disheartening to observe that we have seldom extended this national proficiency into our educational system. Today our schools must teach more basic information and affect the attitudes, values, and social insights of more students with relatively fewer teachers that ever before. The last decade has brought developments that, used wisely, can dynamically improve the effectiveness of what we do in our schools. But unfortunately the public, school administrators, and teachers have traditionally resisted change. Many of our schools are still designed as they were fifty years ago and function as they did at the turn of the century. Much of what we do is structured on the past, not designed for the present and future.

Today one out of every four United States citizens is receiving some type of formal education. With each passing year, as a greater proportion of our students complete more years of schooling, this ratio increases. The net result is a school population ex-

Dr. Diamond is presently Director of Instructional Resources, University College, University of Miami, and was formerly Associate Professor of Education and Instructional Television Program Supervisor at San Jose State College. Originally a mathematics teacher, his first experience with television was as a television teacher for the Mohawk-Hudson Council on Educational Television. He was also Television Coordinator for the Plainedge Public Schools.

panding more rapidly, proportionally speaking, than the population as a whole. Coupled with this increasing enrollment is the growing shortage of qualified teachers. Our colleges simply have not been able to train enough teachers to fill our needs. Not only do we need an adequate number of teachers but we also need well-trained, talented teachers. It is estimated that we will need 200,000 new teachers every year for the next decade and there is little chance that this need will be met.

Moreover, the talents of the teachers that we do have are often wasted. Many teachers spend as much time performing simple clerical tasks, proctoring study halls, and policing lunch rooms as they do in actual teaching. Teachers are so bogged down with unimportant duties that they rarely have enough time to prepare lessons or to work with individual students. Within a single school, several teachers spend time preparing identical materials for identical lessons. In general, our teachers have been given the same general responsibility, regardless of interest or talent. Industry and many of the professions long ago learned that because individuals differ in interests and ability, it is vital to use the particular individual in roles he can best perform.

What makes the problems facing education even more complex is the fact that we not only have more students with relatively fewer teachers, but that our schools must teach more than ever before. Each year finds an increase in the knowledge and understanding required to earn the adjective "educated," and as a direct result our schools must continually increase the amount of information and the number of experiences conveyed to each student.

The traditional alignments and allocations of subject matter are shifting. Subjects once contained in the college curriculum are now part of the high school science or math class; algebra is now commonplace in the elementary school, and the University of California has been experimenting with the teaching of certain fundamentals of calculus in the second grade. Many of our schools are now teaching subjects that would stagger the imagination of those who have been away from the classroom for only a few years—e.g., the chemical molecular theory of evolution, the field concept in physics, and the energy concept of chemical bonding. Not only are new materials being added and concepts being changed, but entirely new bodies of information are being included in the curriculum. For example, many states will be requiring within the next few years that all students take a foreign language as part of their elementary program.

The problem is obvious: given the same amount of time in school, the student of today must learn more information, have more educational experiences, and take more specific subjects than ever before. And this must be done by more students with relatively fewer teachers. And it is also obvious that we can succeed only if our educational system becomes as efficient as possible.

The report by the President's Commission on National Goals states:

> The development of the individual and the nation demand that education at every level and in every discipline be strengthened and its effectiveness enhanced. New teaching techniques must continue to be developed. The increase in population and the growing complexity of the world add urgency.[1]

Encouraged by Federal and private grants, educators are engaged in unprecedented researches in the general area of improving instructional methods, and the results to date have been excellent. The tools and techniques for improving our educational system are rapidly being developed; many are already available and in effective use. But unfortunately the majority of communities, colleges, and school districts have been slow in accepting these materials and approaches for their own use.

Television, as applied to education, has held the center of attention for the past decade. During this period it has been praised, damned, misused, and made the subject of much flamboyant propaganda, both pro and con. But much of the discussion has missed the point: in reality the effectiveness of television depends upon what is televised and how it is applied, for the medium is simply a means of transmission, nothing more. Recently the government has, for the first time, taken an active part in expanding the use of television in our schools by passing legislation designed to increase the number of educational stations. Television is beginning to assume its proper place in instruction as only one part of the answer in effective teaching.

Earlier chapters have demonstrated a broad spectrum of practical applications for television within a wide range of subject areas and grade levels. When used as a simple magnification device within the laboratory, classroom, or large lecture hall, television has made it possible for the teacher to improve student learning while saving himself both time and effort. Many chapters include specific examples of effective staff and resource utilization by television. We find administrative applications in student and faculty orientations, in the administration of standardized tests, and in in-service training. One chapter defines television's role within a comprehensive guidance program, while several describe student training programs associated with the district-operated television studio. In short, the applications of television within any education program are as varied as are our problems and our talents.

[1] *Goals for Americans,* Report of the President's Commission on National Goals, The American Assembly, Columbia University, 1960, p. 6.

THE FUTURE FOR INSTRUCTIONAL TELEVISION

From what we already know about instructional television it is possible to make some estimates of its future and long-range potential in education.

Instructional television will become a basic part of our teaching process. It can be expected that, within the next few years, the television receiver will become a standard part of classrooms and laboratories. Television will be used in many ways and in conjunction with many other teaching tools. The type and amount of television will vary according to the type of material being presented, the environment in which the teaching takes place, the alternate techniques available (programmed instruction, team teaching, etc.), and the abilities and attitudes of students. No one student will receive his entire education via television, but television will contribute to the education of every student.

The single-room television camera will become an integral part of the laboratory and large lecture hall and will be handled in much the same way as other audio-visual devices. Serving as an enlarger and transmitter of both two- and three-dimensional materials, easily operated by the instructor, and priced within the limits of most budgets, the single-room television camera will meet specific needs in many classrooms. It will be used within the laboratory to eliminate the need for repeated demonstrations, allowing the teacher to use his time more effectively. It will be used as a teaching tool along with the filmstrip, overhead and film projectors, the tape recorder and phonograph within the large lecture hall in a wide variety of ways and in many subject areas.

The use of community or educational television stations will increase dynamically. With recent government support it can be anticipated that an overwhelming majority of school districts will be within the range of some educational or community television station within the next few years. The number of districts using programs of the type offered will obviously increase substantially over this period. It can be anticipated that there will be increasing emphasis on evening programming for adult education and on homework assignments for day students, also that in-service training programs especially designed to help teachers use in-school telecasts will increase in numbers. The traditional, inflexible schedule in secondary schools will limit their use of in-school telecasts; television programs for elementary schools will continue to exceed in quantity those planned for the higher levels.

The quality of instructional programming will improve while the number of live programs produced by individual educational or community stations will decline. The need for high-quality programming will necessitate a weeding-out process to eliminate unsatisfactory productions. Superior programs will be made available

195

to stations by such organizations as National Educational Television (NET) (see pages 198–203). Most of these series for national distribution will be produced under grants to individual stations or institutions with outstanding resources. School districts will be offered complete materials prepared under state, government, or commercial sponsorship. Such "packaged material" will contain textbooks, teachers' guides, films, and related materials; television presentation will form only a part of the entire package.

Many school districts will combine the use of the community or educational station with closed- or open-circuit operations of their own. Stations are limited in the number of programs they can televise, and such programs must cover only those content areas where the need is agreed upon by a majority of the participating school districts. While the number of programs being offered and the number of districts using these lessons will increase, there will be a growing need on the part of many schools for programs not offered by already existing stations. As a result, many districts will build and operate their own television facilities. District-produced programs will be designed to fill specific local curriculum needs or to meet unique scheduling, staffing, or other administrative problems. It can be anticipated that many school districts will use inexpensive, low-power, 10-watt transmitters, combined with highly directional receiving antennas that will, in time, be available. This particular technique will allow neighboring school districts to utilize a wide spectrum of open-circuit channels without technical interference.

These district-operated installations will obviously vary greatly in both complexity and cost. It can be expected that school district programming will include administrative and in-service applications as individual districts explore expanded use of existing facilities.

Video tape will play an increasingly important and basic role in instructional television. As the cost of the equipment and tape decreases there will be a multifold increase in the use of video tape within our schools. Complicated demonstrations will be taped and then played back as part of regular presentations. Courses which combine lecture and laboratory will often employ taped lectures which can be viewed by students in the laboratory immediately preceding their individual activity. Portable cameras and video tape recorders will open up new areas in the use of community resources. The recorder's immediate playback potential will have many applications in those subjects where self-evaluation by the student is desired. Its use as a self-evaluation device for teacher in-service training is obvious. Outstanding presentations by the regular staff and guest speakers will be retained for later playback. Video tape will have a dynamic effect in secondary school instruction, where presentation of taped programs several times during the day will overcome the knotty scheduling problems which presently hinder the use of instructional television in our high schools. (See illustrations on pages 205 to 207.)

The number of statewide and regional educational television networks will increase. As the need and desire for instructional television increase, there will be a growing demand for state and regional networks. The majority of these will broadcast on UHF bands (channels 14 to 83). Many such networks will telecast over several channels simultaneously. It can be expected that much of the support for these networks will come from state governments seeking to uplift educational standards on a statewide basis. This,

Control room of the South Carolina Television Center

obviously, will necessitate an extremely cautious developmental process with a maximum of cooperation to forestall the many problems associated with state or governmental control.

It can be anticipated, then, that television will play an ever-increasing role in the formal education of our children. The role itself will vary from subject to subject, from grade level to grade level, and will be dependent upon many factors. Instructional television is but one of a series of techniques that must be used if we are to overcome the basic problems now facing our educational system.

PROBLEM AREAS

Those educators involved in the development of instructional television must find solutions for many problems if the medium is ever to take its proper place in our education system. Since its early conception instructional television has stimulated much contro-

NET (National Educational Television) makes available to its member stations a wide variety of high-quality programs for late afternoon and evening viewing.

"Turn of the Century," with Max Morath and Jan Ferrand (NET)

"An Age of Kings" (NET)

"Heifetz Master Class," with master violinist Jascha Heifetz and, here, Erick Friedman (NET)

"State Department Briefing." Washington Correspondent Merriman Smith interviews Secretary of State Dean Rusk. (NET)

"Art and Man," with French novelist and critic Jean Marie Drot and sculptor Ossip Zadkine (NET)

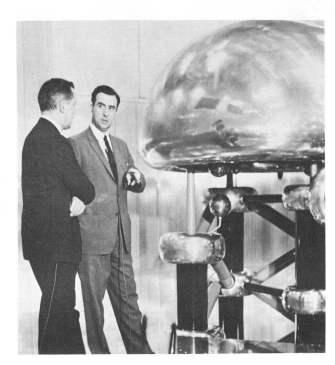

"Challenge." The function of the cyclotron is explained by Dr. Albert Crewe, Director of the Argonne National Laboratories. (NET)

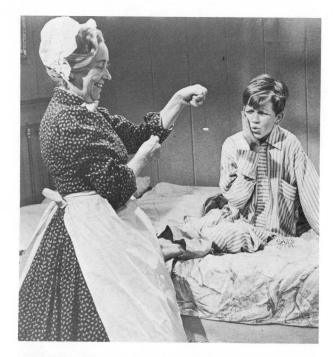

"What's New," a series designed for children, presents the BBC production of *Mark Twain*. (NET)

"The Wild Duck," presented by Associated-Rediffusion (NET)

"The Quiet War," a special documentary on South Vietnam (NET)

"Prospects of Mankind." President John Kennedy and Eleanor Roosevelt discuss the Peace Corps. (NET)

versy. Dick Lewis puts it this way:

> Among many disquieting developments in the relatively deliberate evolu-
> tion of education, television is a significant creator of alarm. Even the ad-
> vent of the teaching machine (which, as a self-instructional device, is so
> often considered an extension of the textbook) is minimally affecting the
> placid security of education. But TV, in a dramatic way, cuts sharply
> across all aspects of an instructional program and prods deeply into the
> traditionally private classroom life of teachers.[2]

In the remainder of this chapter some of the major areas of concern will be explored in some detail.

Teacher attitudes. Research has shown that the attitude of the classroom teacher plays a substantial role in the final success of any
television lesson. A television lesson viewed by the class of a
teacher who is resistant toward television has little chance of being
effective.

It is apparent that we must not only inform our teachers of the
potentials of television but that we must also help them develop a
positive attitude toward exploring the use of the medium within
their own classrooms. This educational program falls into two distinct parts—that which takes place in the prospective teacher's
undergraduate program, and that which is designed for teachers
already in the field.

The college program. Student teachers may learn of instructional
television (as well as other technological developments) in two
ways: first, by a planned orientation program within the regular required curriculum, and, second, by observing proper application of the medium within their own college classes.

Unfortunately, graduates of many teacher preparation programs
are uninformed about instructional television. They know little
about the role it may play in their own teaching or about the
responsibility of the classroom teacher in effectively using instructional television.

The picture our college students receive is often left to chance.
As a result, it tends to be sketchy and inaccurate. It is imperative
that colleges provide carefully planned, fully supported programs
of instruction in new techniques. Obviously, this means that instructors must be kept up to date. Some colleges are now, for the first
time, including specific experiences with television for all their
future teachers. These range from one or two lecture-demonstra-
tions to actual experience in teaching on television, evaluating television lessons, and planning for the use of the medium within their
classrooms.

Perhaps the best method for the future teacher is to be taught
by the new techniques. Most of us teach as we were taught. Yet, in

---

[2] Richard B. Lewis, "TV, or Not TV, That Is the Question...," *Teachers College
Record,* 63 (7):564–569, April, 1962.

The video tape recorder brings to the teacher an entirely new range of effective teaching techniques.

A laboratory demonstration introducing the laboratory activity that will follow is recorded for use within the large lecture hall.

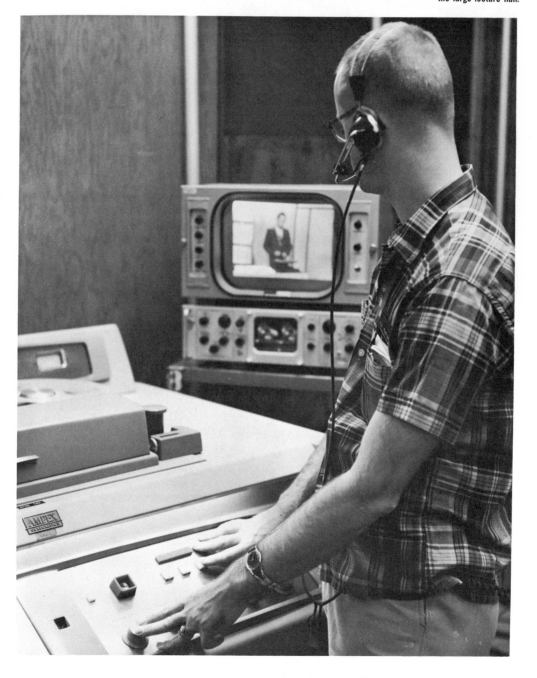

In public speaking, the teacher has the advantage of immediate playback and evaluation.

The advantage of immediate playback in physical education is obvious. In the teaching of diving, a small television camera is focused on the diver and connected to the tape recorder.

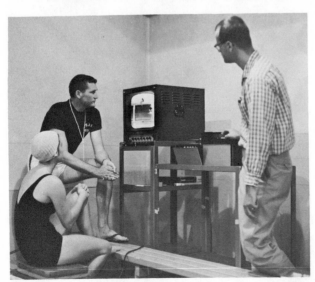

Within a matter of seconds, the dive is played back for comments and suggestions.

The development of compact, lightweight video tape recorders allows for easy mobility and simple operation. Within a matter of minutes, the unit may be moved to another classroom or activity area.

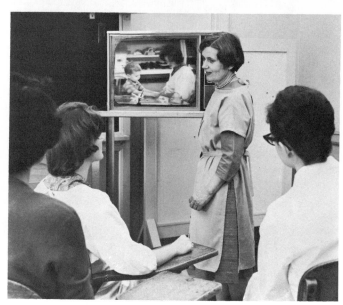

In the training of teachers, the faculty member and the student evaluate the student-teacher's classroom experience immediately upon its completion.

college, "Do what I say, not what I do" is too often the rule rather than the exception. It is within the teacher training programs that we should find our best teaching, by television as well as by traditional methods.

In-service education. While the college program can, over a period of years, affect the teaching that goes on within a school district, the school administrator must rely on teachers already within his district when he wishes to implement change. It is the atmosphere within a district that will, in effect, determine the individual teacher's attitude toward change or experimentation. The responsibility for creating an atmosphere conducive to the introduction of instructional television rests solely with the school administration.

The problems of reaching the in-service teacher are discussed in Chapters 13 and 14, dealing with in-service education by television, and in Appendix A, which offers suggestions for a careful program of teacher orientation. Before any new tool, such as television, is introduced, teachers must be prepared. Too many projects have been doomed before they began by poor teacher attitudes resulting from improper faculty orientation.

Equipment versus education. All too often the money that has been made available for a television project has had behind it technological rather than educational orientation. By the time the equipment has been purchased, the studio designed, and the technicians hired, there is little money left for curriculum analysis, research, and production. As a result, while the equipment has been of the highest quality, the lessons being telecast have not. We have simply spread mediocrity to an extent that would have been impossible without television.

Some school districts have rushed into television without the proper curriculum planning, staff orientation, and technical staffing. Often the decision to use television has been reached before alternative solutions have even been investigated. When we rush blindly into television there can be only one result: disaster, for the best way to sink any instructional project is to produce low-quality education.

Successful studio production takes both time and talent. Any administrator planning his own production center must realize this fact and plan accordingly. While it is possible to plan the technical development in a way that will save both time and money (Appendix B), the thoughtless reduction of time and assistance needed to plan and present the lessons themselves will drastically lower the quality of productions. Teachers and students will accept technical limitations; they cannot accept poor education. During the early phase of a project it is far wiser to produce a few lessons of high quality than to produce many of dubious effectiveness. Ineffectual presentations simply result in loss of support by teachers and by the community.

Before rushing ahead to purchase elaborate television equipment, there are many questions that an administrator must ask. For many school districts a comprehensive studio operation is not practical today and will not be tomorrow. Long before turning to a district-operated television installation, the administrator must have analyzed the particular problems that his district faces and must have included television in his study of alternatives. Are there alternatives other than television that may be just as effective and far less expensive? Are programs already available from a local educational or community station that will do the job? What can and cannot be done with television? In short, each administrator must ask himself this question: Does television fit into my particular situation and, if so, how can it best be utilized?

Trained personnel. Instructional television needs talented, highly skilled personnel with educational backgrounds to assume many of its more important technical roles. If the lessons are to be of the highest quality the producer, the director, and the visualization specialist (graphic artist–photographer) must understand not only television techniques but also the teaching and learning process.

In the early days of instructional television most technical positions were necessarily filled by persons gravitating into the field from the commercial television industry. Many of these people are highly talented; they have done and continue to do superb work. In a number of instances, however, the production staff and the television teacher simply could not communicate; the results were naturally unfortunate. In instructional television the production emphasis must be to assist the teacher in communicating to the student the material being covered, period. Some of the basic rules of commercial television productions cannot be applied to educational programming. While the end result in both cases is good television, the step-by-step process of arriving at the finished program is basically different.

For example, the responsibility of the director in the entertainment field differs from his responsibility in instructional television. In commercial television the director has sole authority for both content and presentation. In the educational field his responsibility is primarily production, while content and interpretation are in the domain of the television teacher. Similarly, the visual specialist must understand the learning process and the need for simplicity of visualization. There have been just as many examples of overvisualized lessons as of lessons which failed to make full use of television techniques.

The colleges might have been expected to assume responsibility for the twofold training needed for work in the field of instructional television. Unfortunately, with few exceptions, such programs have never materialized. Many institutions have an occupational curriculum for the already overcrowded commercial field but, at the time of this writing, less than a handful have comprehensive programs designed to train administrators, producers, directors, and graphic artists especially for the educational field.

As a result, the majority of individuals now involved with instructional television have had to learn by experience, with all the added problems that learning of this type brings. The only way to learn from the experience of others is through extensive reading and personal contact. Unfortunately practical references are still hard to find, while extensive visiting is expensive. We find, therefore, the same mistakes being repeated over and over again.

School districts searching for persons to head or staff a new television operation have nowhere to turn. The two organizations offering placement help, the National Association of Educational Broadcasters and the Department of Audio-Visual Instruction of the NEA, find that they do not have enough specially trained individuals to fill the growing need.

As a result administrators are forced to employ individuals with a minimum of educational experience or to turn to those within the educational field who may have shown no more than a casual interest in the potential of television. The person proficient in television techniques must then be given time to learn about education, or the educator entering the instructional television area must have time to visit successful current projects or to take one or more of the few appropriate college courses now being offered. Superintendents must realize that qualified individuals are simply not available and that instructional television personnel must, of necessity, learn on the job.

Research and evaluation.   As stated in Chapter 15, research in the area of instructional television has been hindered by muddy and unmeasurable objectives, much duplication, little application, and a lack of both breadth and depth.

Often in the comparisons of televised instruction with standard teaching techniques the teacher has simply been moved into the television studio with a minimum of change. Unless the techniques that make television teaching more effective are used (see pages 49 to 55), and unless enough time is devoted to lesson preparation, the true effectiveness of the medium will remain unknown.

Many important aspects of television utilization have yet to be fully investigated. These include, among others, the interrelationships of television teaching, student attitude, and student motivation, and the effectiveness of various types of television application combined with small-group and self-study learning situations under the direction of the classroom teacher. An effort must be made to explore the combination of techniques and configurations that will produce the best results within each and every course, for it can be expected that the most effective combination for one course will not hold true for all others. Before such investigation is possible, each course must be carefully analyzed for its particular objectives; obviously realistic evaluation requires clearly stated, measurable objectives.

Recent findings have opened up a whole series of questions. Is it possible that it is the motivated student who takes advantage of the well-organized, visualized television presentation and, therefore, might we not pretest our students and then "program" each individual into those learning situations in which he will perform most effectively? In several chapters the authors have reported a substantial reduction in the time needed to complete a particular area of study when television was used. Should these courses have their content increased or their allotted time decreased? And then there is the question of course duplication. Many subjects begin with the same basic material and then each, according to the field of study, goes deeper into one particular area. Could not the common information be presented on television? What better way do we have of showing important interrelationships between subjects? In short, we must explore how to best utilize the teacher's time and the student's time for effective learning.

Well-designed, carefully conducted research programs will determine television's role in education. Research rather than intuition is the long-range guide to improved instruction. Only with reliable and valid findings can administrators and teachers present a rationale for how and what we teach. But once these facts do become known it is the responsibility of both teacher and administrator to put the information into practice.

At no other stage of our history have we found education in such a dynamic period of growth and yet, paradoxically, a time of change coupled with conservatism and resistance. Perhaps someday we will consider the mid-1960s as the period in which our school system matured, leaving behind the basic tenets that have been the guiding forces since the "Little Red Schoolhouse," the "self-contained" classroom and the "jack-of-all-trades" teacher. Instructional television, if its potential is realized, can surely be one of the major aids in our striving toward a new, qualitatively higher educational standard in this country.

Appendixes

Your next steps

THIS SECTION is designed specifically for the administrator or teacher who is planning to use television within his school or school district. The technical section on equipment is not intended to be complete but is designed to present to the reader basic information that will save time, effort, and dollars as this area is explored.

In Appendix A, Dick Lewis presents some practical suggestions for the administrator who wishes to introduce some form of instructional television into the school program and must first overcome teacher resistance and inertia.

Appendix B is unique in structure and invaluable to anyone facing the problems of equipment purchase. Equipment covered ranges from studio facilities and portable television units to antenna systems and classroom receivers. In this section Mrs. Martin presents the basic rationale of what to look for and offers some specific guidelines to be followed.

Appendix C discusses in some detail the selection and responsibilities of the television teacher. Emphasis is placed on the often overlooked but extremely important problems that most television teachers will face.

A major area of concern has been the low quality and uselessness of a great majority of the prepared teacher's guides now available. These guides serve as the main, and often only, contact between the classroom and television teacher and the effectiveness of the television lesson is often dependent upon the comprehensiveness of the guide. Appendix D presents to the television teacher a practical outline for the preparation of the grade with a rationale for its contents.

For the administrator wishing to explore the effectiveness of a television project Appendix E includes several types of evaluation forms that school districts have found practical, relating directly to material covered in Chapter 15 by Dr. Brown.

Nurturing TV exploration:
notes on introducing instructional television

Richard B. Lewis

Did you ever tame a bird? To catch and nurture the interest of a school or college faculty and staff in using television is a similar experience. Patience, humility, and competence, as well as sensitive response to feelings, moods, and attitudes, all play parts in the activities of those who would give leadership to the utilization of television in education. If conviction is based upon sound scholarship, if enthusiasm is sufficiently strong, yet carefully controlled, if devotion to the basic purposes of others motivates action, and if necessary basic competence is demonstrated, then—with a little bit of luck—slow progress can be made toward winning teacher understanding and acceptance of television as an ally and a promising tool for teaching.

Since teachers, like birds, tend to be wisely or instinctively skittish in the presence of unknowns, the following points are offered as suggestions for consideration by television enthusiasts and by operating personnel.

Don't snow them! When teachers show curiosity about television, move in slowly. Sudden bursts of conviction and enthusiasm cause protective defenses. Never burst forth with technical information, terminology of the trade, or blasts of implication that you are the key to a great, complex, mysterious technology; remember, they don't need television—they can walk away. In fact, if they don't walk away, they still don't need to know a fader from a cable.

Get them involved! Ten successful minutes before the camera, with a monitor handy to let them see themselves, may do more to eliminate teachers' fears of television than one month of your persuasive telling. Or—with diplomacy—you may discourage poor teachers from appearing on TV, and at the same time create

Dr. Lewis is Professor of Education and head of the Division of Audio-Visual Services at San Jose State College, San Jose, Calif. This chapter is revised from a paper presented at Pennsylvania State University, 1959, and published in *The Role of Production in Televised Instruction,* National Association of Educational Broadcasters, Urbana, Ill.

enthusiastic and even effective users of television. What you do and say will make the difference. The last holdouts against television are those who persist in saying, "I've never used TV; I'm against it."

Promote experimentalism!   Beware of flat and firm statements of finality about how, when, and why to use television. In the first place, you will be wrong—no final answers are in. Then, second, you must nurture an experimental viewpoint toward every aspect of television teaching. There are infinite possibilities in every situation; many of them will work, some better than others. Suggest that everyone should have the opportunity to try different approaches, methods, materials. Defer as long as possible the day when anyone can say, "*This* is the way to teach with television." The natural tendency to freeze methods is a threat to ultimate optimal utilization of the medium. Therefore, create a spirit of "We're all in the same stage of development—try, experiment, try some more." Don't let a failure stop the trying; don't throw out the baby with the bath water.

Avoid closed corporations!   Devise methods of keeping groups with common interests working together. This probably leads to good television utilization; it certainly leads to better human relations. Avoid setting up a martyr or a star performer. Develop teams. If one is on camera, others work with observing students; then have them change places. There is less risk in a mediocre TV lesson than in an embittered target for colleague barbs. TV advances when several teachers help each other, and when TV personnel help them all.

Involve the entire administration!   What are the problems that beset administrators today that TV may help solve? Are the same problems facing teaching personnel? Think this one through in your school, and bring administrators and teachers together. Also, develop procedures for the use of TV for direct administrative purposes, such as testing programs, registration, teacher and student orientation, and institutional interpretation and promotion. Workshops and programs for visiting groups permit the direct involvement of administrative personnel; put them "on the air."

Beware the status seekers!   "BTOs" (Big Time Operators) can destroy the future of television in education, whether they are ambitious teachers or TV production personnel. The production director who insists on being the master teacher, who "controls" the professor, who gets the credits, will be rewarded by rear views of departing potential television enthusiasts. Yet, sure skill on the part of every technical staff member must be evident in teaching programs; the "invisible waiter" in a fine restaurant has skills to be emulated: unnoticed, he applies his talent to the comfort and pleasure and success of his guest. "Tips" for producers will be the support of television in the institution by proud and satisfied teachers. Status-seeking teachers require special, individual attention; fortunately they are few in number.

Avoid creeping complexity! Whether it be in technical matters or production techniques, beware of gradual complication of television presentations and utilization. Work constantly to reduce the strange, madhouse, mechanical, and overcomplicated atmosphere of the commercial studio. Work to simplify equipment and to reduce the number of persons required to produce a lesson on television. Cut confusion, the possibility of technical failures, and the special atmosphere of "studio" so dear to so many producers. Four men closing in on a nervous bird will ensure quick flight; an expert man may make a friend. Technical crews, especially, need to cultivate the "invisible waiter's" techniques.

Focus on teaching and learning! Television is not destined to replace the teacher. Television will not, of itself, ensure learning. Respect the great insecurity felt by teachers when challenged by a new tool; recognize the fact that, badly used, television could do a disservice to education. The sole purpose of using television is to make teaching and learning better than they are without television, to extend the scope and depth of education in the face of a growing population and increasing necessity for the dissemination and assimilation of knowledge. The role of the teacher will be affected by television, and—used wisely—television can help make possible more effective person-to-person teaching in small groups; this idea suggests the many things to be learned about television teaching and viewing, about the schedules and deployment of teaching talent, about making learning an active experience both in the presence and out of the presence of the television screen. Thus, TV personnel must be concerned about education and every aspect of the educational process; thus, too, almost every aspect of television production is subject to analysis in terms of teaching and learning procedures, content, and personnel.

As we initiate, nurture, and promote exploration of television teaching in colleges, we must take great care not to be like children, delighted with the new toy, unable to contain our enthusiasm: many a teacher will tentatively poke his head into the studio and say, "Thought I'd look in and see what you're doing. I have an idea that. . . ." Well, if you figuratively jump out from behind a tripod and shout, "Whoops!"—too bad, not only is the bird gone, but you may have lost him for good.

appendix B

Planning for television:
from objectives to equipment

Gaither Lee Martin

The administrator exploring the purchase of television equipment, whether it be a single television receiver or a complete studio facility, faces many problems. The variety of available equipment is extensive and often confusing. In this section Mrs. Martin offers a series of practical guidelines and a rationale that may save both time and money.

Educators contemplating the installation and utilization of television for instruction are confronted with many problems. However, development of an evolutionary plan will minimize these problems, ensure economy, and encourage efficiency. In order to develop such a plan the educator needs to know:

- Where to go for needed information
- The right questions to ask
- Pitfalls to be avoided

It is the purpose of this section, while not answering all questions, to help develop a planning procedure, and to give some guidelines on how TV systems and utilization of television relate to an instructional program. Emphasis is upon TV equipment and related technical problems as they may be identified in the course of curriculum and administration studies. Answers to specific questions can best be obtained from the many excellent books (see Bibliography) and technical manuals available to educators, and from other sources to be suggested.

SOME SUGGESTIONS FOR PRELIMINARY PLANNING

Since many applications of TV are now operational routine in a wide variety of configurations in educational institutions of all types, careful consideration should be given to the experience of others by:

Mrs. Martin is Coordinator of Instructional Television Services at San Jose State College and for many years has served as a consultant on equipment and facilities to area school districts.

1. Locating programs presently operated by institutions or school districts similar to the one conducting studies (see pages 289 to 293 for a partial list of school districts now using instructional television).
2. Visiting television installations.
3. Obtaining and studying literature prepared by others using instructional television.
4. Exploring the ideas of administrators, architects, engineers, and television personnel who have had experience in planning for and utilizing television (asking them how they started, what they would have done differently if they had the opportunity to begin again, what their major unsolved problems are, and what problems they have solved, and how).
5. Engaging assistance (from initial planning to the end of complex system installation) from agencies or consulting services whose primary function is to supply information.

As preparation for planning, the educator should have at least a rudimentary knowledge of some of the common technical terms used in discussing television. This does not mean that he will need to be an engineer, or have the technical knowledge of experienced television personnel. It does mean that he will need the ability to use proper terminology that will elicit specific and accurate responses when he raises questions. Such knowledge during initial planning will certainly save time, and probably money (see Glossary).

Another suggested preliminary planning activity is the development of a file of information sources. As an administrator reviews available literature, he will find descriptions of different instructional television installations and arrangements, ranging from use of the single-room camera to transmission systems as complex as Airborne Television. Probably he will find installations similar to the one he is planning, and he should find out all he can about these systems. Careful analysis of the uses of television should include study of the instructional objectives of any specific application and an appraisal of the outcomes obtained. Files of agency addresses and names of people from whom assistance and information can be requested, as well as major manufacturers of television equipment, can be helpful for reference when installation planning is in progress.

FUNDAMENTAL USES OF TELEVISION SYSTEMS

Chapters in this book reveal a surprising variety of demonstrated applications of television for purposes of education. The uses of television may be divided into three basic categories:

I. Studio to classroom(s). This use of television may be provided by either closed or broadcast television, or both, for supplementary or enrichment programs to:
A. aid classroom teachers to bring to students resources not normally available

B. aid the district in which there is a shortage of qualified teachers in certain specialized content areas

C. aid the classroom teacher in giving the best possible fundamental instruction to students in a specific curriculum area.

II. Single-room television for laboratory or lecture demonstrations for either small or large groups of students when television equipment can be moved into a classroom, lecture hall, or laboratory, to be used as an image magnification device, a teaching aid for the instructor.

III. Administrative use of television for:

A. Observation to:

1. Provide a means of studying remotely located, hazardous, or other activities inconvenient for group viewing in person

2. Provide appropriate and effective pre- and in-service instruction of teachers in teaching methods, in counseling and guidance, and in technical subject instruction.

B. Communications medium for:

1. Guidance programs

2. Giving standardized tests

3. Conducting faculty meetings

4. Presenting important information to faculty and students

5. Presenting important speakers to a number of individuals or groups in different locations.

Though the broad uses of television are few, its multiplicity of applications to instruction challenges the imagination. Though many applications are treated in detail in preceding chapters of this book, others have been developed, or are being developed, as television is increasingly accepted as a part of the educational system.

When television is used for instruction, it must be integrated within the framework of the curriculum, and its value should, therefore, be assessed in the same objective terms as other resources for instruction. The best appropriate equipment money can buy, and the best overall administrative plan for programming the equipment, will surely fail unless those persons charged with utilization of the instructional program have a thorough knowledge of the techniques of its utilization and an understanding of the benefits television can bring to the learner.

The applications of television offer potential benefits for the improvement of instruction only when effectively used and adequately supported. Capital investments and support budgets for implementing instructional television are major items and should be on a continuing basis. It is neither practical nor economical to buy equipment, employ personnel, and initiate instructional television programming as a short-term project. Before television can be accepted and supported with full justification, the technical and economic factors involved require analysis and careful projection. Planning, therefore, should start with a basic and thorough analysis of educational needs to determine whether and how television can be used in any specific local situation.

RELATING EDUCATIONAL NEEDS TO TELEVISION SYSTEMS

Justification for television equipment installation should be based upon an analysis of educational needs suggested by the following questions:

1. Why is television needed?
   a. To bring supplementary instructional resources to the classroom?
   b. To aid a teacher in giving the best possible instruction to students?
   c. To provide instruction in specialized areas when qualified teachers are in short supply?
   d. To accommodate increasing enrollments?
   e. To help compensate for limited building budgets?
   f. To effect savings in faculty time and energy?
   g. To provide in-service training of teachers?
   h. To improve the structure and content of the school curriculum?
   i. To give the faculty some experience with television with minimal investment?
   j. To acquaint the public with the school program?

If the need for television equipment is justified, then answers to the following questions should determine the appropriate kind of equipment to be installed.

2. What kind of television may meet the identified needs?
   a. Use of instructional programs from local educational television stations?
   b. A simple television system with which to experiment in a few classes?
   c. A basic system that can be expanded in size and scope as the instructional television program is developed and new applications are defined?
   d. A system capable of providing television instruction in or for one or two schools, or for all the schools in a school district?
   e. A system capable of providing observation experiences from remote locations for specified purposes?
   f. A broadcast station facility for open-circuit telecasting to a specific area for instructional purposes?
3. What are the budget considerations involved?
   a. How much money is available to spend on instructional television?
   b. What space is available where television equipment could be installed, maintained, and utilized? What new additional space will be needed? What will it cost?
   c. What professional personnel are available or needed to guide and support the television program for the defined local instructional objectives?
   d. What technical personnel and resources will be necessary to support the instructional television program next year and in five years, if long-range goals are to be met? What will they cost?

TELEVISION SYSTEMS TO MEET EDUCATIONAL NEEDS

When the questions above are answered, even tentatively, consideration will then be given to types of television systems and equipment. All television systems, from the simplest to the most complex, contain three elements:

1. Transmission systems
2. Reception systems
3. Origination systems

TRANSMISSION SYSTEMS

Open-circuit television. Open-circuit television refers to broadcast stations transmitting on (VHF) Very High Frequency (channels 2 to 13) or (UHF) Ultrahigh Frequency (channels 14 to 83). Owning and operating a broadcast television station requires licensing by the Federal Communications Commission (FCC). Rigid controls are maintained by this governing body, and strict adherence to FCC rules and regulations is required. The steps to be followed and the topics to be considered in planning, making application for, constructing, staffing, financing, and operating a broadcast television station are too detailed and technical to be treated in this section.[1]

Low-power transmission. Experiments are being conducted in the use of low-power transmitters for instructional purposes. These projects have been given special FCC permission to operate below the 100-watt minimum now in force.

These low-power stations, usually in the 10-watt range, combine originating equipment with a translator unit and have several basic advantages:

1. Cost is far below that required for 100-watt stations.
2. Under ideal conditions, the station may have a coverage of 300 square miles.
3. Operation and maintenance are economical.
4. Neighboring school districts may use the same channel without interference, with each district covering its own area.
5. New rules and regulations for this type of operation may reduce the cost of test equipment and other devices now needed to comply with FCC rules and regulations.

This type of operation is still in the experimental stage, but it warrants attention for future developments.

[1] For those interested in considering this area of television, materials, including "Broadcast Application Procedures," "List of Printed Publications," and broadcast application forms, may be obtained without charge from the Federal Communications Commission, Washington 25, D.C. Also, the National Educational Television and Radio Center, 10 Columbus Circle, New York, N.Y., serves as a clearinghouse of information and assistance for educators planning broadcast facilities.

Closed-circuit television. Closed-circuit television refers to other than broadcast television, and FCC licensing is not required. A closed-circuit system provides for the electronic transmission of television signals ("RF" or "Video"—see Glossary) from a camera or cameras (originating equipment), over cable (coaxial) or by microwave (a point-to-point transmitting system) to selected receivers (television sets—the reception equipment), permitting private reception of programs only by those receivers included in the circuit.

Closed-circuit television (CCTV) is a private communications system providing simultaneous transmission of picture and sound. It is used by many school systems in a wide variety of applications. Elements of a well-planned closed-circuit system may also permit use of broadcast programming. For this reason the major emphasis of this section will be on closed-circuit systems.

RECEPTION SYSTEMS

If the programs from educational or other stations not operated by a local district will meet educational requirements, then the technical problems for the district are minimal. Equipment to be purchased will include an antenna system, necessary wiring, and receivers. Such a system is called a distribution facility, and is an extension of the "transmission" process from station to classroom viewers; such systems are much the same as those used in hotels, but their design for school purposes will be determined by the ultimate variety of television applications specified by the school system.

Antenna systems. Antennas for receiving broadcast programs in a school are very much the same as those for home reception. They may be of the indoor or outdoor variety, and are usually of two main types: (1) very simple single-conductor unit to pick up all channels, or (2) more complex master-antenna systems, with separate antennas for each channel designed and oriented for optimum signal reception. Antennas should be purchased to meet local conditions, such as the location of the school, the distance and directions of the broadcast stations, and the number of television receivers to be served, and to overcome obstacles such as tall buildings or mountains which may interfere with reception. The number and type of antennas best suited for a school may be determined by consulting television equipment suppliers.

Distribution systems. A distribution system is necessary in order to transmit television programs to a number of rooms. The wiring for such systems is much the same as that provided for several television sets in a home, or for the many rooms in hotels and motels. De-

225

tailed descriptions of distribution systems may be found in many texts and technical manuals, and there are many vendors who specialize in designing and installing such systems; in some areas, local telephone companies will provide television distribution services. A cable distribution system used for wiring rooms within a building may be extended for services between buildings or among schools in a school district. (For some distribution problems, a microwave system may be superior to a cable system.) For the installation of some in-school wiring systems at minimal cost it is possible to use the services of school technical staff members or local technicians.

Though the technical details of designing distribution systems cannot appropriately be discussed here, a brief guide to the types of systems may be helpful.

The two types of closed-circuit television distribution systems in most common use are radio frequency (RF) and video. A third, microwave distribution, will also be discussed.

RF distribution systems are used in the majority of educational closed-circuit television installations. The major advantages of RF systems (on cable) are:

1. Flexibility of the system for a variety of programming objectives.
2. Multichannel capability (all standard television VHF channels 2 to 13) may be utilized on RF distribution.
3. All channels may be used simultaneously (different receivers in the same or different rooms may be tuned to desired channels).
4. Amplifiers may be added to the cable, where necessary, to maintain a high-quality signal level. Special splitters may be added to main trunk lines to extend feeder lines to new locations as the occasion demands. Thus, the system can be extended whenever new facilities or locations are designated.
5. One cable carries both audio and video signals together for all channels used.
6. Economical standard home receivers, or special school receivers, may both be used.
7. The cable system for RF distribution may be extended when necessary to reach additional viewing areas.
8. A two-way cable system, called a "round robin," or a "distribution and pickup system," can be provided, using RF to allow each receiving room to become also a potential originating room for programs.
9. Federal Communications Commission licensing is not required. Operating costs are low, maintenance is minimal, and reliability is high.
10. If the system is designed as a "wideband" system, it is possible to add a special high-resolution channel for transmission of complex data, should the need arise.
11. RF systems provide "space" on the same cable for transmission of special signals, in addition to the television picture, to control a variety of functions, such as automated receivers and student response systems.

In a school system, all classrooms designated to use television should be interconnected by shielded, coaxial cable or some other appropriately wired system. The cable usually starts at a central point where the signals are inserted into the system at the origination point (see figure below). The coaxial cable may be run through conduits, ducts, or crawl spaces; when wiring within a district, messenger wire to support the coaxial cable may be strung overhead on poles.

In classrooms, plug-in outlets may be mounted in boxes placed either inside or on the surface of walls, and "isolation" devices (splitters) may also be permanently installed in the boxes. This plug-in allows for the connection of a television receiver to the system and, because of the splitters, any receiver connected to the system may be operated independently and on any channel without affecting any other receiver.

The tremendous flexibility of RF distribution systems cannot fail to be recognized when it is apparent that several open-circuit broadcasts and one or more closed-circuit programs initiated within the school may be simultaneously transmitted over the same system. The several-channel capability in standard RF systems thus vastly increases the potential applications of television. Proper planning for a distribution system will permit such flexibility.

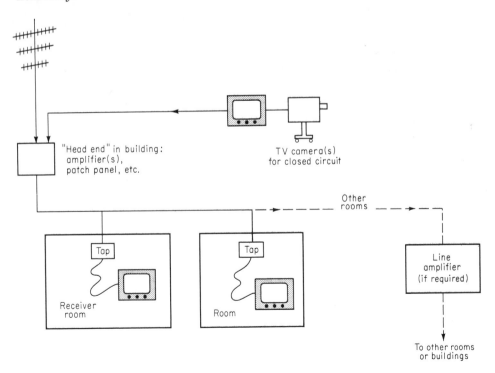

Schematic of a typical distribution system

1. Cables normally used are coaxial; generally, the larger the cable, the less line loss. Therefore, fewer amplifiers may be needed. RG 59 U cable, about ⅜ inch in diameter, is often used for short runs; RG 11 U, about ½ inch in diameter, will conduct TV signals over greater distances with lower loss. New developments in cables (such as Jerrold JT 200 type) should be explored at the time of system design.
2. Conduit for TV distribution cable systems should be installed in new construction. Though both system design and construction methods affect conduit plans, here are a few guidelines based on current experience:

Normal conduit size, in.	*Comments*
½	Impractical.
¾	Barely adequate for one large cable. Sometimes used from a trunk line to a single tap.
1	Often satisfactory for two-cable runs of coaxial plus an intercom cable.
1½	Desirable. Permits wide range of future adaptability of the system to changing needs.
2–3	Usually specified for distribution feeds between floors and between buildings, and for camera cables.

Special consideration must be made of curves and bends in conduit when coaxial cable is used; cable manufacturers specify minimum radii of cable bends.

Installers of cable must be aware of potential cable damage caused by excessive strain during "pulls" through conduit.

3. Often conduit may not be necessary for TV cable installations if proper suspension and protection from physical damage can be provided in crawl spaces and areas over corridors. Access to taps and splitters must be provided and excessively long "pulls" avoided.
4. Continuous runs should be arranged to loop through rooms rather than be provided as separate runs to each room.

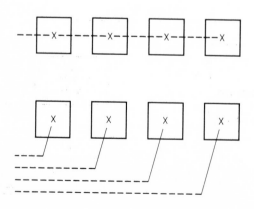

Video distribution systems also use coaxial cable to carry the video signal (picture only) directly from TV cameras to a special video receiver called a monitor. Video systems are superior to RF systems in that:

1. Picture quality and definition are high.
2. Less amplification is necessary to maintain high signal levels.

But the disadvantages must also be considered:

1. Only one channel may be used on a cable at one time.
2. Separate cable must be used for each video signal if several programs are to be carried simultaneously.
3. Audio lines must be run separately if voice is to accompany picture.
4. Video monitors are much more expensive than standard RF receivers—perhaps double or more in cost.

RF and video distribution methods can be designed for dual applications by providing a switching procedure from one system to the other. This approach can be valuable in instruction where very high definition pictures are occasionally required, as in some laboratory teaching in engineering, science, and industrial arts classes. Therefore, video systems, or special RF channels, may be considered when very detailed picture resolution is required, such as for demonstrations of small precision operations or special skill techniques, and for making very small objects large, as in microscope techniques.

Microwave distribution is a line-of-sight or point-to-point signal transmission system for picture and sound requiring FCC licensing. This system may be used in conjunction with ground, building, or district-wide distribution systems where it is impractical to make cable runs because relatively long air line distances are involved. Channels for their use must be licensed by the Federal Communications Commission, and in some areas may be difficult to obtain, though special channels for education may be available at the time of application. Each microwave link carries a signal in only one direction, and a licensed engineer is required for its operation. Microwave equipment is often used in conjunction with standard broadcast station-transmitter operations, but seems impractical for most local school uses. Decisions to use microwave for interschool distribution must be based upon careful prior study of all alternative types of available closed-circuit distribution systems and their relative feasibility and costs (see page 230).

Intercommunication systems are used to provide two-way talking facilities between TV origination points and reception points. In closed-circuit systems, it is desirable to pull multipair audio cable along with coaxial cable when the distribution system is installed. This communication facility is inexpensive, requires minimal service, and permits conversations between any points on the distribution system. Although educators disagree regarding the necessity for a two-way communication system between classroom and television teachers, the costs are so modest (if audio lines are installed with the coaxial cable) that this added function can be available if desired. If video distribution is used and sound is to accompany televised pictures, then audio lines must be installed in addition to lines for separate technical or instructional conversation.

Television receivers. In school situations, television receivers serve a large number of viewers in many different locations and under varying viewing conditions. Therefore, television receivers for school use should meet such criteria as these:

1. Sturdy construction: receivers will be moved, stored, pushed into corners, and handled by students and teachers. Dark wood finishes will show mar, scratch, and chip marks more readily than light, hardwood, or metal cabinets.
2. Receivers should be portable if they are to be transported from room to room. They can be mounted on metal rolling stands approximately 46 inches high, with swivel wheels at one end, and fixed, locking wheels at the other end. Soft, oversized rubber tires are desirable and allow the stands to be moved with ease and with minimal vibration. Also desirable

A microwave link with the high-frequency radio transmitter (left), sending audio and video signals in a directional line-of-sight "beam" to a receiver (right).

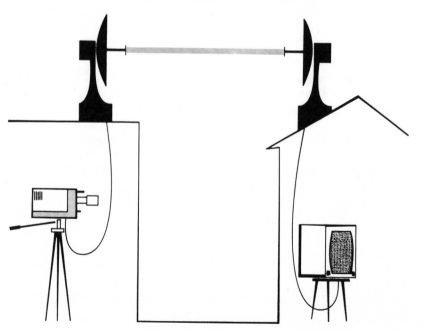

is a 1-inch lip around the top of the stand to prevent the receiver from sliding while being transported. A rubber pad under the receiver will also help keep it in position. The top of the receiver screen should be 4½ to 7 feet above the floor level; it should be tilted slightly forward, and it may have a hood across the top, if necessary, to keep out the overhead light reflections. Because the greatest light-reflection difficulty may be experienced with light coming from side windows, receivers should be placed with their backs toward windows, or in corners away from window reflections.

Where permanent installations are possible, receivers should be wall- or ceiling-mounted for better visibility, less risk of damage or unauthorized tampering, and reduction of theft hazard (see illustrations, pages 233 to 235).

3. The nominal picture size for the average classroom should be a minimum of 21 inches, and the 23-inch size is preferred. A 24-inch nominal screen size would be desirable, were it not for the cost, but often it is found more economical to standardize on 23-inch receivers and to use several, as required, rather than to use larger viewing screens.

4. Speakers should be front-mounted in receivers so that the sound projects toward the viewers. Speakers mounted on the side, top, or rear of the receiver tend to project sound by reverberation, which reduces audibility.

5. Receivers should have power transformer–type circuits. Without this type of circuitry, one side of the chassis can become one side of the power line, and the shock hazard is very great and dangerous. Receivers with power transformer circuits are usually carefully constructed and reliable.

In the viewing classrooms one 23-inch receiver should be used for each group of 30 to 50 students; a 21-inch receiver is generally adequate for 18 to 25 students; 19-inch receivers are adequate for 15 to 20 students. For individual instruction or 1:1 ratio between instructor and student for extremely intricate skill technique demonstrations, a 17-inch portable receiver for each student or pair of students is adequate.

Television receivers for school use are manufactured by many television equipment companies and usually may be purchased at substantial educational discounts through local or regional distributors.

ORIGINATION SYSTEMS

At the point of program origination in closed-circuit television there may be found a great variety in both equipment and types of systems employed. They may vary from a simple single camera on a stand to highly complex combinations of equipment including many cameras, a switching system, and special cameras and accessories for using films and other visual materials. Furthermore, closed-circuit television systems must work under widely varying application conditions which determine the types of cameras and accessories required. To plan and design a closed-circuit television system requires a knowledge of the capabilities and limitations of various types of television equipment and combinations of equipment, and an ability to relate this knowledge to the requirements of the intended applications.

At this point some careful decisions must be made regarding camera (originating) equipment based on immediate and future applications:

1. Will the camera system be permanently installed or portable?
2. Will it be operated manually or by remote controls?
3. Will it be standard (meet EIA standards and therefore be suitable for both closed-circuit and on-the-air broadcast programming) or nonstandard?
4. Will it be nonstandard but capable of being modified to meet EIA standards by adding components as programming requirements expand?
5. Will systems be combined or separated for different applications?

If the immediate educational need is to give teachers some experience with television applications at minimal investment, or to orient students to television, or to provide a laboratory device for image magnification (making small things large), then the purchase of a simple television system is practical. The simplest workable television origination equipment includes a camera, camera control, and receiver(s). This may be a nonstandard, vidicon, industrial-type system (see figure, page 234), including tripod, lenses, and cable. It may be purchased for about $1,200. This system is basically an audio-visual tool, but it does send a picture over a coaxial cable directly from a camera to one or more television receivers. It is easy to operate and maintain, and has a number of instructional applications (see Part I).

1. In some systems the controls are in the camera itself; in others, controls are in a separate unit.
2. A separate small receiver to be used by the instructor is optional, depending upon teaching conditions.

If the educational needs require one presentation to be viewed in a number of classrooms, or to meet similar educational objectives, a simple basic system that can be expanded as the instructional television program evolves would be in order (see figure, page 235). Such a system should meet or be capable of meeting, with minor additions or adjustments, the EIA standards for broadcast television equipment. EIA standards ensure that an installation may proceed from a simple to a more complex system for more extensive programming without loss of investment, flexibility, or efficiency.

(Opposite) Receivers may be mounted in various ways, depending upon the particular design of the room being used and the program being televised.

For some rooms a side-wall mount is practical. Note the forward tilt of the receiver to reduce the glare from windows and overhead lights.

The portable receiver unit designed for the Anaheim School District (Anaheim School District)

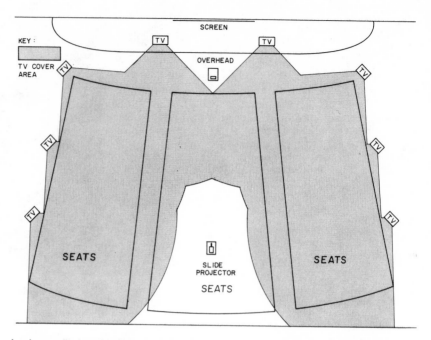

In a large auditorium eight 23-in. receivers are used along with both overhead and slide projectors. Since the room was used for many other activities, the two front receivers were on movable carts to facilitate easy removal. The extremely high ceiling and balcony made overhead mounting impractical. Note poor viewing in the rear of the middle section.

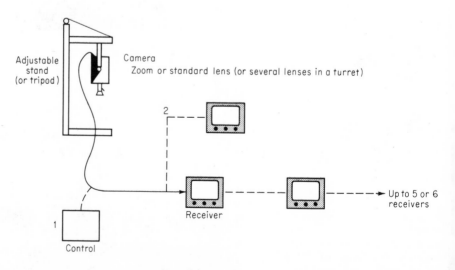

A single-camera in-room image magnification system

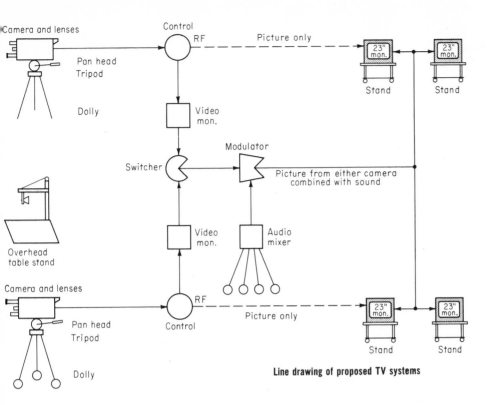

Line drawing of proposed TV systems

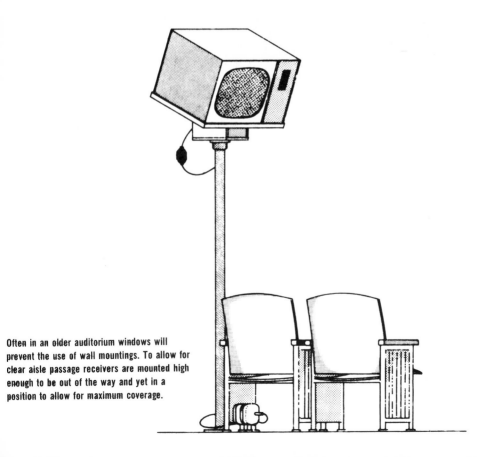

Often in an older auditorium windows will prevent the use of wall mountings. To allow for clear aisle passage receivers are mounted high enough to be out of the way and yet in a position to allow for maximum coverage.

235

Equipment list for two-camera system

Originating equipment	Transmission equipment	Receiving equipment
Manually controlled		
Camera and camera control (with vidicon tube) with or without viewfinder.	Modulator, to mix the picture and sound as a composite RF signal to be sent to standard TV receivers.	TV receivers, standard school model (23 in.).
		Rolling tables for TV receivers, if they are to be portable.
Turret, for 3 or 4 fixed lenses.	Coaxial cable, RG 59 U for intraroom runs; RG 11 U or equivalent low-loss cable for intraroom and long runs; for transmission of signal from camera equipment to rooms, between rooms, or between buildings.	
Lenses: 1 in. (25 mm-*f*1.9)		
2 in. (50 mm-*f*1.9)		
3 in. (75 mm-*f*1.9)		
Lens adaptors and close-up extension tubes. Zoom lens.		
Tripod with pan/tilt head.	Intercommunication cable, to be pulled at the same time as the coaxial cable; for two-way communication between all receiving areas; power supply, headsets, and accessory equipment.	
Dolly.		
Camera cable and connectors.		
A switch for 2-camera operation.	Tap-off kits, boxes, connectors, etc., for termination of cable at each reception location.	
Video monitor (at the bridging output of the switcher).		
Lights (simple, clamp-on) and portable studio type.		
Audio mixer, to feed microphones, allows use of 2 or 3 microphones.		

Remotely controlled

Camera and camera control (same as for manually controlled).

Remote-controlled pan/tilt head.

Remote-controlled iris/focus.

Remote-controlled turrets with fixed lenses or remote-controlled zoom lens with necessary attachments.

Remote-control panel with necessary cables.

Tripod/dolly (same as for manually controlled).

Monitor (same as for manually controlled).

Lights, portable on standards, or additional room lighting.

Same as for manually controlled.

Same as for manually controlled.

Note: Additional and necessary:
1. Microphones, lavalier-type.
2. Small tools for adjustments and simple maintenance.
3. Operating funds available for tube and engineering supplies and/or to obtain outside maintenance on the systems.
4. Tabletop camera stand, desirable for use with the single-room camera system for image magnification.

237

A flexible and basic two-camera system is described as an example of one that might be used initially in an installation that may need to be versatile at the outset. This system has the following capabilities:

1. Each camera system may be used separately with one or more television receivers for image magnification within classrooms.
2. The two camera systems may be used together with a simple switcher for two-camera studio-type programming. Each camera will be mounted on a tripod and dolly with a manual pan/tilt head. (A remote-control system may be provided for one camera.) Cameras to pick up films and slides may be provided.
3. The following equipment list (see table) provides for configurations to include:
   a. Single manual camera unit
   b. Dual manual camera unit
   c. Remote-controlled camera unit
   However, items are listed in such a way that the systems may initially be simplified or may be augmented in accordance with EIA standards.

Three different systems of operating originating equipment are presented in the following table, with notations suggesting the characteristics of each. Though the technical characteristics of equipment for each system are similar, there are distinct physical configurations that facilitate their convenient use for particular instructional applications.

If programs are to initiate from a permanent central studio, equipment packages are designed for the purpose; if equipment is to be transported from room to room, or from building to building, then portable equipment must be considered. For some applications, such as for observation techniques, remotely operated (portable or fixed) equipment is available. It is pertinent to note, too, that in some studio installations where staff is limited and programming is uncomplicated, remotely controlled cameras have proved advantageous, though less flexible than manual studio cameras. A review of the following table suggests factors to be considered in equipment selection.

Lighting for television.　All television systems require adequate light for good picture quality. But lighting requirements vary depending on the type of television equipment, where it is used, how it is used, and on the program presentation requirements. The basic principles of lighting used for photographers, motion pictures, and the theater apply to television. This topic has received thorough coverage in many published works. Educators planning a television installation should become familiar with lighting procedure, and with requirements for the type of television equipment to be installed and the applications anticipated.

Three modes of TV origination*

Central studio	Portable equipment	Remotely controlled equipment
Equipment is concentrated in one area.	Equipment may be moved from area to area without moving participants from convenient locations.	Equipment is flexible. Cameras are usually small; may be remotely controlled in all operational functions.
Lighting can be controlled conveniently.	Light conditions cannot be controlled without supplementary lighting equipment.	Same as portable.
Audio systems can be controlled conveniently.	Audio systems are difficult to control and optimum audio pickup is difficult to achieve.	Same as portable.
Noise can be controlled by acoustical treatment.	Noise cannot be controlled.	Same as portable.
Adequate space permits efficient camera movement.	Restricted space often makes camera movement difficult.	Space no problem if cameras are remotely controlled, equipped with satisfactory lenses, and mounted on wall or on pedestals.
Additional media (film, 2- by 2-in. slides, transparencies, rear screen projection) may be used as an integral part of a lesson without interruption.	Use of additional visual media may be restricted.	Same as studio.
Graphics and other instructional materials can be handled efficiently and effectively.	On-the-spot activities can be televised (extracurricular activities and special presentations).	Same as portable or studio.
No distractions or interruptions by an audience.	An audience may cause distractions and interruptions.	Depends on the type of programming. In observation situation participants may be less disturbed by remotely operated equipment than by presence of camera operators.
Maintenance cost is less because equipment is permanently installed.	Maintenance cost may be increased if equipment is moved often.	Same as portable.
Cameras, cables, and accessories do not deteriorate as rapidly.	Camera cables deteriorate more rapidly in studio use because of handling.	Camera cables may deteriorate rapidly because of long runs, and storage or support problems.
Air conditioning and/or ventilation should be provided.	Air conditioning and ventilation may not be available.	Same as studio.

* New technology has provided television systems that can function in all three of the above-described modes of TV origination. Compact, portable systems can be used for studio presentations, disconnected, and moved from one area to another, or can be equipped with remote controls and operated remotely. The above table is suggested as a guide in determining the advantages, disadvantages, and requirements for operating originating equipment.

To lower the cost of equipping the studio, many techniques may be used. In the Plainedge Public Schools and San Jose State College studios the overhead grid system has been built with regular garage-door tracks under which movable crossarms with integral electrical wiring are hung.

Vidicon cameras, in general, operate especially well under lighting that exceeds 150 foot-candles of incident light. In studios, a variety of spot- and floodlights is needed; standard studio lights are available in a wide variety of types.

In some studios, a system originally designed for motion-picture production work is proving economical and flexible. These systems use compact and lightweight lamp units and boost voltage to the lamps through use of a transformer-converter from standard 120- or 240-volt power receptacles. A variety of lamp configurations and accessories is available.

For some applications standard room lighting will permit adequate televised pictures. In some instances standard fluorescent lights are augmented by very-high-output fluorescent units to raise light levels.

One feature available in some camera systems is automatic light-control circuitry that automatically adjusts picture transmission for varying light conditions.

Facilities for television. Television as it is used by many schools today imposes a new medium on an old teaching system. This in itself creates a multitude of problems, but separate problems are created by the mechanics of television, the equipment, and the working and storage space required, as well as by the personnel involved and their specialized functions. Unfortunately, minimum (in some cases inadequate) facilities are available, even when instructional television programming is heavy. Although it is often difficult to incorporate an adequate television facility in existing space, it can usually be done largely because the television equipment for school use is both flexible and compact.

In recent years newly constructed buildings and older buildings recently renovated are often designed to allow for the installation of various kinds of instructional communications media. It is a fortunate educator who has developed his plans for an evolutionary program of television before planning and constructing a new building. Thus he has the opportunity to use a "systems planning" approach toward developing the television installation and allowing adequate space for studio(s), control room(s), workrooms, auxiliary rooms, storage, and offices. During construction he can provide for adequate power, conduits, duct work, air conditioning, acoustical treatment of walls and ceilings, and proper grids for lighting.

If existing facilities are used, serious compromises must often be made either in equipment or programming. It should be emphasized that the amount and kind of space needed for television operations, whether in new or old facilities, depend upon the amount and kind of programming currently undertaken or planned for the future. As an example: if a classroom is to be an originating "studio," one kind of space problem is posed; if a mobile or portable unit is to be used, a different space problem is created; if programs are to originate from a central studio, requirements for appropriate space and auxiliary facilities must be met. Some general specifications for using existing and new facilities when planning television space are given in the following table.

Considerations of existing and new facilities for studio presentations

Existing facilities	New facilities
Unobstructed activity or classroom space can be used. Cameras need 10 to 15 ft of space for movement in front of the teaching area.	Inside ground-floor area, with unobstructed studio space, allows for flexibility in programming. Where 1 studio is provided, the size must be adequate for back-to-back programming. Space, however, in the long run may be more economical than extra personnel required for quick changes of teaching resources in a studio; 2 or more smaller studios, each of adequate size, are essential for extensive direct teaching programming.
Control room adjacent to studio area: space required depends on complexity and size of equipment and the number of operating personnel. Allow space around equipment for maintenance and repair.	A control room, or a combined control room, for each studio adjacent to each studio area, enclosed, or with glass partitions, should be large enough to house all control equipment and operating personnel.

Existing facilities	*New facilities*
Auxiliary equipment housed in a control room requires ventilation and cooling; air-conditioning units are required. Concentration of equipment in a small area (especially the power supplies) may generate extreme heat which causes equipment to operate improperly and to deteriorate at a rapid rate with increased maintenance costs.	It is desirable to have an auxiliary equipment room adjacent to the control room, with adequate space for maintenance, repair and adjustment of equipment, and air conditioning, if possible.
Space for a film chain can be in a large control room or adjacent room. Film chains can be operated remotely from the studio control console, allowing flexibility in location.	A film chain and projection equipment room adjacent to control room must be readily accessible to operating personnel and control room(s).
Maintenance, repair, and workshop space near studio area should be provided.	Adequate maintenance, repair, and workshop space are necessary near studio area.
Storage space for set pieces, auxiliary equipment, engineering supplies, and test equipment is required.	Storage space for set pieces, auxiliary equipment, engineering supplies, and test equipment is needed.
Air-conditioned, dust-free space is required for kinescope and/or video tape recorder(s) if included, also racks for tapes or films. Dust-free cabinets are necessary for spare parts. Space for editing, maintenance, and operation of equipment is needed.	Air-conditioned, dust-free space for kinescope and/or video tape recorder(s), and racks for tape or film are required, with dust-free cabinets for spare parts, and space for editing, maintenance, and operation of equipment if program "storage" is undertaken.
Studio ceiling height should be at least 11 ft, but up to 15 ft is desirable to allow room for pipe grid for hanging light fixtures.	Studio ceiling height should allow room for lighting grids, fixed or movable, to be installed at time of construction. Fifteen feet from floor to ceiling is minimum.
Window walls (in space converted from classrooms) may be shielded by heavy drapes on continuous track, or by panels of a special type of seamless display paper high enough to cover windows and provide a background for camera field of view.	In normal studio space, flats or backgrounds high enough to fill the camera view at all times are used; walls may be unfinished and acoustically treated.
Studio and control-room ceiling and upper portions of walls should be acoustically treated.	Both studio and control-room walls and ceilings should be adequately treated for sound control.
All operations areas should be air-conditioned. The cooling capacity is determined by zone, type, and extent of lighting, and by type of equipment used.* Studio lighting equipment adequate to produce acceptable television pictures will contribute greatly to temperature rise.	Air conditioning of all operations areas is an absolute necessity and should be installed during construction, with capacities determined by analysis of loading estimated. Temperature and humidity control of film and tape storage areas is necessary.

* It should be noted that with new technological developments, television equipment is changing at a rapid rate. Transistorized camera units are increasing in popularity and partially transistorized units are available. These units are smaller in all dimen-

Existing facilities	*New facilities*
Electrical power requirements depend on the type and amount of television and lighting equipment installed. Power to operate a 3-camera studio with film chain and associated components should have a minimum of 220-volt AC input at 200-amp service. This power may not be sufficient to operate heating, ventilation, or air-conditioning equipment in addition. Numerous electrical outlets should be provided in the studio and control rooms to allow for set and equipment arrangements.	Power requirements are the same as for existing facilities but should be installed during construction.
Conduit, ducting, electrical and power outlets must be planned to serve the existing facility. Coaxial cables have low-current, low-voltage lines and for this reason they are often run outside of conduit. Check local electrical codes. Cable may be run in existing ducts and in overhead ceiling space. It gives better protection for the cable and helps eliminate signal interference if cable is run through proper conduits. Determining where and how cable may be run should be in charge of an electrical engineer.	TV and electrical power conduits, ducts, and outlets should be included during building construction, with careful specifications to allow for flexibility and proper location of termination boxes.
Intercommunication systems should be maintained between the control-room and operational areas. Audio lines should be parallel with coaxial lines to achieve two-way communication between all viewing and originating areas.	Intercommunication systems should be installed at the same time as coaxial cables. All originating and viewing areas should be provided with intercommunication facilities.
Studio floor should be hard-surfaced, smooth, and level. Rapid movement of cameras over uneven, rough floors causes poor camera work.	Studio floor should be hard-surfaced, smooth, and level. The centralization of as many functions as possible will reduce the number of personnel necessary to operate the facility.

Program storage devices. At this time (and the expression is used advisedly when writing about television developments), available television program recording equipment is of two kinds: sound-on-film recorders and television tape recorders.

A kinescope recorder is a means of obtaining a permanent record on sound film of a television program. This recorder employs a special synchronized film camera that photographs images from

sions than earlier all-tube systems, require little power to operate, and generate little heat. Where costly and expensive renovation of existing facilities is necessary to provide studio and control-room space, it is wise to investigate the possibility of purchasing transistorized or partially transistorized equipment as an initial investment. Further, for portable or mobile operations transistorized equipment offers attractive economies in space, convenience, and maintenance.

the face of a high-definition television monitor. One moderately priced type of kinescope recorder uses a modified single-system sound motion-picture camera and a standard video monitor. Kinescope recording film is processed in the same manner as any motion-picture film. For school use, 16-millimeter kinescopes (films) are useful because they can be run on regular classroom-type 16-millimeter sound motion-picture projectors.

TV tape recordings (video tapes) are made on magnetic tape in the same manner as an audio tape recording. Immediate playback, repeated playback, and erasure and reuse of tapes are possible. The initial cost of video recording equipment has been extremely expensive (between $30,000 and $60,000) and tape used in the machine, though it may be reused many times, is an expensive item, costing from $100 to $200 or more for one-hour programs.

Recently, the sale of relatively low-cost tape recorders (about $12,000) with proportionate savings in tape cost have opened new prospects for the educator.

These machines, unlike their more expensive and more professional cousins, are thus far suitable only for closed-circuit television applications and may not be used for on-the-air broadcasting. However, they have exceedingly great potential value for educational purposes. The possibility exists that, in time, recordings made on these machines can later be converted for broadcast if the need arises.

Television program recording can affect numerous aspects of television planning: the variety of applications, efficiency in use of personnel, conservation of space, the amount of programming possible with limited facilities, and the cost of television operations. Careful cost analysis may make early investment in video tape recording advantageous both economically and educationally. An extensive program of direct teaching by television cannot realize its inherent efficiency and economy without television recording.

SUMMARY

This is a review checklist for taking first steps toward adopting television for instruction:

1. Educational problems and needs identified ( )
2. Specific objectives for television utilization identified ( )
3. Information gathered:
   a. Reviewed literature, especially that about comparable districts (see Bibliography) ( )
   b. Learned rudimentary TV terminology (see Glossary) ( )
   c. Developed file of sources of information, names of places, people, companies that seem promising sources of help (consult NAEB, NET, NERTC, and NAB) ( )

d. Visited existing installations ( )
e. Discussed problems and solutions with experienced educational and technical personnel ( )
f. Analyzed objectives in relation to proposed program and equipment requirements ( )
g. Explored alternative choices of equipment types, configurations, and costs ( )
h. Explored available facilities, space, and construction requirements for alternative equipment suitable to meet objectives ( )

Before you buy equipment, answers to some questions must be sought:

1. Is it to receive and distribute off-the-air programs?
2. Is it to provide image magnification services?
3. Is it to permit both image magnification and simple studio-type presentations?
4. Is it to set up a complete studio facility to achieve programming objectives?
5. Is it for any number of combinations and alternatives that hold promise of educational benefits and economic feasibility?

Finally, remember that you will need some personnel with technical knowledge either conveniently available, if you start television on a conservative basis, or on your own staff, if more elaborate programming is anticipated. And you can be sure that each next step is a potential challenge that can be a stimulating prospect, if thorough groundwork is done on paper before you buy equipment.

appendix C

The television teacher

Robert M. Diamond

Two teachers determine the final success of any instructional television program; one is in the classroom, the other is on television. The role and importance of the classroom teacher have been discussed within many chapters of this book. It is the purpose of this section to cover, in some detail, the role and selection of the television teacher.

The television teacher has several basic responsibilities: selecting and designing the program content, writing the study guide (see Appendix D), preparing the production outline,[1] and finally, presenting the lesson itself on television.

In fulfilling these functions the teacher will have assistance. However, it can be anticipated that there will be a direct relationship between the number of students viewing the program and the amount of aid, both human and material, that the television teacher will receive. When televising over open circuit or within a large closed-circuit operation, the teacher will usually be assisted by a producer-director, a graphic artist, and often curriculum specialists to assist in material selection, program design, and guide writing.

In smaller operations the role of the producer-director is often assigned to another teacher, students in the art department prepare the graphic materials, and the individual teaching in this situation will soon, of necessity, become an expert improviser. In many cases the teacher will have full responsibility for selecting and preparing all the charts, graphs, slides, and photographs that will be used.

---

[1] The production outline briefly summarizes what is going to be said, what the teacher will be doing when he says it, and what visuals are to be used and when (see page 250). It is from this outline that the director prepares his production script, designs the studio layout, and anticipates any technical problems that may arise.

TEACHING ON TELEVISION TAKES TIME

Obviously, to do a good job, the television teacher needs enough time. It is here that we find one of the major weaknesses in many of the existing television projects. From experience we find that the teacher will need, depending on format and content, between ten and twenty hours to prepare for each fifteen- to thirty-minute presentation. Chicago City Junior College figures that the television teacher needs seven hours for every one that would be taken to prepare and present the same lesson in the classroom. This time is divided between guide writing, selecting the program content, finding necessary resource materials, rehearsing, and presenting the lesson. Not included are the many hours often spent in meeting with teachers, administrators, and parents to discuss past and future programs. (A kit of materials prepared for television instructors at San Jose State College will be found on pages 251 to 253.)

In surveying existing projects, however, we find teachers are often being released for only one hour a day to present as many as two or three television lessons per week. Some teachers are actually carrying their television assignment as an overload above their regular teaching load. In some cases programs have been presented without a single studio rehearsal; the teacher simply brings in his materials, hands the director his production script, and then hopes and prays that what *should* be seen will be seen. As Dr. Murray states on page 103, it is truly remarkable that so many of our television teachers have done as well as they have under such conditions.

The talented teacher, given enough time to prepare and aided by all the advantages inherent in teaching on television (see pages 49 to 56), can present certain information in a manner that cannot be matched by the teacher in the classroom. Only when the teacher is handicapped by lack of preparation time and assistance do we hear the question from the classroom teacher: "What can television do that I can't do as well myself?" Under proper conditions this question will not be heard after the first few televised lessons.

SELECTING THE TELEVISION TEACHER

There is no set formula for selecting the television teacher. Simply stated, the creative classroom teacher who has the ability to communicate with students and an enthusiasm for the material being taught will usually make an excellent television teacher. Persons in the field have spent endless hours discussing which traits are most important. The only conclusion that can be drawn is that the individual rarely exists who has them all. As a result the problems of selecting the television teacher are many, and compromises common. Usually the process includes interviews, multiple recommendations, and brief television auditions.

Most lists of desirable traits for a television teacher will include the following:

1. A thorough knowledge of the subject
2. Classroom teaching experience
3. The ability to communicate
4. Creativity
5. Well-organized work habits
6. The ability to work with others and to take criticism
7. A sense of humor
8. The ability to improvise

Most of these points are self-explanatory. Several, however, deserve special attention.

The importance of subject-area knowledge and teaching experience cannot be overrated. The television teacher must make many subject and content decisions that will directly affect the teaching in every classroom using the telecast.

The teacher will find that television presentation accentuates two basic problems common to all teaching: proper pacing and proper vocabulary. In the classroom situation the teacher can adjust immediately to facial expressions and student reactions. Obviously this is impossible with television. Visits to classrooms viewing the programs (possible with taped or filmed lessons), meetings with classroom teachers, and the use of feedback questionnaires (see Appendix E) help greatly, but the television teacher must rely on past experience for that sixth sense of timing and word usage.

To assist the television teacher, many experiments have been tried in which a class is present in the studio during the telecast. Almost without exception this method was discontinued immediately. Two things tend to happen: first, with students in the studio, the teacher loses eye contact with the students in the viewing audience, and second, the entire logic behind a program is often lost when the teacher attempts to pace his presentation to the students in the studio. One major advantage of television—and this has been mentioned as often by students as by teachers—is the ability of the television teacher to complete a body of information without interruption. With a class in the studio this becomes extremely difficult.

One television teacher, with a helpless smile, stated that the major problem she faced when teaching on television was—people. "When you appear on television," she explained, "everyone becomes your critic." That is an undeniable fact of life for the TV teacher.

While the majority of self-appointed critics are well-meaning, and often the suggestions excellent, the constant and wearing barrage of advice must be lived with and expected. No longer protected by the walls of the classroom, the teacher can now be seen by fellow teachers, students, parents, and often the public at large. Notoriety has its advantages and disadvantages.

In those fields where disagreement exists as to what should be taught and when it should be covered, the television teacher may become the focal point for all the emotions that have been building up through the years. Since the medium has often been used as a major force to facilitate change, it is always wise to involve as many individuals as possible in the early planning stages to reduce the amount of negative reaction that may be expected.

The television teacher must work closely with the entire production staff over a long period of time. He will need to adjust to teaching on television, which is not, and should not be, the same as teaching in the classroom. He will feel the stress of working under constant deadlines, and in most instances there is no such thing as talking past the bell. At the end of a given segment of time the teacher must be finished, period. It is imperative that the television teacher have the understanding and the flexibility to function well under these conditions.

The ability to think on one's feet will also be an important asset for the teacher. While this is true for all teachers, it is especially true on television, where the unexpected can be anticipated. No matter how well a program is planned, things will happen: an experiment misfires, an animal runs loose, an articulate guest becomes tongue-tied. The television teacher must be able to work effectively in such situations. Fortunately many television teachers have been able to use the unexpected not only to enhance their lessons but also to build a stronger rapport with the student in the classroom.

ADDITIONAL PROBLEMS

Obviously the excellent television teacher is hard to find. Unfortunately, even when we have found the ideal teacher, we often have difficulty getting him on television.

Besides the reluctance of administrators to release their staff members to teach on television, which has been discussed previously, some teachers simply do not want to teach on television. The problems and pressures mentioned earlier in this section certainly make this understandable. However, quite often their decision is based more on a fear of the unknown than on anything else. Such fears can be overcome when the individual is introduced to television teaching on a gradual basis. Some of the finest television

249

teachers are those who at first were hesitant to try. Perhaps the best salesman for teaching on the medium is the teacher who has had the experience. Despite its many problems, there are few individuals who have not enjoyed television teaching and found it to be one of the most exciting and rewarding experiences of their teaching careers. As video tape becomes more common many of the basic fears are negated by the ability to redo a program, and the various pressures that come with "live" televising are substantially reduced.

In conclusion, if instructional television is ever to reach its potential we need our best teachers, backed by all the resources that go with teaching on television. The teacher must be given enough time to do the job and to do it well. It is the school administrator, therefore, who must make the decisions that will, in the long run, determine the success or failure of any television project.

SAMPLE PRODUCTION OUTLINE

Program: "Seashore Life" (Part 1)
Date: December 6
Time: 11:30 A.M.
Station: KNTV
Instructor: Dr. Frank Gale

Video	Audio	Running time
Gale at table with salt water aquarium	Introduction	30 sec
cu* Puts ink in jar of water, adds mussels	Let's set up an experiment	1 min
	The ocean serves three purposes:	3 min
S1	1. Aesthetic	
S2	2. Recreative	
	3. Economic	
To aquarium		
cu Pismo clam [super]		5 min
cu Long-neck clam	Compares 2 types of clams	
cu Mussel		
cu Abalone		
Gale moves to easel with cards	Tides:	7 min
C1 Chart of intertidal region	High tide	
S3	Low tide	
S4		
C2 Tidal zones	The tidal zones:	10 min
	Spray zone	
	High-tide zone	
	Middle-tide zone	
	Low-tide zone	

Video	Audio	Running time
	Shorelines:	12 min
S5	1. Rocky coast	
S6	2. Sandy beach	
S7	3. Bay and estuary	
Gale moves to easel with large charts	Causes of tides	
		14 min
cu Large chart A		
cu Large chart B		
Moves tide		
		17 min
To aquarium		
cu Jar of water		
Returns to experiment	Introduces next telecast	

* Key: cu—close-up
       S—slide
       C—card
       super—name shown over picture

MATERIALS PREPARED FOR TELEVISION TEACHERS

Memo to: Television Instructors
From: ITV Program Supervisor

The following material has been prepared to save you time and effort in the preparation of your telecast.

First planning meeting: approximately 3 weeks before actual telecast; time required, 1 to 2 hr.

At this meeting the production script for the telecast is prepared. Techniques and visuals that will be used are discussed and selected.

For a list of the types of materials that we will prepare for you and some indication of the types that are well suited to the medium, please see the attached material prepared by our graphic artist.

You might find it helpful to outline your material in the following format:

Video: what you wish the audience to see	*Audio:* what you are saying
Chart of _____	A. _____
Slides of _____	1. _____
Show object _____	2. _____
	B. _____
etc.	etc.

Walk-through: approximately 3 days before telecast; time required, ½ to 1½ hr.

The telecast is reviewed with all visuals in finished condition and all materials present that will be used. Final format and set design are discussed. Instructors are given the opportunity of manipulating all materials that will be used.

Between walk-through and rehearsal final changes are made in visuals where needed.

Rehearsal*: approximately 1 day before telecast; time required, 1 to 2 hr.
After a brief walk-through the entire telecast is rehearsed with cameras.

* Special schedule for open-circuit in-service telecast
Rehearsal and brief walk-through: Friday, 3 P.M.
Final rehearsal: approximately 1 hr before telecast. Time will differ according to the complexity of the individual telecast.

Memorandum

To: Instructional Television Instructors
From: Margaret Murray, TV Graphics Specialist
Re: Visual Materials for Television

You will find that the ideas you wish to convey through the use of TV will be made even more effective by utilizing the visual aspects of that medium. Your available art work probably will not have been constructed within television requirements; however, most materials are adaptable. When choosing which visual materials will be successful over TV, consult the list of "desirables" below. If in doubt, bring them to the planning session.

If you do not have graphic materials already prepared or wish to supplement those existing, consider the possibilities suggested in the list "Sources related to your topic." Notice on the list the contributions that we can make to your presentation. We are anxious to help in any way and hope you will take advantage of our services.

I. The desired form

A. Format (see illustrations 1 and 2 following)

All graphic materials (slides, photographs, flat materials, etc.) should be in a $3:4$ ratio, horizontal format. The smallest symbol to read must be at least $\frac{1}{25}$ of the smallest dimension of the art work. All material to be read (words, numbers, etc.) must be included in the essential area because of differing adjustments on home TV receivers. Some receivers may not show or may highly distort the "supplementary" area; however, be sure the supplementary area is included in the total presentations.

B. Points of information

Discussion points to be emphasized are most successfully handled on television by the use of an outline form. Since the speaker is relating the information in detail, the outline serves to reinforce—not to duplicate—the verbal information. Also, it is well to keep in mind that a list, graph, etc., can only be seen by the viewer when the camera is "on" it. The camera is "on" it when the speaker's remarks involve the visual; therefore, much extraneous information (defining a chart in terms of time, place, and cause) may be eliminated. Headings, instead of full sentences, 3 to 4 words per line, and 4 to 5 lines per chart, work very well.

C. Contrast

Don't depend on color differences. TV is only sensitive to values, not tones or hues. Extreme contrast (black against white, etc.) or shiny items (glare, reflection) cause technical problems.

D. Style

The simpler the style, the better it is for TV. Art work of limited detail—strong, bold, simple statements—project the best (similar to highway-sign approach).

II. Sources related to your topic

You can:

Books, magazines:
  Graphs and statistics
  Drawings or photos of people,
    facilities, and events involved

Copy them photographically or reconstruct them graphically to suit specific needs.

Films, filmstrips, slides

Use "clips" (short movie scenes) or slides directly on television film chain.

In the field:
  Specimen
  Facilities
  Example of topic

Shoot slides (preferred) or short movie clips on location (needs more time, must be planned 4 to 5 weeks ahead).

Models:
  Live specimen
  Models which break down
  Mounted examples, etc.

Work excellently used directly.

Your ideas or sketches of mechanisms:
  Specimen
  Relationships
  Abstract concepts

May be visualized in several forms which fit TV requirements. The illustrations may be constructed from discussions at planning meetings.

Appendixes

Illustration 1

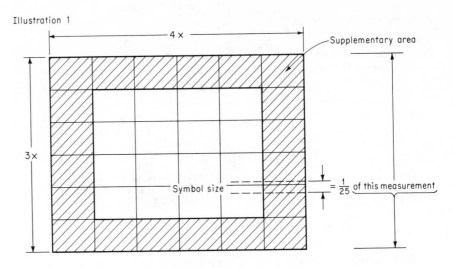

Illustration 2

The essential area is determined by dividing each side into six parts and drawing lines through the total area. The outside border of boxes is considered the supplementary area; and what is left, the essential area. This is called the rule of one-sixth.

254

appendix D

The teacher's guide

Robert M. Diamond

The television teaching guide serves two purposes: first, it is the basis on which classroom teachers or administrators decide *if* a particular presentation is to be used; second, it assists the classroom teacher in using a televised lesson to its best advantage.

It is therefore important that the guide be carefully prepared and designed in such a way as to be most helpful to the teacher. It is the purpose of this outline to serve as an aid in the planning and preparation of an effective teaching guide.

Details of teaching guides will naturally vary from course to course and from program to program, but the basic objective of each guide or series of guides will be the same: to assist in the selection and in the use of an instructional television presentation.

Guides themselves generally fall into two types:

1. *The teacher's manual,* composed of a series of individual outlines, one for each telecast in the series. The manual is usually extensive and is available before the start of the school year. This is made possible when the entire series is on tape or film with the manual being written after the programs are completed. Usually a brief introduction covers information pertinent to the entire series and is followed by a detailed guide to each telecast (see sample, page 259).

2. *The single-program guide* is a complete teacher's guide prepared for each telecast. These guides are usually designed to reach the teacher on a weekly basis no later than two weeks before the actual telecast and are common for the wide majority of programs that are not recorded far in advance. Obviously these guides cannot be as comprehensive as those prepared after the program has been completed. The reasons for this are twofold: first, the television teacher is usually emphasizing the preparation of the lesson and has little time to devote to the guide, and second, there is always the possibility that the lesson will change after the guide has been completed. Guides of this type are inclusive, containing the general series information as well as information pertinent to the particular telecast.

WHO SHOULD PREPARE THE GUIDE?

The television teacher, obviously, is the key individual in this task. However, it is often wise to assign an additional person to work with the television teachers in preparing the material; such extra help can ensure a superior product, and many districts have found that a good, comprehensive teacher's guide not only helps to sell the particular series, but also has a positive effect upon the entire curriculum.

HOW SHOULD THE GUIDE BE WRITTEN?

There are five basic axioms for the writing of the teaching guide:

1. The guide is directed to a fellow teacher or an administrator—in other words, to an experienced and talented professional. Classroom teachers resent any writing that smacks of a patronizing attitude.
2. The guide must be brief, concise, and clear. Neither administrators nor classroom teachers have enough time to wade through reams of paper.
3. A check should be made to ensure that everything of importance is included. The teaching guide serves as the main contact between television teacher and classroom teacher, and it is extremely important to the final success of any TV program. It should not be written hastily, as an afterthought, so to speak. Enough time must be taken to do a good job.
4. The guide must be done in time. It must be completed far enough in advance to allow for printing delays and the mechanics of distribution. All guides should be in the teachers' hands at least two weeks before the actual presentation of a program.
5. The program must be known *before* the guide is written. Whenever possible the program should be well under way before the guide is prepared. As programs develop, they have a tendency to change for various reasons; e.g., certain aspects of the material are often found more adaptable to television than others. (The writer is aware of the potential conflict between items 4 and 5. Yet it is vital that both needs be borne in mind and met as far as circumstances permit.)

WHAT PRELIMINARY INFORMATION SHOULD THE GUIDE CONTAIN?

The classroom teacher or the administrator must be given information to help him decide

1. *If* a particular program should be used
2. *How* a selected program can be used to its best advantage

Before such a decision can be adequately reached, certain questions must be answered. It is just as unfortunate to have the wrong classes watching a program as it is for the program not to be used in classes where it might make an excellent contribution. The teacher's manual or guide should, therefore, cover the following points (in the manual, points 1 and 2 are contained in the general introduction):

1. The day, time, and length of the presentation. (Is it going to be physically possible for classes to view the program?)
2. For whom is the program or series designed? (Is it for students in the same grade and at the same stage of development as ours? Is it designed for the slow, average, or fast student?)
3. What are the objectives of the lesson? (Does the lesson relate to work we are doing in our classes? Does it contain material that can be covered more effectively and more efficiently by the televised lesson than by other methods?)
4. Are the contents of the program important to the class? (Is the program worth the time that it will take to use it well?)
5. How is the program designed to be used? (Is it presenting a new concept, reinforcing an old one, or providing extra but not essential material?)

To assist the classroom teacher in taking full advantage of a program, the guide must also contain the following additional information of a preliminary nature:

1. What concepts is the television teacher assuming the class already knows?
2. What activities are suggested for use before, during, or after the program?
3. What related material can be found or made that will assist the classroom teacher in using the program?
4. Are there recent developments that are related to the program that the classroom teacher may not be aware of?

Various formats have been successfully used. An outline for a single-program guide will be found on page 258. While the terms used are common, the value of the information contained under each heading has ranged from superior to useless. To assist in the preparation the following guidelines are offered.

GUIDE CONTENT

Objectives. Under this section there should be listed the specific and measurable things the program is trying to do. The importance of clearly stated objectives is covered in Chapter 15, pages 165 to 166. As mentioned by Dr. Brown, an excellent guide to writing the objectives is Robert Mager's *Preparing Objectives for Programmed Instruction* (San Francisco: Fearon Publishers, Inc., 1961).

Content. Here we find what will be done during the program, words that will be defined, experiments or demonstrations that will be carried out, problems that will be solved: in other words, a brief outline of the program.

Single-program guide outline

Title of program _____

Date _____ Time _____ Length _____ Channel _____

Television teacher _____
                (name)   (position)

Guest(s) _____
                                  (if any)

This series is designed for grade(s) _____

This series is designed for students of _____ ability.

Objectives

Content

Preprogram activity suggestions

Suggested activities during telecast (if any)

Postprogram activity suggestions
  Assignments

Related material

Preprogram activity suggestions. This section contains two bodies of information:

1. A list of any concepts and important words that the television teacher is taking for granted the students *already* understand. It is important that the students do know what the television teacher assumes they know. We find that we need only to use one term that is not understood to lose an entire audience.
2. A list of any activities that the classroom teacher should carry out before the program. If a new topic is being introduced, this section may be omitted. An important thing to remember is that most teachers will be extremely limited in time, so these activities should be selected very carefully. It is often a help to suggest different activities for students of varying abilities.

Suggested activities during telecast. Under certain conditions the students may participate actively *during* the telecast. This type of activity is often overlooked and yet, when used, can be extremely effective. This may mean the simple use of paper and pencil or, under some conditions, the actual use of equipment. In such cases it is imperative that the teacher be told what to expect and also be informed as to what materials the students will need.

Postprogram activity suggestions. Again, as in the preprogram suggestions, those activities that will be of greatest benefit to the students should be listed. These are suggestions, and it is best to select those activities that are of greatest value. If some of the suggestions are rather new and include some materials that the teacher will have to prepare, it is wise to include concise instructions that will simplify things for the teacher. Quite often the suggestion may be to repeat some activity performed during the program. It is of benefit to list once again activities for students of varying abilities.

Assignments. If the telecast is one in a regular teaching series, there may be added a list of suggested assignments and, where necessary, some correcting information for the teacher. This information must be practical, using texts that are easily available, with a selection of alternate assignments. Once again the teacher should not be overloaded with work.

Related materials. Quite often this section of the guide is one of the most beneficial to the classroom teacher. The television teacher is in touch with many outstanding resources and will be continually informed of new developments in his teaching field. Since the classroom teacher has difficulty in finding time to keep up with the newer developments, the guide can perform a great service in this area. A listing of free materials that are related to the program, and sources from which they can be obtained, is also invaluable to the teacher. Quite often the distributor of the material will gladly send a supply that can be given to the teachers using the program. This section should also contain a listing and brief description of any books, pamphlets, film clips, and films that are suggested as related material for the teacher to use.

SAMPLE TEACHER'S GUIDE

Title of program: "What Makes Rockets Go"
Date: May 15 **Time:** 10 A.M. **Length:** 20 min **Channel:** 13
Television teacher: Robert Hassur, Assistant Professor of Science Education

For grades 5 to 8
For students of average to high ability

Objectives. At the completion of the telecast the students will be able to:

1. List six ways in which the action-reaction principle is involved in everyday life
2. Describe how the action-reaction principle functions in a jet or rocket engine.

Content. The lesson will center on the action-reaction principle as developed by Newton. This topic will be introduced by analyzing several ordinary activities, e.g., walking and skiing, which are action-reaction situations. Special films and demonstrations will be used to show how we use action-reaction in almost every common activity. A "thrust-mobile" (see page 262) will be used to show the relationship between the total energy (mass X acceleration) and an action and its corresponding reaction. The discussion will broaden to include jet and rocket engines and how they function as action-reaction devices. Factors such as gravity, atmosphere, weightlessness, fuel consumption, orbital velocity, and escape velocity will be discussed in relation to their influence on successful rocket flights. The program will conclude with an experiment designed to summarize the concepts involved in action-reaction. In this experiment the instructor will propel himself across the studio floor using a carbon dioxide fire extinguisher.

Suggested preprogram activities.   (In these activities it is not necessary for the teacher to give any answers or to say whether an answer or conclusion is right or wrong. Let the students puzzle and think. The telecast will help them answer some of the questions, but further research and thought will be needed to answer them all.)

1. Discuss the history of the development of the laws of motion as first set down by Newton.
2. Do some simple experiments involving action-reaction such as:
   a. Release the air from an inflated balloon and note the results (stress careful observations). Now add weight by taping some paperclips to the inflated balloon, and repeat the experiment. Careful observation will reveal that the balloon in the second trial moved more slowly. Discuss the apparent relationship between energy, weight, and speed in the two balloon flights.
   b. Construct or borrow a wooden platform on wheels (e.g., furniture dolly). Have a student stand on the dolly and *carefully* step from it to the floor (again, careful observations). How is this related to walking? Try stepping from the cart slowly and then quickly. Note any differences? Why does it take more energy to run than to walk?
3. Have the students use a common brick and a piece of balsa wood or styrofoam cut to the same size. Have the students lift, propel, and slide the objects with equal force and with varying forces, and describe what they observe. Ask them which is heavier, which has the greater mass. Discuss the relationship between weight and mass. Weight is relative; mass is constant. Ask them if the brick will weigh as much in orbit or on the surface of the moon. How about the styrofoam?
4. Discuss the history of rocketry. An American, Robert Goddard, was a pioneer in the rocket field. He is often called the "Father of Rocketry." Discuss how rockets have influenced the course of history and are influencing our lives today.

Suggested postprogram activities

1. Have some students construct a "thrust-mobile" (see example, page 262), described in the telecast, and a "miss fire" rocket (see example, page 263), and continue the experiment by ejecting objects of various weights

(masses) and recording the thrust (reaction). Construct a thrust graph to show the relationship between thrust (reaction) and weight (mass) of the objects ejected from the cart.

2. Discuss the concept of gravity and centrifugal force and perform some of the activities outlined in *Journey into Space* and *What Is Space* by Vessel and Wong.

3. Have students help in constructing a bulletin board comparing the size and use of some of our operational rockets. Indicate the payload and fuel capacity of each. (The ratio of payload to fuel is an index of rocket engine efficiency.) Indicate which missiles are suitable for manned flight and why.

4. Have students set up a display (on science table or in showcase) of toys and household devices that utilize the action-reaction principle in their operation. Examples: balloon toys, water rockets, windup cars (wheels act on surface through friction, reaction drives car ahead), propeller aircraft, paddle-wheel boats, etc.

Related material

1. Plastic model construction kits of many current rockets, manned space capsules, satellites, and space stations. Available from any hobby shop.

2. Small carbon dioxide cartridges. Inexpensive, available at hobby and sport shops. Can be used to power rockets, race cars, boats, and planes. They develop considerable thrust, which can be controlled by varying the size of the hole that is punched in the sealed end of the cartridge to release the gas.

3. Water rocket. Available at toy shops or department stores. Uses water and compressed air as propellants. Air is compressed into the water-filled rocket with a small pump. When released, the compressed air forces the water out at a high velocity, driving the rocket to a height of about 30 feet. Two- and three-stage models are available.

4. Alpha I. Available at toy shops or department stores. Carbon dioxide gas generated within the rocket from baking soda and vinegar propels the rocket. With everything in its favor, the rocket will reach a height of 50 feet.

5. Jetex—solid fuel rocket, miniatures of JATO units (jet-assisted takeoff) used on military aircraft. Perhaps the most sophisticated of those listed here, recommended only for older students under the supervision of parent or teacher. These units develop tremendous thrust for their size. They can carry a 24-inch model airplane 500 feet into the air with an 11-second burn time. The entire unit, including an airplane and fuel supply, can be purchased at hobby shops for under $5.

6. Films and references:
   Man in Space (motion picture), Walt Disney Productions.
   Convair Division of General Dynamics Corp., San Diego, Calif.: *Space Primer*, 1959. The best single reference available on the subject.
   Vessel, M., and H. Wong, *Journey into Space*. San Francisco: Fearon Publishers, Inc., 1959.
   ———, *What Is Space*. San Francisco: Fearon Publishers, Inc., 1959.
   Bendick, J., *The First Book of Space Travel*. New York: Franklin Watts, Inc., 1953. Grades 4 to 6.
   Branley, Franklyn, *Experiments in the Principles of Space Travel*. New York: Thomas Y. Crowell Company, 1955. Grades 6 to 8.

Ley, Willy, *Adventure in Space.* New York: The Viking Press, 1957. A series of books.

Neurath, Marie, *Rockets and Jets.* New York: Lothrop, Lee & Shepard Co., Inc., 1952. Grades 4 to 6.

Lehman, Milton, "The Strange Story of Dr. Goddard." *Reader's Digest,* November, 1955, p. 147.

Pratt, Fletcher, *All about Rockets and Jets.* New York: Random House, Inc., 1955.

Sootin, Harry, *Isaac Newton.* New York: Julian Messner, Publishers, Inc., 1955.

Williams, Beryl and Epstein, *The Rocket Pioneers.* New York: Julian Messner, Publishers, Inc., 1955.

Yates, Raymond, *Model Jets for Boys and Girls.* New York: Harper & Row, Publishers, Incorporated, 1952. Ages 10 to 14.

Zim, Herbert S., *What's inside of Engines.* New York: William Morrow and Company, Inc., 1953. Primary.

THE "THRUST-MOBILE"*

This device consists of a mousetrap on a wheeled cart. The trap is used to eject objects of varying mass from the cart in order to demonstrate action-reaction.

Materials needed:

♦ Mousetrap
♦ Scrap lumber
♦ 4 wheels (could be cross sections of a broom handle drilled in the center)
♦ Objects of varying mass, e.g., flashlight battery, ping-pong ball, block of wood, 8-ounce lead fishing sinker, etc.

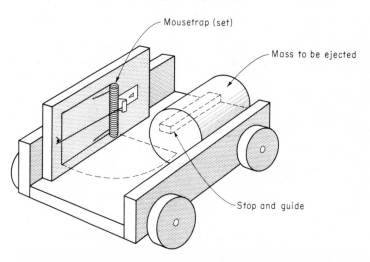

*The following section, while highly useful to the teacher, is often omitted owing to lack of available preparation time on the part of the television teacher—Ed.

Construction details are not critical. The arrangement of the components is given in the illustration. The function of the stop and guide is to stop the motion of the trap yoke and guide the objects as they are ejected from the cart.

In operation, the trap is set in the usual manner: the object to be ejected is placed on the end of the wagon and the position of the cart on the table is marked. The mousetrap is set off by tapping the treadle with a pencil. (The stop will prevent the pencil from being caught by the yoke.) The thrust can be measured in terms of how far the cart is moved from its original position. After several trials using objects of varying mass, it will be noted that the maximum thrust is obtained with objects whose mass approaches that of the wagon itself. The distance that the cart moves with each mass can be plotted on a graph and a curve can be developed. By interpolation, specific thrust can be predicted for any given mass. The energy of action and reaction can be altered by building a duplicate cart containing a rattrap. This modification will produce an engine that in effect consumes fuel at a higher rate. The same mass will produce greater thrust with the rattrap than with the mousetrap because of the higher rate of reaction.

THE MISS FIRE

This is a safe rocket for class use.

Too often one reads in the paper about some youngster or teacher who was injured while attempting to fire a homemade rocket. The "Miss Fire" rocket was designed to enable teachers to reap the instructional benefits of an actual rocket and to do it safely.

The rocket is constructed of a paper tube obtained from the roll-type paper toweling used in many schools and industries. It was selected because of its convenient size, strength, and easy availability. If a paper tube is not available, it can be constructed by rolling sheets of paper smeared with glue over a dowel of proper diameter. Smear the dowel with wax or petroleum jelly to aid in removing it after the glue is dry. The power source is a small compressed carbon dioxide cylinder. There is no fire hazard; the gas is not harmful and the cylinders are safe to handle even with the roughest abuse. Shots of up to 80 feet or more in elevation have been made with such a rocket. The shots can be made on any schoolground or park during non-rush hours. If shots are made nearly vertical, they can be carried out in surprisingly small areas.

Materials needed:

- Paper tube, approximately 12 inches by ⅞ inch inside diameter
- Two corks to fit snugly the inside diameter of the tube
- Wire, soft iron, 1 foot

- Manila folder
- Rubber stopper, shaped for nose cone
- Glue (airplane glue or white casein glue)
- CO_2 cylinders (available at hobby shops)
- CO_2 puncturing gun
- Wire-type spark plug gauge
- Stopwatch with second hand

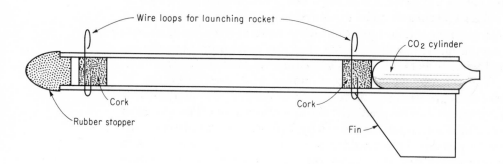

Directions. Wrap the entire outer surface with a sheet of paper (ditto will do) spread with white glue. This will stiffen the tube and the rocket will last longer. Slip the CO_2 cylinder into one end of the tube and let it project out far enough so it can be easily removed. Mark that position and cement a cork in place so that it will serve as a stop for the cylinder. Reduce the inside diameter of the tube where the cylinder is to be placed, until it will fit snugly. This is done by cementing strips of cardboard or paper to the inside of the tube. Glue a cork in the opposite end of the tube about 1½ inches from the end. Shape the rubber stopper with a razor blade so that it will serve as a nose cone. Cut three fins from a manila folder and cement these to the tube 120° apart. Drill a small hole through the tube at the location of the corks. Insert a piece of soft iron wire through the holes, bending one end in a U shape and forcing it back into the cork (see figure above). Form a loop on the other end about ¾ inch in diameter. The wire loops should be placed in line with each other and between a pair of fins.

A 3- to 4-foot length of ½-inch inside diameter steel or aluminum tubing slipped over the upright rod of a ring stand will serve as a launching pad. The wire loops of the rocket will slip down until the lower loop or the fins touch the base of the ring stand. Trajectory can be adjusted by a small block of wood at one end of the ring stand base.

Firing. The rocket is fired by puncturing the lead seal in the end of the cylinder with an ice pick or a commercially available puncturing gun. The size of the hole produced will determine the altitude and the efficiency of the rocket. The larger the hole, the greater

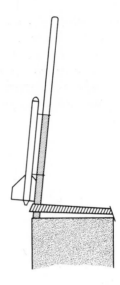

the thrust. The altitude attained by the rocket can be calculated by timing the duration of flight. Using a stopwatch, simply start the watch when the rocket is fired and stop it when the rocket strikes the ground. Make an immediate record of the seconds shown by the watch.

Having determined the time of descent (½ total time), you can get an approximation of the maximum altitude reached from the equation

$$h = \tfrac{1}{2}gt^2$$

where h = maximum height by the rocket, ft
$\quad t$ = time of descent, sec
$\quad g$ = acceleration of gravity, 32.2 ft/sec²

Because atmospheric drag has not been taken into account, the results will always be too large. The method, however, is a reliable means of comparing a number of rocket shots if the rockets are of similar design and construction and were shot in the same general location.

A more precise determination can be accomplished by accurately determining the maximum altitude from azimuth and elevation readings from two locations along a measured base line. A surveyor's transit or alidade is used to make the measurements, which are then used to calculate the altitude using geometry or trigonometry.

The hole size in the end of the cylinder is easily measured with a wire-type spark plug gauge (select one that contains a large variety of sizes). Simply insert the wires into the opening until a snug fit is obtained. Plot the maximum calculated elevation and the corresponding hole size on a graph. After a number of trials, a curve can be determined and the hole size needed to attain a specific altitude can be obtained by interpolation on the graph. A test shot can be made with a specific puncture size and the accuracy of the graph can be tested. The commercial puncturing gun can be adjusted to produce a desired hole size. The carbon dioxide cylinders and the puncturing gun are available at small cost at any hobby shop.

Sample evaluation forms

TV EVALUATION FORM*

Lesson _____ Taught by _____

Date _____ Grade _____

Person rating _____

Please rate each question on the following scale:

1. Objectives

| | Lowest | | | | Highest |

a. Were the objectives clearly
   stated?

$\quad$ 1 $\quad$ 2 $\quad$ 3 $\quad$ 4 $\quad$ 5

b. Were the objectives feasible for
   the level of students being
   taught?

$\quad$ 1 $\quad$ 2 $\quad$ 3 $\quad$ 4 $\quad$ 5

2. The lesson

a. How adequately was the lesson
   planned to achieve the
   objectives?

$\quad$ 1 $\quad$ 2 $\quad$ 3 $\quad$ 4 $\quad$ 5

b. In your opinion how effective
   was the lesson planned for the
   level of students in your class?

$\quad$ 1 $\quad$ 2 $\quad$ 3 $\quad$ 4 $\quad$ 5

Please rate the following aspects
of the lesson:

	Lowest 1	2	3	4	Highest 5
Verbal presentation					
Use of visual aids					
Timing					
Appropriate use of demonstrations					
Effectiveness as a TV instructor					

* Roscoe C. Brown, Jr.

3. Teacher activities from this lesson

a. Were any activities used to follow up the lesson?
Yes _____ No _____ Not indicated _____

b. If yes, which activities were provided?
Making things: Yes _____ No _____ Not indicated _____
Practicing skills: Yes _____ No _____ Not indicated _____
Specific projects: Yes _____ No _____ Not indicated _____
Collateral activities: Yes _____ No _____ Not indicated _____
Others: Yes _____ No _____ Not indicated _____
Please list the specific activities below; be brief.

1. _____

2. _____

3. _____

4. _____

5. _____

c. Was any evaluation of the lesson attempted with the pupils?

Yes _____ No _____ Not indicated _____
What evaluation activities did you use?

_____

_____

_____

4. Teacher evaluation

a. In your opinion to what extent did this lesson achieve the stated objectives?

Lowest　　　　　　　　　　*Highest*
1　　2　　3　　4　　5

b. What were the weaknesses of the lesson?

_____

_____

_____

c. Is this area of instruction adaptable to TV instruction?
Yes _____ No _____ Not indicated _____

d. Should this lesson be:
Required _____
Supplemental _____
Not used _____

e. Are the topics covered in this lesson a part of the regular curriculum?
Yes _____ No _____ Not indicated _____

TELEVISION QUESTIONNAIRE*

To All Teachers, Central Park Road School:
We would like you to take a few minutes to complete the following questionnaire about the television project that we have been

* Roscoe C. Brown, Jr.

conducting at Central Park Road School. Please feel free to make any comments that you think are pertinent to evaluation of the television project. Thanks for your help.

What is your opinion about the television instruction project at Central Park Road School?

- Valuable in all areas where used   ——
- Valuable in some areas where used   ——
- Of doubtful value in all areas   ——
- Not worth the time and effort taken from regular classroom teaching ——

If left up to you, where would you use instructional television?

- In all areas of instruction   ——
- In some areas of instruction   ——
- Which ones:

_____ _____

_____ _____

_____ _____

Would not use it in any areas of instruction _____

Why? _____

_____

In which of the areas of instruction where instructional television was used at Central Park Road School do you think television was most effective?

_____ _____

_____ _____

_____ _____

Why? _____

_____

Which of the areas of instruction could just as well have been taught without television?

_____ _____

_____ _____

_____ _____

_____ _____

Why? _____

_____

What suggestions do you have to improve television instruction on the following points?

Planning for television instruction (including areas selected for TV instruction) _____

_____

The television instructors _____

_____

The methods used on television _____

_____

The follow-up of television instruction _____

_____

None _____

Please make any other comments that you have about television instruction.

_____

_____

_____

SOUTH CAROLINA EDUCATIONAL TELEVISION CENTER
2712 Millwood Avenue
Columbia, S.C.

INFORMATION SHEET

Teacher _____   Date _____

School _____

Number of students in classroom _____   Subject _____

TEACHING

Introduction: Good ____   *Comments:*
                Fair ____
                Weak ____

Summary: Effective   ___
         Ineffective   ___

Content: Right amount   ___
       Too much   ___
       Too little   ___

Sequence: Logical   ___
        Unrelated   ___

Vocabulary: Good   ___
          Too difficult   ___
          Too easy   ___

Visuals: Right amount   ___
      Too many   ___
      Too few   ___

Pacing: Right   ___
      Too fast   ___
      Too slow   ___

Teaching technique: Strong points _____

                    Weak points _____

LEARNING

Student attention: Strong ___ Average ___ Poor ___
Student response to telecast: High ___ Average ___ Low ___
Learning retention from telecast: Large ___ Average ___ Small ___
Student reaction to telecast: Favorable ___ Average ___ Adverse ___

TECHNICAL

Picture: Clear   ___   *Comments* (describe trouble):
       Hazy   ___

Sound: Distinct ___
      Poor   ___

FEEDBACK QUESTIONNAIRE
Hagerstown, Md.

School _____ Grade ___ Subject _____
Classroom teacher _____ Number of students ___ Lesson date _____
Level of student ability: Above average ___ Average ___ Below average ___

1. Sound: Distinct ___ Audible ___ Not clear ___ Describe difficulty _____

2. Video: Clear _____ Interference _____ Describe difficulty _____

3. Introduction: Stimulating _____ All right _____ Dull _____

4. Development: Clear _____ Interesting _____ Weak _____

5. Visuals: Enough _____ Too many _____ Too few _____

         Shown long enough _____ Not long enough _____ (which one) _____

         Effective _____ Didn't make the point _____ (which one) _____

6. Speed of lesson: Right _____ Too fast _____ Too slow _____

7. Vocabulary: Right _____ Too difficult _____ Too easy _____

8. Level of lesson for students: Too difficult _____ Satisfactory _____

     Too Elementary _____

9. Amount of student participation during TV lesson: Inadequate _____

     Adequate _____ Too much _____

10. Summary: Effective _____ All right _____ Omitted _____   T _____

11. Length of telecast: Right _____ Too long _____ Too short _____   P _____

12. Amount of student participation after telecast: Inadequate _____

     Adequate _____   E _____

13. Student interest: _____

        —USE OTHER SIDE FOR SUGGESTIONS AND COMMENTS—

ANAHEIM CITY SCHOOL DISTRICT

Telelesson reaction form

School _____ Teacher _____ Grade _____ Lesson date _____

Subject _____ Lesson title _____

1. What technical qualities (audio-video), if any, caused children to lose attention?

_____

2. How did children react to this lesson? _____

_____

     A. Was the purpose of the lesson accomplished? _____

     B. What successful related classroom activities resulted from this lesson?

_____

_____

3. What were the strengths and weaknesses of this lesson?

	Strength	Weakness
A. Opening		
B. Development of lesson		
C. Visual materials used		
D. Summary of lesson		
E. Student participation		
F. Motivation for additional learning		

4. What in your opinion would have made this a better lesson?

_____

_____

_____

_____

DIVISION OF RADIO AND TELEVISION EDUCATION
Administration Building
Parkway at 21st Street
Philadelphia 3, Pa.

Television evaluation report

School _____ Teacher _____ Grade _____

Program title _____ Date _____

Number viewing _____ Where viewed _____ Size of screen _____

These are the general aims of the television programs which are planned to implement approved curriculum philosophies.
(Each series varies in its purpose as indicated in monthly schedule.)

1. To contribute to the outcomes of education: the knowledges, skills, attitudes, and appreciations
2. To supplement the work of the teacher
3. To demonstrate teaching techniques
4. To stimulate pupil interest
5. To acquaint parents with our schools

To help us realize these aims, your comments and suggestions, as noted below, are necessary.

We suggest that the teacher, in order to utilize the program most effectively:

1. Make sure, well in advance, that the set is in good working order.
2. Settle her class in good time for comfortable and not-too-crowded viewing.
3. Consult the monthly television schedule for _topic_ and _grade level_. Descriptions are purposely kept brief. Extensive preparation on the teacher's part should not be necessary.
4. Give class opportunity to discuss program under teacher's guidance.

Please mark the points which apply to the programs you have viewed. Use other side for additional comments.

1. Quality of reception: Good _____ Poor _____ (If poor, indicate nature of difficulty)
2. General interest shown by children _____
   (Encouragement of good listening and audience habits is an influential factor.)
3. Any preparatory period? _____
4. Appropriateness of program for recommended grades:
   Satisfactory _____ Too advanced _____ Immature_____
5. Has program served as resource material? _____
6. Has program given teacher any teaching technique? _____
7. Has it increased pupil interest and understanding in this area? _____
8. Has it fostered any desirable attitude or appreciation? _____
9. Has it provided opportunity for any development of skill or creative activity? _____
10. Please indicate any in- or out-of-class follow-up activities which resulted.

11. Comments and suggestions.

12. What other topics or activities would you like to have presented on television?

Please mail this form after each telecast or at the end of each week to Miss Martha A. Gable, Director, Radio-Television Education, Board of Education, Administration Building, Room 230, Parkway at 21st Street, Philadelphia 3, Pa.

Glossary

Antenna A conductor or system of conductors with which radio or television signals are received or transmitted through space. May be formed of suspended wires, metal rods, or, as in a microwave system, a parabolic reflector or dish. (P. Lewis)

Audio The sound portion of a television presentation. (Kendig & Martin)

Audio filter or equalizer A means of selectively adjusting sound frequencies to produce special effects or to minimize unwanted sounds.

Audiofrequency signal An electrical signal whose frequency lies within the limits of audibility; approximately 20 to 15,000 cycles per second. (Kendig & Martin)

Camera chain A television camera connected to a control unit and viewing monitor. (P. Lewis)

Camera monitor A video monitor that is an integral part of the control unit for a television camera, usually located in the control room for use by director and engineers. It is electrically interconnected with the camera circuits and normally includes a waveform oscilloscope.

Channel The assigned frequency for a radio or television transmitter or closed-circuit modulator.

Closed-circuit television The use of television, transmitted from cameras to receivers over cable, or by microwave, permitting private reception of programs only by those receivers included in the circuit. (Kendig & Martin)

Coaxial cable Special cable consisting of a center conductor concentrically positioned within an outer shield used to provide low-loss transmission of video and/or radio frequency signals. (Kendig & Martin)

Commercial television Programs initiated by broadcast stations operated by private organizations primarily for profit. It involves the use of advertising, entertainment, and programs in the public interest. (Kendig & Martin)

Community television station A nonprofit station supported by public subscription that sells television time, at cost, to educational institutions or school districts for part of its daily program. Falls under the category of an "educational station" for FCC licensing.

Cut A production term for an instantaneous transition from one television picture to another.

Direct television teaching Presentation of the major portion of a course of study, by the television teacher, supplemented by individual study and small-group discussions under the direction of a classroom teacher.

Dissolve A production term for a gradual transition in which one television picture gradually fades out while another fades in.

Dry run A complete rehearsal without cameras or lights. Often called a walk-through.

Educational television   A broad term usually applied to cultural and community broadcasting which may include some programs for in-school use.

Educational television station   A nonprofit station owned and operated by an educational institution or school district as part of its ongoing educational program. For FCC licensing this term refers to *any* nonprofit television station.

EIA (RETMA) standards   A set of criteria and standards which are the basis for commercial broadcast equipment—both transmission and reception. All equipment used for conventional telecasting purposes must meet these requirements. The Electronics Industry Association (EIA), formally known as RETMA, was responsible for activating the research committees that set these standards. (P. Lewis)

Fade   A production term for a gradual transition in which the television picture gradually goes to or comes up from black (no picture).

FCC   The Federal Communications Commission, the governmental agency responsible for the regulations of radio and television in the public interest. (Kendig & Martin)

Film chain   An equipment arrangement in which one or more projectors (usually 16-mm. film and/or 35-mm. slide) are designed for image pickup by a television camera.

Film chain multiplexer   An arrangement of half-silvered mirrors or prisms that combines the beams of light from several projectors and directs them into the lens of a single television camera.

Film clips   Short sequences of motion-picture film inserted into a television presentation. (Kendig & Martin)

Focus   The optical or electrical adjustment of a camera or lens to obtain a sharp picture.

Gain control   An electrical adjustment for either increasing or decreasing sound volume or picture contrast.

Image orthicon   A highly sensitive television camera used extensively in commercial television; usually considered an unwarranted expense for the normal instructional application.

Instructional television   Television used within the formal classroom context on any educational level.

Kinescope recording   A motion picture made directly from the images appearing on a special television monitor.

Lens turret   A revolving lens mount on the front of a television camera.

Line amplifier   An amplifier used to boost the strength of video signals that have been attenuated (reduced) by traversing long coaxial circuits. (Kendig & Martin)

Microwave link   A special high-frequency radio transmitter and receiver capable of carrying audio and video signals in a directional line-of-sight "beam."

Patch panel   A device on which incoming cables terminate in connectors in order that the various circuits may be interconnected at will by patching short lengths of cable between connectors. (Kendig & Martin)

Picture definition   The sharpness of detail on a reproduced image.

Radio frequency signal   An electrical signal whose frequency lies above the limits of audibility (20,000 cycles per second). (Kendig & Martin)

Rear projection   An arrangement whereby scenes (film, slides, etc.) are projected from behind on a translucent screen; the television camera picks up the projected image from the screen side opposite the projector, allowing the instructor to be in front of the projected scene and to point directly to it. This technique eliminates the extensive lighting problems associated with front projection.

Remote unit   A mobile television facility providing for both audio and video. Used to pick up and transmit events outside a studio.

Resolution (also Definition)   The number of alternate black and white lines that may be resolved across the entire width or height of a television screen regardless of its size. A measure of the ability of a television system to reproduce fine detail.

RF amplifier   An amplifier that boosts the strength of a radio frequency signal. (Kendig & Martin)

RF monitor (TV receiver)   The standard black-and-white home receiver capable of displaying radio frequency signals from open-circuit transmitters and closed-circuit modulators on the standard frequencies (channels). Receives both audio and video. Usually capable of displaying slightly in excess of 300 lines resolution.

Signal multiplexing   A device for mixing several signals for transmission over a single system. (P. Lewis)

Single-room television   Television used as a simple magnification device within the classroom or laboratory. The camera, receivers, and controls are located within the single classroom and are of simple design, usually with the camera controls built into the camera unit.

Super   A video special effect in which two television signals are fed into a switcher-fader so that one is superimposed upon the other.

Supplementary television   The use of television lessons that are directly related to the course of study and are presented on a scheduled basis to augment the classroom offerings.

Switcher-fader   A control device which allows the director to cut, fade, and dissolve between two or more television cameras.

Synchronizing generator   A device which generates precision electrical timing pulses used to coordinate various functions throughout a television system. (Kendig & Martin)

Team teaching   The teaching of a single lesson or course segment by several teachers working cooperatively.

Television modulator—closed-circuit   A miniature television transmitter which accepts video and audio signals from separate sources for purposes of combining them into a signal which can be transmitted on a cable at radio frequencies. These radio frequencies usually fall in a standard television channel and are fed to a television receiver.

Total teaching by television   The teaching of an entire course by means of television.

Translator   A small electronic device which receives a signal from a television station at a given VHF frequency (channel) and converts it to another frequency (usually UHF). This signal, on the new frequency, is then transmitted into an area not reached by the original signal.

Ultrahigh frequency (UHF)   A frequency of 300 to 3,000 megacycles per second; includes channels 14 to 83.

Very high frequency (VHF)   A frequency of 30 to 300 megacycles per second; includes channels 2 to 13.

Video   The picture portion of a television presentation.

Glossary

Video monitor   A high-definition television receiver connected directly to the camera output. Does not incorporate channel selection or an audio signal.

Video switcher   A device used to select a desired video signal from the potential choices and connect it to an output circuit. If specially adapted to fade one picture into another or to superimpose pictures, it is called a "switcher-fader."

Video tape recording (VTR)   The recording of both the picture and sound of a television presentation by electronic impulses on a special magnetic recording tape which can be played back when desired.

Vidicon   A camera pickup tube of much smaller physical size than the image orthicon; it requires more light but is less expensive in cost and operation. The normal tube for instructional television, industrial, and broadcast film applications.

Waveform monitor   An oscilloscope designed to measure the voltage or "level" of the video signal. Used to set video level to certain prescribed limits so that the signals from several cameras have the same brightness and contrast.

Zoom lens   A variable-focal-length lens which, by simple mechanical adjustment without physical movement of the camera, can vary the field of view without losing the clarity of focus.

Annotated Bibliography

In preparing the following bibliography an attempt has been made to include those materials that an individual exploring the potentials and applications of instructional television will find most helpful. To facilitate use, the materials have been divided into the following categories:

General: A wide range of publications that are concerned with instructional television's role and related fields. Includes information for teachers and administrators.

Research: Several reports and studies that are basic reading for anyone investigating television's role in education and planning to design an experiment within this general area.

Equipment, facilities, and production: Some excellent source material for administrators and staff who will be actively involved with planning and producing for instructional television.

Program and materials sources: Listings of television series now available on film or tape for school use.

Periodicals: Journals and other publications devoting space, on a regular basis, to instructional television.

Applications: A partial list of school districts and related agencies who have actively used television, with the type of utilization specified.

General

Allen, William H.: *Television for California Schools.* California State Department of Education, Sacramento: State Printing Office, 1960.
    Conclusions and recommendations based on a study in (1) the importance of the new educational communication media to instruction; (2) the findings of research on instructional television; (3) relationship of instructional television to educational television; and (4) implications that the potential uses of these media may have for education in California (particularly in terms of a statewide educational television system).
Brown, James W., Richard B. Lewis, and Fred F. Harcleroad:
    Audio-Visual Instruction: Materials and Methods. New York: McGraw-Hill Book Company, Inc., 1959.
    The most complete reference book of its type. Comprehensive chapters on the many techniques and materials available to the classroom teacher with specific suggestions and techniques, including one chapter on television.

283

Current Developments in Educational Television. Washington, D.C.: National Educational Television and Radio Center, Fall, 1961.

An occasional publication that presents results of surveys: current activities, new programs (e.g., Airborne), closed- and open-circuit, legislation affecting educational television, FCC, etc. The information is presented in a concise, clear manner.

Educational Television, The Next Ten Years. Stanford, Calif.: Institute for Communications Research, Stanford University, 1962.

A dynamic discussion of educational television in the United States. Articles by top leaders in educational and commercial broadcasting which detail educational television problems, describe educational television's future and make recommendations to facilitate its rapid growth in proper directions. Of particular interest to administrators will be the chapters which deal with "The Problem of Financing, 1961–1971," and "The Problems of Resources and Facilities, 1961–1971."

Fletcher, Leon C.: *Instructional Television Review 1959–1961.* Menlo Park, Calif.: Pacific Coast Publishers, 1961.

Answers briefly a multitude of common questions concerning instructional television. Particularly valuable to educators who are pressed for time and wish to be briefed on the broad issues and aspects of the medium's use in education and still be provided with some specific answers for embarrassing questions.

Foshay, Finette P. (ed.): *Interaction in Learning: Implications for Television.* Washington, D.C.: DAVI, NEA, 1959.

This pamphlet, prepared by a group of distinguished educators for the NEA, examines in detail the components of interaction and the need for it. Especially worthwhile is the second half, which discusses in detail techniques for achieving interaction when using television.

Fund for the Advancement of Education: *The National Program in the Use of Television in the Public Schools.* A report of the first year. New York: 1959.

A nationwide experiment involving, in 1957–1958, 40,000 students in 200 elementary schools. Summaries of reports, projects from Atlanta; Cincinnati; Dade County, Fla.; Detroit; Jefferson County, Ky.; Milwaukee; Nebraska; Norfolk; North Carolina; Oklahoma City; Philadelphia; and Wichita.

Kendig, Kathryn Dye, and Gaither Lee Martin: *The ABC's of TV, A Handbook on Instructional & Public-service Programming for Educators & Community Leaders.* San Jose State College, 1957.

This guide was one of the first of its kind to appear. Shorn of technical vocabulary and covered throughout with practical illustrations, it has proved its worth for the experienced as well as inexperienced since its publication. For those contemplating the use of instructional television, it gives step-by-step instructions for the administrator, producer, teacher, and technical workers. A glossary of terms and bibliography is appended.

Purdue University: *International Seminar on Instructional Television.* Seminar Report, Lafayette, Ind., Oct. 8 to 18, 1962.

The latter sections of this report contain some fine information on the role of the classroom teacher, and report research with some emphasis on facilities and special applications of the medium.

Siepmann, C. A.: *TV and Our School Crisis.* New York: Dodd, Mead & Company, Inc., 1958.

The various "crises" problems in education in 1958, particularly as they related to survival of the western world, were presented and examined by the author. His suggestion is that television holds promise for solving some of the problems noted, if adopted and used properly by the educational system. Of particular interest to educators are the chapters which spell out how the inherent characteristics of the television medium lend themselves to the solution of these problems. Information on television in England and France is presented.

Smith, Mary Howard (ed.): *Using Television in the Classroom.* New York: McGraw-Hill Book Company, Inc., 1961.

While designed for the teachers participating in the Midwest Program on Airborne Television Instruction, this information is practical for all teachers using television within their classrooms. Includes brief history of instructional television, and introduction for classroom teachers, and illustrations of how teachers are using this new medium. Bibliographies follow each chapter.

The Superintendent's Viewpoint on Educational Television. New York: Thomas Alva Edison Foundation, Inc., 1959.

Panel discussion before the National Association of Educational Broadcasters. Verbatim speeches of superintendents from Washington County, Md.; Newton, Mass.; Pittsburgh; Philadelphia; and New York City.

Tarbet, Donald G.: *Television and Our Schools.* New York: The Ronald Press Company, 1961.

Discusses the role of educational television in the curriculum. Describes the techniques essential for direct teaching by television and offers program ideas for school, college, in-service, and adult education purposes. Examples of actual programs are cited throughout the book. Usable, easy reading.

Teaching by Television. New York: The Ford Foundation and the Fund for the Advancement of Education, 1961.

A report in digest form of the significant television projects on the college and public school levels in the United States up to January, 1961, including more than 100 school systems and 100,000 students and teachers. The research purist will not find enough detail for his satisfaction, but the busy teacher and administrator will find the generalizations concerning the capabilities of television in education (based on the projects described) useful in learning what television has and has not been able to do in actual educational situations.

Teaching with Television—Guideline for the Classroom Teacher. Anaheim City School District, Anaheim, Calif., 1963.

A guide for teachers emphasizing the importance of the classroom teacher for effective television utilization. Defines role of and presents suggestions for teacher-directed activities. Defines role of the Anaheim Television Project within specific subject areas.

Teaching with Television: Guideline for the Resourceroom Teacher. Anaheim City School District, Anaheim, Calif., 1963.

Defines the role of the large-group teacher within the Anaheim "Redeployment Plan." Designed to assist the teacher in becoming more effective within this situation and in the use of related television instruction.

Trump, J. Lloyd, and Dorsey Baynham: *Focus on Change: Guide to Better Schools.* Chicago: Rand McNally & Company, 1961.

This volume presents clearly and concisely the logic behind team teaching. Strongly recommended for any administrator who is exploring team teaching and television for large-group instruction. It offers specific suggestions with rationale.

Research

Holmes, Presley D., Jr.: *Television Research in the Teaching-Learning Process.* Detroit: Wayne State University, 1959.

A comprehensive survey, with summaries, of research in educational television to date of publication. Basic reading for anyone exploring the potential of television.

Kumata, Hideya: *An Inventory of Instructional Television Research.* A project of the Institute of Communications Research at the University of Illinois. Ann Arbor, Mich.: Educational Television and Radio Center, Dec., 1956.

The first review of instructional television research and "must reading" for anyone planning a research project in this area.

Mager, Robert F.: *Preparing Objectives for Programmed Instruction.* San Francisco: Fearon Publishers, Inc., 1961.

Presents guidelines on how to write specific and measurable program objectives. A must for television teachers and individuals involved in television research.

Schramm, Wilber: *The Impact of Educational Television.* Selected studies from the research sponsored by the National Educational Television and Radio Center, 1960.

A review of studies conducted with the support of the National Educational Television and Radio Center. Also contains a series of interesting general articles. Covers the impact of television on children.

Schramm, Wilbur, Jack Lyle, and E. B. Parker: *Television in the Lives of Our Children.* Stanford, Calif.: Stanford University Press, 1961.

A report of the first major study in the United States concerned with the ways in which television operates in the lives of children. It represents three years of research on 6,000 children and information obtained from 2,300 parents, teachers, and school officials, summing up everything so far discovered by research (1961).

Equipment, facilities, and production

Bretz, Rudy: *Techniques of Television Production,* 2d ed. New York: McGraw-Hill Book Company, Inc., 1962.

A comprehensive description of the tools of television production, their capabilities and limitations, and the techniques for operating them. Helps the layman understand, in simple but accurate terms, the workings of electronic montage, the optics of lenses, the methods of synchronizing film projectors with television scanning rate, and the other technical facets of television production. A reference rather than a text, presented in non-technical, comprehensive language, as valuable to the commercial broadcaster as it is to the educational broadcaster.

Bretz, Rudy, and Edward Stasheff: *The Television Program: Its Direction and Production.* New York: Hill and Wang, Inc., 1952.

A comprehensive text on television production and direction techniques. Well illustrated. Recommended for production personnel.

Cavert, C. Edward: *Producing Your Educational Television Program.* Schenectady, N.Y.: Mohawk-Hudson Council on Educational Television, 1961.

An excellent guide designed to serve those responsible for producing their educational television program or series. Extremely well illustrated and practical. Contents include techniques for the director, teachers and production staff, with appended glossary of terms.

Costello, Lawrence, and George N. Gordon: *Teaching with Television.* New York: Hastings House, Publishers, Inc., 1961.

How to produce and use televised instruction on all educational levels, both closed- and open-circuit.

Design for ETV, Planning for Schools with Television. Prepared by Dave Chapman, Inc., Industrial Design for Educational Facilities Laboratories, New York, 1960.

A superbly illustrated report showing how to plan new schools or adapt existing schools for teaching by television. Excellent material on room arrangement for television. It presents the conclusions of a study conducted by industrial designers in conjunction with educators, psychologists, architects, engineers, etc. While the equipment section needs updating, it is highly recommended. Free on request.

Kemp, Jerrold: *Planning and Producing Audiovisual Materials.* San Francisco: Chandler Publishing Co., 1963.

A comprehensive guidebook for beginners and experienced persons on the planning and production of photographic picture series, slide series, filmstrips, overhead transparencies, and motion pictures. Techniques described apply directly to visual materials for television.

Lewis, Philip: *Educational Television Guidebook.* New York: McGraw-Hill Book Company, Inc., 1961.

An excellent guide for administrators who contemplate the purchase and use of television systems for schools. Lewis' criteria for the selection and purchase of equipment are excellent. Diagrams and explanations are complete but not cluttered with unnecessary detail. The guidebook is so organized that it is at once an inventory and a simplification of technical detail. Includes case studies, bibliography, and glossary.

Spear, James: *Creating Visuals for TV.* Hagerstown, Md.: National Education Association, 1962.

An extremely practical book on the preparation of visuals for television. Includes a variety of techniques. Well illustrated.

Stasheff, Edward, and Rudy Bretz: *The Television Program: Its Direction and Production,* 2d ed. New York: A. A. Wyn, Inc., 1962.

A comprehensive explanation of the nature of the television medium with specific, practical explanations of the duties, art, and science which become the craft of the television producer and director. It is basic reference with precise directions "how to" for the prospective and practicing television producer, director, or teacher-performer.

Program and materials sources

A Guide to Films, Kinescopes, and Videotapes Available for Televised Use. New York: National Instructional Television Library, Spring, 1962.

The guide describes a total of 169 television courses available for use by educators in the United States. It is also a catalog of sample materials available from these courses. Each sample contains a 16-mm film of one representative lesson and two sets of related printed materials.

National Educational Television and Radio Center, 10 Columbus Circle, New York 19, N.Y.

The coordinating center for the National Educational Television Network. May be contacted for information concerning NET membership stations and available television series.

NET Film Service Catalogue. Bloomington, Ind.: Audio-Visual Center, Indiana University, 1962.

This is a catalog of additional NET educational films available to educators over and above those listed in the *NET Instructional Television Materials Guide.*

1962–1963 Catalogue of MPATI Courses. Purdue, Ind.: Midwest Program on Airborne TV Instruction, Inc., 1962.

The booklet describes 24 courses which are available from MPATI, each covering a school semester or a full academic year of instruction in a subject. It contains information about the content of each course, the intended grade level, and the television teacher, plus details about rental charges and how sample taped resource-material units may be obtained for preview.

Periodicals

Audiovisual Instruction. Department of Audiovisual Instruction, National Educational Association, 1201 16th Street, N.W., Washington 6, D.C.

A major audio-visual publication that devotes much space, and often entire issues, to the use of television within instruction.

AV Communications Review. Department of Audiovisual Instruction, 1201 16th Street, N.W., Washington 6, D.C.

A bimonthly publication, containing research abstracts, book reviews, and major articles on the audio-visual field.

Educational Screen and Audiovisual Guide. 415 North Dearborn, Chicago 10, Ill.

A monthly publication in the audio-visual field that regularly carries articles on varied applications of instructional television.

Journal of the SMPTE. New York: Society of Motion Picture and Television Engineers.

A monthly publication. It is the best single source of current authoritative information concerning technical developments in motion-picture and television production devices and systems. It is technical, written from the engineer's point of view, but is not beyond the comprehension of a layman.

NAEB Journal. Urbana, Ill. National Association of Educational Broadcasters.

A bimonthly publication containing articles relating to all aspects of educational broadcasting. These are contributed by outstanding educators and educational broadcasters throughout the United States. Its treatment of research is light, but in all other areas of educational broadcasting it is considered by many to be the best single source of current educational television information available. Its style makes easy and interesting reading.

Television Factbook. Washington, D.C.: Broadcasting Publications, Inc.

An annual publication. A comprehensive source of operating information about television stations in the United States. Particularly valuable are transmitter coverage maps and ownership-operating personnel lists for each station. Other listings of interest include program production, production facility, consultant, advertising, public relations, etc., organizations associated with the commercial broadcast industry.

Applications*

The following is a partial list of school districts and related agencies who have actively used television within their instructional program. The majority of these have printed information available on request.

Alabama

Birmingham Public Schools
2015 7th Avenue, North
Birmingham 3, Ala.
Att: Producer-Coordinator, TV-Radio
(Production center for state ETV network; all grade levels, in-service and adult education)

Arizona

West High School
2910 North 19th Street
Phoenix, Ariz.
(CCTV, single-room, magnification at secondary level)

California

Anaheim City School District
412 E. Broadway
Anaheim, Calif.
Att: Project Director
(Production center for CCTV; elementary-level and in-service education)

Carlsbad Elementary School District
801 Pine
Carlsbad, Calif.
(Production center, OCTV, CCTV, used at elementary level)

---

* Editor's note: The majority of school districts with substantial television projects have published reports on their particular operation. For anyone interested in materials of this type it is suggested that they write the school district directly. Unfortunately, the great majority of published and printed information on instructional television is in paperback form and therefore not available in most libraries. An excellent source of information is the college television center exploring uses of the medium and offering courses in the subject.

Fontana Unified School District
9680 Citrus Avenue
Fontana, Calif.
(In-service classroom observation)

Fresno County Schools
2314 Mariposa Street
Fresno 21, Calif.
Att: Radio-TV Consultant
(County coordination OCTV, CCTV, production centers using local commercial station; elementary, in-service, and adult education)

Los Angeles County Superintendent of Schools
155 W. Washington Boulevard
Los Angeles 15, Calif.
(Commercial station used at all grade levels and for in-service education)

Mt. Diablo Unified School District
1936 Carlotta Drive
Concord, Calif.
(Use of educational station at elementary level)

Colorado

Denver Public Schools, School District No. 1
414-14th Street
Denver 2, Colo.
Att: Director, Dept. of Radio and Television
(Educational station used at elementary level and for in-service and adult education)

Florida

Dade County Public Schools
1410 NE 2nd Avenue
Miami 32, Fla.
Att: Director, Radio and Television Education
(Educational station used at elementary and secondary levels)

Georgia

Fulton County School Office
2580 DeLowe Drive
East Point, Ga.
(Production center, CCTV used for elementary, in-service, adult education and single-room magnification)

Illinois

Wright Junior College
3400 N. Austin Avenue
Chicago 34, Ill.
Att: Dean in Charge, TV College
(OCTV, CCTV, use of local education and commercial stations at all levels and for in-service education and single-room magnification)

Evanston Township High School
1600 Dodge Avenue
Evanston, Ill.
(CCTV, OCTV, educational and commercial stations used for secondary and
in-service education)

Indiana

Marion Senior High School
Marion, Ind.
Att: Principal
(CCTV senior high school)

Midwest Program on Airborne Television Instruction
Memorial Center
Purdue University
Lafayette, Ind.
(Production center, OCTV used at all grade levels and for in-service
education)

Iowa

Des Moines Public Schools
1800 Grand Avenue
Des Moines 14, Iowa
Att: Director, Educational Television
(Production center, OCTV used at all grade levels, in-service, and adult
education)

Kansas

Wichita High School
701 W. 33rd Street South
Wichita 7, Kans.
(OCTV, CCTV, commercial station used at all grade levels and for single-
room magnification)

Kentucky

Jefferson County School District
2301 Clarendon
Louisville 5, Ky.
(Educational and commercial stations used at all grade levels and for in-
service and adult education)

Maryland

Closed-circuit Educational Television Project
Washington County Board of Education
Hagerstown, Md.
(Production center, CCTV used at all levels and for in-service education)

291

Annotated bibliography

Michigan

Detroit Public Schools
9345 Lawton Avenue
Detroit 6, Mich.
Att: Supervisor, TV Teaching Project
(Production center, OCTV, educational station used at all grade levels and for in-service and adult education)

Minnesota

Minneapolis Public Schools
807 N. E. Broadway
Minneapolis, Minn.
(OCTV educational station used at all grade levels and for in-service and adult education)

New York

Corning City School District
291 E. First Street
Corning, N.Y.
Att: ETV Office
(Production center, CCTV used at all grade levels and for in-service and adult education)

Cortland Public Schools
241 McLean Road
Cortland, N.Y.
Att: Television Studio
(Production center, CCTV for all grade levels and for in-service and adult education)

Great Neck Public Schools
345 Lakeville Road
Great Neck, N.Y.
(Production center, CCTV used for all grade levels)

Plainedge Public Schools
Wyngate and Peony Drives
Massapequa, L.I., N.Y.
(Production center, CCTV and OCTV [low-power] used for all grade levels)

Rochester City School District
410 Alexander Street
Rochester 7, N.Y.
(OCTV, CCTV, commercial station used for all grade levels and adult education)

Scarsdale Public Schools
Post Road
Scarsdale, N.Y.
(OCTV, CCTV, production center, single-room magnification for secondary level)

Schenectady Public Schools
108 Union Street
Schenectady, N.Y.
(CCTV and OCTV, commercial and educational stations used for all grade levels and for in-service education)

Ohio

Cincinnati Public Schools
608 E. McMillam Street
Cincinnati 6, Ohio
(Educational station used for all grade levels, in-service and adult education)

South Carolina

South Carolina Educational Television Center
2712 Millwood Avenue
Columbia, S.C.
(Production center, statewide CCTV for secondary and in-service education)

Texas

Snyder Public Schools
Snyder, Tex.
(CCTV, single-room magnification at secondary level)

Utah

Weber County School District
1122 Washington Boulevard
Ogden, Utah
(Production center, OCTV [low-power] for elementary level)

Virginia

Hampton Road ETV Association
735 Pembroke Avenue
Norfolk, Va.
(OCTV, educational and commercial stations, used for all grade levels and adult education)

Wisconsin

Milwaukee Public Schools
5225 W. Vliet Street
Milwaukee 8, Wis.
(Production center, OCTV, educational stations used at all levels and for in-service education)

Index